Praise for
Guerrilla Marketing for Writers

"This book teaches the marketing tools every writer needs to know today."
—John Gray
author of *Men Are from Mars, Women Are from Venus*

"This book is clear and simple and every writer will benefit from the strategies—I wish I had this book when I started writing."
—Jack Canfield
co-author of *Chicken Soup for the Soul* and
Chicken Soup for the Writer's Soul

"Writers create babies called books and then orphan them. Read this book and make your book a bestseller . . . and that's the right idea!"
—Mark Victor Hansen
co-author of *Chicken Soup for the Soul* and
Chicken Soup for the Writer's Soul

"Whether you sell to a publisher or publish yourself, the author must do the promotion; publishers do not promote their books. Fortunately, now there is a Guerrilla Marketing book for the writer. Enlist now and requisition your weapons. Don't go into the publishing jungle unarmed."
—Dan Poynter
author of *The Self-Publishing Manual*

"If you want your book to bounce off the shelves, read *Guerrilla Marketing for Writers*. It is filled with powerful insights and proven techniques!"
—Roger Crawford
author of *How High Can You Bounce?*

"*Guerrilla Marketing for Writers* is a primer for primal promotion. The advice is smart, savvy and sensible. The writing is clear, concise and easy to follow. Most of all, *Guerrilla Marketing for Writers* guides and motivates new and established writers alike."

—Drs. Richard and Rachael Heller
authors of *The Carbohydrate Addict's Lifespan Program* and
The Carbohydrate Addict's Diet

"As a veteran author myself and president of a PR firm specializing in author promotion, we know what it takes to promote a book. Every author on the planet should read *Guerrilla Marketing for Writers* and devour every word. In this age of lightning-strike attention spans, this book will keep you glued to every page. If you write a book, be sure to read this one first."

—Robyn Spizman
president of The Spizman Agency and
author of more than sixty how-to books

"When Jay, Rick and Michael talk, every writer should listen. These three power-packed pros will give you advice and council you can't find anywhere else—listen to them. I've benefited and so can you. This is a must-buy book!"

—Sheila Murray Bethel
author of *Making a Difference: 12 Qualities That Make You a Leader*

GUERRILLA MARKETING
FOR
WRITERS

JAY CONRAD LEVINSON,
RICK FRISHMAN & MICHAEL LARSEN

WRITER'S DIGEST BOOKS
CINCINNATI, OHIO

Dedications

JAY To my daughter Amy who teaches me about writing by example. She is my masterpiece.

RICK To my wife Robbi

MIKE To Elizabeth, my one and only

FROM ALL OF US To the writers this book helps earn the recognition and rewards they deserve.

Visit our Web site at www.writersdigest.com for information on more resources for writers.

To receive a free weekly e-mail newsletter delivering tips and updates about writing and about Writer's Digest products, send an e-mail with "Subscribe Newsletter" in the body of the message to newsletter-request@writersdigest.com, or register directly at our Web site at www.writersdigest .com.

04 03 02 01 00   5 4 3 2 1

Library of Congress Cataloging-in-Publication Data

Frishman, Rick
  Guerrilla marketing for writers / by Rick Frishman, Michael Larsen & Jay Conrad Levin-son.—1st ed.
    p. cm.
  Includes bibliographical references and index.
  ISBN 0-89879-983-X (pb : alk. paper)
    1. Authorship—Marketing. I. Larsen, Michael. II. Levinson, Jay Conrad. III. Title.

PN161.F75   2000
070.5'2—dc21   00-063326
                                                                     CIP

Edited by David Borcherding and Jessica Yerega
Designed by Sandy Conopeotis Kent
Cover design by Stephanie Redman
Production coordinated by Sara Dumford

Acknowledgments

First many thanks from all of us to the folks at Writer's Digest Books: Jack Heffron for having enough faith in us to take the book on, Dave Borcherding for his patience and acumen, Richard Hunt for his marketing support, and the rest of the staff for their help in making the book as good as it can be.

This book draws on the knowledge of other authors, especially those in the Guerrilla Hall of Fame, and to them we express our gratitude for helping to light the way for you and us.

JAY

In my heart, I owe acknowledgments to my coauthor, Mike Larsen, and to his partner in life and literature, Elizabeth Pomada, for all the wondrous things that have happened in my life after writing my first book. Thanks also to Rick for enriching the book with his knowledge and experience. Lots of people, from editors to my wife, Pat, and my daughter, Amy, should also be singled out. But in truth, Mike and Elizabeth get the lion's share of credit for transferring my words from my head to books that now appear in 18 languages. They did the real heavy lifting.

So did Bill Shear, President of Guerrilla Marketing International, who arranges speaking gigs for me around the world. Without him, the books would have been remaindered. With him, they have sold over one million copies. Every nonfiction needs a Bill Shear, but I've been blessed to have him. All writers need allies. These are mine.

MIKE

The first thank-you has to be for Jay both for giving me the opportunity to be part of the franchise he created by collaborating on the book, and also for being a friend and client since 1977. My second thank-you goes to Rick. Like Jay, he's one of the most knowledgeable people on the planet about what he does and a pleasure to work with. My gratitude also goes to Charles Rubin for his advice about online marketing and to Sharon Donovan of Conari Press for sharing her excellent publicity materials. To my ace proofreader, assistant and friend Antonia Anderson, a huge thank-you for her help in getting the words right and everything else she does to make our lives better. My deep appreciaton goes to Adele Horwitz and Devra Hall for reviewing the manuscript and making helpful suggestions. Special thanks must also go to Orvel Ray Wilson for all he has done through his books and his seminars to build the guerrilla brand. For their help and support, thanks also go to John and Shannon Tullius of the Maui Writers Conference, Barnaby and Mary Conrad, Frances Halpern, Margaret Brownley, and Sharon Goldfinger and Robert "Captain Bob" Smith. As always, Ray and Maryanne Larsen and Rita Pomada have been wonderfully supportive. I bow toward you with great gratitude. Last and most, thanks to Elizabeth, my be-all and end-all. I'll never be able to repay everything that she does for me personally and professionally. Helping her get back to Nice is as close as I can come to it.

RICK

The first thank you goes to my wonderful co-authors Jay and Mike. Working with you has been a joy. I have to acknowledge Mike (Manny) Levine, who founded Planned Television Arts in 1962, and was my mentor and partner for over 18 years. You taught me that work has to be fun and meaningful and then the profits will follow. To my exceptional management team at PTA: Hillary Rivman, David Hahn, David Thalberg and Margaret McAllister. Your professionalism, loyalty and friendship means more to me than you will ever know. To the staff of PTA, you are the best in the business. Thank you to David and Peter Finn, Tony Esposito, Richard Funess and all of my colleagues at Ruder Finn. It is an honor to be part of this amazing company. To my friends Mark Victor Hansen and Jack Canfield. Making the journey with the two of you has been incredible, and your friendship and advice has been invaluable. To Harvey Mackay, for the lessons about networking and for your amazing support. You are in a class of your own. To my mother and father, for keeping me out of the fur business and helping me discover my own destiny. And to my brother Scott, for being such a great golf buddy—because he sometimes lets me win. To my children Adam, Rachel and Stephanie. Watching you grow into fine young individuals is the highlight of my life. And to my wife Robbi—you are my strength.

Table of Contents

Part III
WEAPONS GALORE TO HELP YOU SELL MORE

CHAPTER 12

Weapons Made Possible by Your Ability to Write   148

CHAPTER 13

Weapons Made Possible by Your
Ability to Enlist Allies   162

CHAPTER 14

Weapons That Deliver Free Advertising   174

Part IV
WEAPONS THAT ARE ALL ABOUT YOU

INTRODUCTION

WHY YOU NEED THIS BOOK AND HOW TO GET THE MOST OUT OF IT

 A professional writer is an amateur who didn't quit.
—RICHARD BACH

ONLY YOU

Your passion, your books, your career, your life, your ability to overcome adversity, your willingness to promote your books, and your potential as a writer and a human being are all embodied in one unique individual: you.

ON OUR PREMISES

Guerrilla Marketing for Writers is based on the following premises:
- You want to build a successful career as an author.
- You want to sell your books to a major publisher.
- You know little or nothing about publishing and promotion.
- You want the recognition and rewards you will earn by becoming a successful author.
- You are writing adult fiction or nonfiction or children's books.

Guerrilla marketing is not new, but *Guerrilla Marketing for Writers* is. Authors have been using the techniques in this book, but this is the first time these weapons have been assembled and integrated into a comprehensive approach to selling books both to publishers and book buyers.

Because we are not experts on children's books, we asked Andrea Brown, a literary agent who specializes in children's books, to make sure the ideas in the book can also help authors of children's books. She concluded that while the book will help them, publishers don't expect these writers to have plans as ambitious as those they want to see for adult how-to books with large potential readerships.

We believe that the one hundred weapons in the book can be adapted to help authors promote any kind of book from poetry to textbooks. It will also benefit speakers, consultants and other service-based entrepreneurs.

A WHAT-TO BOOK

You will find practical advice throughout the book. But *Guerrilla Marketing for Writers* isn't a how-to book, it's a what-to book.

The goals of this book are to

- make you aware of how important promotion is to your books and your career
- show you the range of free and low-cost weapons you can use to be a guerrilla marketer and, in turn, make your books successful
- be an enjoyable reading experience

The book has boxed "War Stories" about guerrilla marketing in action. We hope that you will E-mail your experiences on how you are using the weapons in the book and creating new ones. The www.gmarketing.com Web site will share readers' wisdom and war stories. We also share bits of "Guerrilla Intelligence" and "Guerrilla Wisdom" for you to have in your duffel bag when you need them.

Guerrilla Marketing for Writers will help you promote your first book, but its value will grow with every book you write. The more books you write and the more weapons you use, the more powerful guerrilla marketing becomes.

This is why we use the phrase "your books." You'll see the word "your" often because the books you write are yours no matter who publishes them, and we want you to feel pride of ownership for them and accept responsibility for what happens to them.

The best editor, publisher and contract can make an enormous difference in what happens to your books. But ultimately, how well you conceive, write and promote them will be the most important factors determining their fate—long before and forever after the pub date.

ARE YOU FICTION OR NONFICTION?

The longer we worked on the book, the clearer it became that we were shoehorning two books into one. We tried to describe the guerrilla weapons in the order of their importance, keep related weapons together and discuss fiction and nonfiction simultaneously. Not possible.

The information an author shares in a nonfiction book is more important than how the book gets written. Does it make sense for a retired doctor who has only a memoir in him to go through the long apprenticeship required to become a professional writer? Should posterity be denied his wisdom simply because he lacks the skills of a professional writer?

His asset is his experience and his ability to promote his book. How he writes his book is his business. He can use an editor, a collaborator or a ghostwriter.

However, the essential element of fiction is also what makes it hard to promote: the author's ability to tell a story. Giving readings and discussing their work is important for novelists both for maintaining their relationships with their fans and for making new ones. But the ability of novelists to use style, as well as story, setting and characters to keep their readers turning the pages, is more important than their ability to talk.

For writers of how-to books with national appeal, the commitment to travel around the country giving talks and selling books is usually essential if they want to sell their books to New York publishers.

If you want to see how different the lists for fiction and nonfiction look when the weapons are listed in order of importance, please see appendix one.

DOLLARS AND SENSE

One of this book's goals is to make sense of your role in promoting your books and to show you how to save money and make it in the process:

- Sixty-three weapons in the book are free.
- Twenty are low cost, meaning either that they cost less than one hundred dollars or they cost only as much as you can afford to spend on them before you use a substitute.

  For example, over time, printing and mailing your media kit will cost more than one hundred dollars. However, you can spend only what your budget allows and E-mail just your news releases when you exhaust your budget.
- Seven weapons in the book are expensive, so you will have to use your "guerrilla greenbacks" (see page 81), your ingenuity or your patience until you can afford them.
- Twelve weapons can help you earn a living. If, for example, you can build your speaking career well enough, you won't have to worry about royalties.

THINKING LIKE A GUERRILLA

Chapter six discusses "minting" a new form of currency, guerrilla greenbacks, to help you minimize expenses. But until you write your breakout book, you will have to take Theodore Roosevelt's advice to "do what you can with what you have where you are."

Even if your promotional budget is limitless, you still don't want to waste money, and you still want your promotional campaign to have maximum impact. Whatever the size of your budget, this book will help you get the biggest bang for your buck.

One goal of your promotion plan is to convince potential publishers of your commitment to your books. But you also need to prove that you're a professional who knows what you're doing.

The most important thing this book can do for you is hidden between the lines: inspiring you to think like an entrepreneur. Don't think like a writer who has something to say; think like an author who has a lifetime of books, products and services to sell—a writer who knows what it takes to make books sell and will be totally committed to doing it. Then you will be a guerrilla marketer.

Hundreds of thousands of entrepreneurs around the world, who started businesses of all kinds with more hope, commitment and ability than experience, have adapted the weapons in this book to make their businesses succeed.

We are confident that if you follow our advice with all of your books, using more weapons as you go along, your profits will repay the cost of this book thousands of times over. We're counting on you to prove we're right (so you won't take us up on the money-back guarantee on page 147!). Welcome to the guerrilla family.

GETTING WHAT YOU NEED ASAP

Like you, your books are unique. So how can you find what you need from this book as quickly as possible? Here are six suggestions that may help you:

- Read the book, checking off the weapons you can use.
- Skim the book to get an idea of what the weapons are.
- Go through the table of contents to see which weapons you think you can use and read those first.
- Forget about logic and read the weapons in any order you wish.
- Pick the weapons you want to use in your promotion plan, then devise a strategy for promoting your book following the advice in chapter six.
- Visit www.gmarketing.com if you have questions or suggestions for the next edition, or if you figure out a faster way to do it. We live to serve!

Part I

GUERRILLA MARKETING: THE RIGHT IDEA AT THE RIGHT TIME

CHAPTER 1

WHY YOU HAVE TO BE A GUERRILLA MARKETER

The book didn't sell because I didn't promote it.
—THE MOST VISIBLE HUMAN BEING ON THE PLANET*

he United States is in the midst of an entrepreneurial explosion, one of the most hopeful signs for the country's future. As a writer, you are an entrepreneur. Every book you write is a separate enterprise with its own fate and its own reckoning that balances income against expenditures. For guerrillas, the only business criterion that counts is profits.

Marketing is anything done to sell a product or service and maintain relationships with the people who make the business possible. Fortune 500 companies spend millions to market their products.

But like most entrepreneurs, authors don't have millions to spend. They have to be guerrilla marketers. They have to use unconventional weapons and tactics that substitute time, energy and imagination for money. That is the essence of guerrilla marketing.

THE DIFFERENCES BETWEEN GORILLAS AND GUERRILLAS

What are the characteristics of guerrilla marketing as opposed to traditional marketing? Guerrilla marketing differs in twelve ways:

---

* President Bill Clinton, author of *Between Hope and History: Meeting America's Challenges for the 21st Century*

1. Traditional marketing uses as big a budget as possible; guerrilla marketing substitutes time, energy and imagination for money.
2. Traditional marketing is geared to big businesses; guerrilla marketing, to owners of small businesses with a big dream but not a big bankroll.
3. Traditional marketing measures effectiveness with sales; guerrilla marketing, with profits.

WAR STORIES

"On October 26, 1809, the *New York Evening Post* carried the following announcement, 'Distressing—Left his lodgings some time since and has not since been heard of, a small, elderly gentleman, dressed in an old black coat and cocked hat, by the name of Knickerbocker.'

Then, two weeks later, an item appeared saying that a man fitting that description had been spotted on a stagecoach heading for Albany. Ten days later, the paper carried a news story that the Columbian Hotel had found a handwritten manuscript he believed to be written by the mysterious Knickerbocker. Seth Handaside, the hotel manager, decided to sell the manuscript in order to settle the bill the elusive boarder had failed to pay.

Months later, the book, a two-volume set, appeared in bookstores (selling for $3), bearing the title *The History of New York*, by Diedrich Knickerbocker. It was a huge success. The author of the book and the elaborate hoax was Washington Irving, who wanted to create a unique publicity campaign for the book and have a little joke on the reader. The name (Died/rich) Knickerbocker was his private joke."

—*The Writer's Home Companion*,
James Charlton and Lisbeth Mark

Jay started teaching guerrilla marketing for the University of California at Berkeley Extension in the seventies, but Washington Irving had perfected it long before him.

4. Traditional marketing is based on experience and then judgment that involves guesswork. Guerrilla marketing is based on psychology—the laws of human behavior that determine buying patterns.

5. Traditional marketing recommends that businesses increase their production and then diversify by offering allied products and services. Guerrilla marketing recommends that you maintain your standard of excellence by focusing on writing your books, and diversify only if you can create synergy that helps sell your books without lowering their quality.

6. Traditional marketing encourages linear growth by adding new customers. Guerrilla marketing also encourages attracting new customers but recommends that you grow your business exponentially by using service and follow-up to create more transactions, larger transactions and referrals from your present customers.

7. Traditional marketing advocates destroying competition; guerrilla marketing urges you to cooperate with competitors and create win-win opportunities with other authors.

8. Traditional marketing believes that one marketing weapon alone can work; guerrilla marketing believes in the synergy created by a combination of weapons.

9. Traditional marketing urges businesses to count their monthly receipts to see how many sales they've made; guerrilla marketing recommends that you count how many relationships you make each month because each relationship can generate many receipts.

10. In the past, traditional marketing didn't encourage using technology because it was too complicated, expensive and limited; guerrilla marketing has always embraced technology because it's simple to use, reasonably priced and limitless in its potential.

11. Traditional marketing identifies a handful of marketing weapons that are relatively costly; guerrilla marketing begins with a base of one hundred weapons, more than half of which are free, and urges you to create others.

12. Traditional marketing intimidates small-business owners because it is enshrouded in mystique and complexity; guerrilla marketing removes the mystique and puts you in control.

THE FIFTEEN MOST IMPORTANT MARKETING SECRETS

I have no fans. You know what I got? Customers.
—MICKEY SPILLANE

Just by learning the following words ending in *ent*, you will be 80 percent of the way to success with your marketing.

You must create your books with the understanding that your promotional efforts can only be as effective as the content of your books enables them to be.

1 Content: Publishers waste millions of dollars a year buying and promoting books that fail.

No amount of money or marketing can overcome a book that doesn't deliver. So your first challenge is to write a book that your networks assure you is as good as you want it to be. The content of your books will determine how you sell them to publishers and promote them to book buyers. Content precedes commerce.

2 Commitment: You must make a commitment to your marketing program.

Talent isn't enough. You need motivation—and persistence, too.
—LEON URIS

Once you decide on the best promotion plan for your books, and your networks agree with you, make the commitment to stick with it.

The only time you can safely stop promoting your books is when you're ready to stop writing them. Before then, commit yourself to **The Rule of Five:** do five things every day to market your books. Think of it this way: a diamond is a piece of coal that stuck to the job.

3 Investment: You must think of marketing as an investment in your future.

Most best-selling authors don't strike gold with their first book. Their sales grow with a succession of books until they write the breakout book that catapults them onto the best-seller list where they stay for the rest of their careers.

Until your promotional efforts pay off and you become a successful author, consider the money you spend on promotion as an investment that will pay for itself many times over.

4 Consistent: Your marketing must be consistent.

You must make your promotion consistent so that, over time, the media and your readers become more receptive to you and your books. One of the weapons in chapter eighteen is the marketing calendar that you will create and tweak as needed every year. But once you're convinced about the most effective way to promote your books, don't change your approach. Make your promotion, like your books, consistently first rate.

Also be consistent about the frequency with which you write your books and when they are published. One book a year is the usual pace.

5 Confident: You must make potential readers confident in you.

Consistency creates familiarity, familiarity builds confidence, and confidence is the most important factor in determining what makes consumers buy. It's more important than quality, selection, price and service.

6 Patient: You must be patient with your marketing.

If you're doing all you can for your books, take two more steps:
- Follow up on your efforts.
- Have patience with your promotion plan, the sales of your books and the development of your career.

7 Assortment: You must use an assortment of weapons to ensure the success of your marketing.

Small businesses shouldn't try to use all the weapons in their arsenals at once, but should unleash them over time with a well thought-out plan.

Unfortunately, this is a luxury writers don't have. Unless publishers make a commitment to a book, they test-market it with the first printing. To sustain your publisher's belief in your book's future, you have to create maximum promotional firepower for it during the crucial four-to-six-week launch window when it's published.

Firing as many weapons as you can integrate effectively into your plan is the best way to accomplish this. If your book doesn't gain momentum fast enough, your publisher will give up on it and go on to other books.

Make it your goal to use at least sixty weapons. The wider the assortment of weapons you use, the wider the grin on your face will be when your royalty check arrives. However, if you can't use a weapon effectively, don't use it at all.

A Web site alone will not make your books successful, nor will a media kit. Regard every weapon as 1 percent of your promotion plan. The best way to guarantee the success of your books is to use as many weapons as you can.

The more weapons you unleash on publication and the more completely you integrate them, the more powerful each of them becomes. Unity and variety are two of the keys to victory in the publishing wars. The bigger your arsenal, the greater your victories.

A bookseller who was chosen to receive the *Publishers Weekly* Bookseller of the Year award was using seventy-four guerrilla marketing weapons (and he was still trying to figure out how to use the other twenty-six!).

8 Subsequent: You must base your promotion on the belief that real profits come subsequent to the sale.
The difference between guerrilla marketers and unenlightened authors is that the latter think promotion is over when someone buys their book. The reality is that 80 percent of lost business is lost because of apathy after the sale.

A sale is either part of a never-ending circle of business and communication with a reader, or it is a straight line heading out of your life in the direction of chapter eleven.

Guerrillas know that the sale of their books to new readers is only the end of the beginning. They understand the immense potential value of every reader, so their goal is to create customers for life. Guerrilla marketing is based on the belief that the customer is everything, the sale only chump change.

If readers like your first book, they may create an endless circle that they complete every time they buy something you offer. What your readers buy after reading the first book is what will produce the greatest profits for you.

9 Convenient: You must run your business so it is convenient for those you serve.

Convenience is an advantage you have over the CEOs of the Fortune 500. Thanks to technology, the CEO of your enterprise can be accessible to the people you need and who need you: your editor, your publicist, the media, speaking bureaus and the rest of your professional networks—and most important, your fans.

You need all the allies you can find in your quest for success. To benefit from their help, you must make it convenient for them to reach you.

Knowing that they can always reach you fast will be an incentive for people to call you instead of competitors. When your business grows big enough, you will have someone filtering your communications, so you receive only those calls which only you can respond to.

GUERRILLA WISDOM

Life, like art, consists in drawing a line somewhere. Don't fall prey to a hazard of working at home by sacrificing your personal life or your leisure time for the sake of availability. Set hours that are convenient for you and the people who want to reach you, and except for emergencies, stick to them.

10 Amazement: Put an element of amazement in your marketing.

Your marketing has to communicate what will most excite potential readers about you and your book. You can use what excites you about your books and what they can do for your readers.

Make the Amazement Factor one criterion for choosing ideas to write about. What can you use in promoting your books that will amaze book buyers? Guerrilla publicist Jill Lublin calls this "The Ooh-aah Factor."

What amazes us about guerrilla marketing for authors is that there are so many ways for you to promote your books, and most of them are either free or you can get paid for using them. You can get paid for promoting your books by giving seminars, you get paid again for selling your books at your seminars, and then you get paid royalties for the books you sell! Ah, the joys of working for yourself!

And the technology you need to build and run your business keeps getting more powerful and less expensive. If you use technology creatively and effectively, it's like riding a rocket instead of a turtle to reach your goals.

11 Measurement: You must use measurement to judge the effectiveness of your weapons.

If you do a publicity tour, you can measure its effectiveness by how many media interviews you had, how important they were, the responses of your live audiences and how your efforts affected sales.

When you are creating the promotion plans for your books, establish how you will measure the effectiveness of your weapons. At the end of the year, you will use this information to help you set up your promotion calendar. A preview: eliminate what fails and double up on what works.

12 Involvement: Create and sustain involvement between you and your readers.

If readers love your first book, you have the opportunity to make them lifetime fans of your work and your related products and services. Guerrillas know that it costs six times more to attract new fans than it does to sell to satisfied readers. So when you add new readers to your network of fans, do whatever you can to enlist them in your publishing network for life.

The real payoff from readers only comes if you can make them lifetime fans who

- buy all of your books for themselves and their friends and tell everyone

they know that they must read them
- come to all of your talks and book-signings
- can't wait to purchase whatever you create

You can't pay someone to do that. It can only happen because of their passion for your books and their pleasure at being involved with you and your career. Your Web site is the perfect weapon for staying involved with your readers and they with you.

Every time new readers buy one of your books, they are investing in you. If they invest the time to read your book and like it, you have the opportunity to invest your time in them and start an enduring relationship.

Use your biography or a page in the back of the book to invite them to become involved with you as a member of your literary community by
- attending your talks
- contacting you at your Web site
- writing you at the address in your books
- calling you at the (preferably toll-free) phone number in your books

You can show your involvement with your fans by being cordial when you contact them, by being helpful to them, and by asking about them.

GUERRILLA TACTICS
Keep a list of all of the places your contact information appears online and offline so if any of it changes, you'll know where to send the new information.

13 Dependent: Learn to be dependent on other businesses and encourage them to be dependent on you.

It may seem paradoxical for you to be an independent entrepreneur but remain dependent on others for the success of your business. But you depend on your suppliers, including your publisher, as they depend on you for something to sell.

You and your readers depend on each other. They depend on you to provide them with good reading and the related products and services you offer. You depend on them for the profits they generate. Guerrillas thrive on the power of teamwork and win-win dependencies that enable everyone to achieve their goals.

14 Armament: You must have the armament of guerrillas–the technology and the skills needed to promote your work.
The growing sophistication of laptops, pagers, cell phones, toll-free numbers, fax machines and Web sites enables you to take your office with you, so you can work and communicate around the globe. When wireless satellite transmission is perfected, you will be able to reach anyone, anywhere.

The electronic miracles that keep tumbling out of our high-tech centers will continue to provide you with the arsenal of a twenty-first-century guerrilla.

15 Consent: You must gain the consent of those to whom you want to market.
A guerrilla who operates a camp in New York runs small ads in camp directories and in the classified sections of many magazines. She also takes booths at trade shows. She doesn't sell anything, she just offers a free video. The video doesn't sell anything either; it just asks for a personal visit.

It's at the visit that she sells the camp to the parents, not only for their children, but for relatives and classmates. Gaining consent minimizes her marketing costs and maximizes her profits.

By being a source of information or entertainment through your books, talks and Web site, you are gaining consent to market to your readers and audiences.

WHY ONE EQUALS FOUR

Every business is four businesses:
- an enterprise that creates a product or service
- a marketing business that sells what it produces

THE GUERRILLA MARKETING HALL OF FAME

Besides being dedicated guerrillas, the following people are sources of information and inspiration to writers. Their ideas and can-do spirit made their way into this book. They inspire writers to launch their careers. Because of their willingness to help writers, they will have a lasting, positive impact on publishing. If you are writing publishable books and you supplement this book with their advice, we guarantee your books will succeed.

We are delighted to give well-earned recognition to:

- Jack Canfield and Mark Victor Hansen, coauthors of the Chicken Soup series. They set the standard for what authors can achieve starting with nothing but their goals, creativity, commitment, speaking ability, willingness to ask for what they want, and a book that delivers.
- Tom and Marilyn Ross, cofounders of the Small Publishers Association of North America and coauthors of *The Complete Guide to Self-Publishing* and *Jump Start Your Book Sales.*
- Jerrold Jenkins of the Jenkins Group, publisher of *Independent Publisher* and coauthor of both *Publish to Win* and *Inside the Bestsellers.*
- John Kremer of Open Horizons, editor in chief of *Book Marketing Update* and author of *1001 Ways to Market Your Books.*
- Jan and Terry Nathan, executive and assistant directors of Publishers Marketing Association, sponsor of PMA's Publishing University.
- Dan Poynter of Para Publishing, author of *The Self-Publishing Manual.*

- a service business that understands that service is whatever customers want it to be
- a people business that makes the first three possible

The larger the business, the harder it is to establish and maintain personal relationships with customers, suppliers and employees. Although they may be poor in capital, guerrillas can be rich in human capital through their relationships with the people in their networks.

One advantage you have over big businesses is that you can establish and maintain warm personal relationships, online and offline, with your readers and other allies in your assault on the citadel of fame and fortune. In the age of multinational conglomerates, consumers appreciate more than ever relationships with businesses that provide them with impeccable service and personal involvement.

According to Amazon.com founder Jeff Bezos, one of Amazon's goals is to be the world's most "customer-centric" company. They want to establish relationships with customers that are so satisfying customers won't be tempted to start from scratch and build relationships with competitors. For a guerrilla author, being the world's most reader-centric writer is a worthy goal.

Although guerrilla marketers are committed to the success of their businesses, they value people more than sales. They pursue their goals ethically and whenever possible, by providing more than what they promise.

THE REAL DOUGH IS OUTSIDE OF THE COOKIE CUTTER

Your creativity—your ability to use your imagination to create new ways to promote your books—will impress publishers because they show little creativity when they promote their books.

Large houses publish hundreds of books a year, so they can't devote enough time or money to creating the most effective marketing campaigns for every book they publish. Even the big books that receive far more attention than the rest of the list are victims of the cookie-cutter syndrome. As each book winds its way through the publishing maze, it is granted the time and attention warranted by its importance to the list.

You and your publisher will have identical interests but not identical agendas. You both want to make money on your book, but your book will only be one of the hundreds of books a large house publishes. They have to pay attention to the whole list; you don't.

If yours is one of the few big books on your publisher's list, your book will be looked after as well as possible given your publisher's time, money and creative limitations.

Authors, like their publishers, are prisoners of the system. The publication of any book is a complex enterprise that, at a large house, involves the fleeting attention of more than a hundred people as the book passes before them on the conveyor belt that connects writers at one end of the publishing process with readers at the other.

Publishers publish far too many books to do all of them justice even if they wanted to. The skill, creativity and commitment with which books are published vary enormously depending on how much love or money or both motivate the publishers and their overworked, underpaid staff. The result: cookie-cutter publishing.

Limited by time and money, publishers fall back on the old standbys. Trade promotion precedes consumer promotion to book buyers. Four common tools for trade promotion are

- publishers' catalogs in which big books take up two pages and little ones take up a page or half-page
- trade advertising in *Publisher's Weekly*, which for most hardcover and trade paperback books consists of being part of a list ad that includes all of the books published during one of large houses' three four-month-long seasons (This is all the advertising most books receive.)
- for the books with enough potential, sending ARCs (advanced reading copies with a letter from the publisher on the first page and the promotion plan on the back cover) to booksellers, key media people and subsidiary rights buyers (If it's a fall book, the publisher may give copies away at Book Expo America (BEA), the annual booksellers' convention.)
- inclusion on the house's Web site, which promotes books to the trade

Some publishers are experimenting with a creative innovation: pre-publication tours for their most promising novelists so they can meet reviewers and booksellers.

Publishers' catalogs are free on request. They're also in your library. When you go through them, you will see the same kinds of consumer promotion techniques again for a house's big books over and over:

- ads in *The New York Times, USA Today* and, perhaps, in book-review sections in major markets, possibly supplemented by follow-up ads
- tours of major markets
- satellite tours in which authors give five-minute print, radio or television interviews to media around the country

• making authors available on publishers' Web sites

The more publishers have invested in a book, financially or emotionally, the more they will try to design a promotion campaign tailored to the book. But they usually fall back on tried-and-true techniques.

Large publishers spend $25,000 or less to acquire most of their books. This doesn't give them a financial incentive to promote them. So unless they love a book or think they can build it over time, the fate of the book is in the hands of the author.

Apart from the big books for which publishers pull out all the stops, a list will include books that publishers think have best-seller potential but for which they don't have the necessary ammunition to position as big books. However, pre-publication reviews, sub-rights sales and in-house passion can convince them that the books can be built over time, so publishers will try to build these books by

• sending ARCs to the media and booksellers
• starting with printings of 25,000 to 35,000 copies
• taking small ads with quotes that rave about the books
• waiting for reviews and early word-of-mouth that will justify their faith in the books
• perhaps sending the author on a short tour

The *The Bridges of Madison County, Snow Falling on Cedars, Emotional Intelligence* and *Angela's Ashes* began their ascent to best-sellerdom this way.

Unless a publisher pays a fortune for your book, a promotion plan that convinces the publisher about your ability to devise and carry out creative, economical and effective ideas for reaching your potential readers will impress them. The more impressed they are, the more willing they may be to help you carry out your plans.

The long-term payoff: everything you do to promote your books also helps sell you, your future books and all of the products and services that you will have to offer.

 The future belongs to those who see possibilities before they become obvious.

—THEODORE LEVITT, AUTHOR

GUERRILLA TACTICS

Six facets of thinking like a guerrilla:

- Think new. Try to come up with fresh ideas that haven't been done before. People like to try new things. New ideas can excite people more than ideas that have been done before even if they were successful. If you and your networks can't dream up something new, use your creativity (discussed in chapter five) to give old ideas a new twist.

- Think inclusively. Create ways to bring people together in a way so enjoyable they will tell friends about it before and after the event.

- Think big. Look at the promotional opportunities your books create with the same breadth of vision you use to look at your books: in the largest possible way. Then pare your ideas down to what you can accomplish. Promotion, like politics, is the art of the possible.

- Think ideas through. Balance the time and energy you need to execute ideas against the potential gain in sales and publicity.

- Think of a way out. Set benchmarks in time and energy to see if you're making the progress you need to make an idea worth implementing. If in the course of trying to follow through on an idea, you become convinced that the payoff won't justify the effort, let it go and move on to the next idea.

- Think of ways to be a giving enterprise, not just a taking one. Make a virtue of commerce by helping your community while you promote your book. Schools, libraries and charities always welcome help raising funds. You will feel better about your efforts, and so will others involved with them. And the media are more likely to cover a charity event than a purely commercial one.

One reason now is such a great time to be a writer is that you can use the books you love and the authors you admire as models for creating your books and your career.

You can bring your vision, passion and creativity to promotion, your unique ability to do the same things differently and better than they've been done before. One way to know you're succeeding: other authors use your ideas.

Guerrilla marketing can do for you and your books what it does for

GUERRILLA WISDOM

I will study and get ready and some day my chance will come.
—ABRAHAM LINCOLN

The more skills and interests you have, the more possibilities they will create for promoting your books. So develop your skills, knowledge and creativity as much as you can in as many fields as you can. They will serve you well.

hundreds of thousands of diverse businesses around the world. How much it helps you and your books depends on how closely you follow this advice:

The Guerrilla Writer's Marketing Commandments
1. Create books, products and services that you can market with pride and passion.
2. Remember that you are in the service of your ideas, your books and your readers.
3. Establish an annual marketing budget that reflects your belief in the importance of marketing and enables you to carry out your promotion plan.
4. Devote the same time, energy and imagination to promoting your books every day that you devoted to writing them.
5. Foster and sustain warm, giving relationships with your networks.
6. Maintain the perspective of a one-person multimedia, multinational conglomerate when you make decisions about writing and promoting your books.
7. Be a lifelong learner in your field and in learning to market your business so you remain competitive.
8. Use state-of-the-art techniques and technology to serve your readers better.
9. Recommend competitors' books if they will meet readers' needs in ways that yours don't.
10. Practice "co-opetition" by seeking ways to benefit from collaborating with your competitors.

11. Make your marketing efforts creative and consistent enough to position yourself as one of the top authors in your field.
12. Welcome change as an opportunity to find ideas and improve your business and your life.
13. Make selling your books to new readers the start of a lifelong relationship.
14. Encourage readers to contact you, and regard this as an opportunity to serve them, to help attract new readers through word of mouth and to publicize everything you can offer them.
15. Welcome the chance to say thank you and reward those who help you.
16. Let your decisions reflect harmonious short- and long-term personal and professional goals that make you eager to get up in the morning.
17. Ask the people involved with your books and your business to help you keep these commandments.
18. Strive to create harmony between what you think, say and do, without crossing the line between being righteous and self-righteous.

Add your own commandments to this list, and share them with us so we can add them to the list. Good luck!

CHAPTER 2

A WRITER'S GUIDE TO AN INDUSTRY ON THE EDGE OF TOMORROW

 Our earth is degenerate in these latter days; there are signs that the world is speedily coming to an end; bribery and corruption are common; children no longer obey their parents; every man wants to write a book; indeed, the end of the world is approaching.

—AN ASSYRIAN INSCRIPTION, 1500 BC

Humanity now publishes as many words every week as it did in all human history up to 1800.

—THE NEW YORK TIMES, 1993

ichael Korda believes that "Book publishing, like any other business, needs to be shaken by a revolution from time to time." The four most momentous revolutions in the history of human communication are the invention of speech, the invention of writing, Gutenberg's invention of movable type in the fifteenth century and the creation of computers in the twentieth.

You are writing books, getting them published and promoting them while publishing is in the throes of the most profound yet promising upheaval in its two-hundred-year history. Experts predict that business will change more in the next five years than it has in the last five hundred.

TRANSFORMING ONES AND ZEROS INTO DOLLARS

 The New Yorker once ran a cartoon showing a computer talking to its owner and saying, "I can be upgraded. Can you?"

Now is an amazing time to be alive. Capitalism, competition, consolidation, technology and the globalization of culture and commerce are accelerating the transformation of civilization.

We are on a wildly exhilarating ride into an impossible-to-predict future. Nobody's in charge of the vessel, and no one knows where it's going, so hang on tight and enjoy the ride.

Here's part of the significance of technology to you:

- Technology is reinventing publishing. It
    — has all but ended the physical drudgery of writing—voice-recognition software enables you to dictate your books into your computer or a microcassette recorder, which then dictates them into your computer
    — offers new ways for you to generate income and publicity for you and your books
    — is creating new options for publishers, booksellers and you to sell your books by downloading them into e-books and other handheld devices, and by making them available online and through print-on-demand technology
    — can multiply your productivity and effectiveness as a writer and a guerrilla (You can use your computer for teaching, communicating with your readers and the rest of your networks, researching your books and the competition, checking on your books' sales, selling them yourself, and of course, promotion.)
    — enables you to collaborate with other writers and your editor as well as connect you with your fans around the world; connections beget profits
    — is vastly enlarging the possibilities for using an essential weapon that only you possess: your creativity
    — is moving books off bookstore shelves where they often languish and onto digital shelves where they can remain indefinitely until they are needed

- Technology has collapsed time and distance. Business goes nonstop around the clock in 180 countries. This globalization is opening new markets for your books and services
- Technology is creating a growing army of powerful marketing weapons, some of which are discussed in chapters eight and ten

Two more points:
- At some point in the first half of this century, it will be possible to put the 17,000,000 documents in the Library of Congress on a disk the size of a sugar cube.
- You are lucky to be writing in English, the principal language of culture and commerce on the net.

In addition to the bounty that technology promises, here are three bottom-line reasons for you to be excited with the changes in the industry:

GUERRILLA TACTICS

Until the day when the high-tech tools you need are as easy to use as your phone, car and refrigerator, you face the challenge of learning about technology.

If you can become an expert on technology, go to it. If not, you need to find a techie you can rely on to
- help you decide what hardware and software will best suit your needs
- install and troubleshoot equipment
- show you how to use the equipment
- advise you when to upgrade your equipment

You may need the help of more than one person, but between your networks and their teenage offspring, you should be able to find the help you need.

Part of what makes the Web so exciting is that we are all inventing it as we go along. Let this freedom inspire you to
- search continually for effective ways to use technology
- not just imitate others, but be better than the best
- strive for continual innovation (Keep improvising unbound by tradition. We look forward to learning about your adventures in cyberspace.)

- The continuing consolidation of the business has triggered an outburst of small new publishers who may offer you the best option for getting your books published.
- The end of the Cold War warmed up China and Eastern Europe as markets for your work. Next up: the Middle East.
- The upside for your books can be far greater than ever. Between royalties and subrights income, if even one of your books wins the best-seller lottery, your share of the profits can reach eight figures.

THE BLADES, NOT THE RAZOR

As technology keeps getting more powerful, it keeps getting less expensive and more accessible to frugal guerrillas. Technology companies understand that the biggest long-term profit is in the blades, not the razor; in using technology, not selling hardware; in the content, not the pipes it goes through. That's why AOL merged with Time Warner.

WHY PUBLISHERS PROMOTE BOOKS

HarperCollins publishes twelve hundred books a year. That's more than three books every day of the year. Can HarperCollins promote all of these books?

Can cows fly?

New writers assume that if publishers buy books, they'll promote them, a reasonable assumption that is usually wrong. Publishers will promote a book if

- they have paid a greater advance than they can afford to lose
- the author's previous book does well enough to convince the house that promotion will enable the next book to do even better
- the agent was able to negotiate a promotion budget
- it has to pump up a book as a lead title to help sell the rest of the season's list
- everyone in the house who reads the book loves it
- editors are passionate enough about it and have enough seniority or a solid enough track record to sway the judgment of the powers that be
- it generates enough subsidiary-rights income to prove its commercial potential

- the book has already been a best-seller in Europe
- the reps go crazy over the book when they read it before the sales conference, where they voice their unbridled enthusiasm
- the reps sell so many more copies than expected that the publisher is convinced the book will be a hit
- the book receives a starred review in *Kirkus Reviews* and a starred, boxed review in *Publishers Weekly* before publication
- Amazon.com sells enough copies before publication to propel the book high enough on its best-seller list to persuade the publisher that the book is worth promoting
- it receives glowing reviews in major markets when it is published
- the timing makes it a potential winner
- a competitive book has done well
- the book hits regional best-seller lists (San Francisco's list is known for being prophetic.)
- new management or a dry spell induces the house to prove it's alive and kicking

It usually takes several of these justifications to prod publishers to promote a book. For more than 95 percent of trade books, none of them happens.

Where does that leave writers?

In need of guerrilla marketing.

FROM THE PUBLIC EYE TO THE PUBLISHING AYE

Michael Korda's *Another Life: A Memoir of Other People* is essential reading if you want to be a successful author. Michael brings the story of publishing in this century to life by telling the saga through a remarkable cast of characters brought to life as only an accomplished novelist can.

He encapsulates the predicament facing self-help and how-to writers who want to be published by a big house:

By the end of the Sixties, the decision about whether to buy certain kinds of books—self-help titles, diet books, exercise books, and so on—was being made on the basis of the author's appearance, telegenic appeal, and ability to get his or her points across convincingly on-screen, and authors in these categories were soon to find that a videocassette of their performance on television weighed more heavily with the publisher than an outline of their ideas. Charm, [a] smile, appearance, energy, the ability to sell while looking natural and to sum up a whole book in a sentence or two became all-important in publishing certain categories of books, favoring those authors who were natural salespeople.

Those authors already in the public eye—whether actors or politicians—are usually astute at promoting their books, since it's just an extension of what they normally do every day.

This is part of the reason agents reject close to 100 percent of the thousands of submissions they see a year. Rejecting books is easier than ever. Like editors, agents only read far enough to decide if they can sell a book to a major house or love it so much it doesn't matter.

Your agent will make sure that your work is as close to perfect as you can make it before it is submitted. Your agent will know where to send your book, but it is the quality and commerciality of your proposal or manuscript that will determine the editor, publisher and deal for your book.

What publishers pay for books usually determines how they publish them. So what you submit must be flawless, because if anyone on the editorial board that makes the house's buying decisions can think of a reason to say no to a book, it's toast.

One reason now is a fabulous time for you to write books is the wealth of opportunities for having your books published, including

- a large New York house or a medium-sized publisher in or out of New York (*Guerrilla Marketing for Writers* is predicated on the notion that this is your first choice.)
- a small press
- a niche or specialty publisher
- a university press
- self-publishing
- publishing or self-publishing online
- publishing books as e-books

- using print-on-demand technology to print your books when buyers request them

If a big house doesn't publish your book, but the book succeeds anyway, agents and publishers will come eagerly looking for you or your publisher.

THE SIX SISTERS

 The only major difference between the movie business and the book business by [the 1970s] was that in the book business the numbers were smaller.
—MICHAEL KORDA

Most industries in the United States are controlled by less than ten conglomerates. As we're writing this, six global multimedia, multinational conglomerates dominate English-language trade publishing:

- AOL Time Warner, which owns Warner Books and Little Brown
- Bertalsmann AG (Germany), owner of Random House, which includes Knopf, Ballantine, Crown, Pantheon, Vintage, Bantam Dell, Broadway Doubleday, Villard and the Literary Guild
- Rupert Murdoch's News Corporation, which owns HarperCollins, Avon and William Morrow
- Pearson, Penguin (United Kingdom), owner of Penguin Viking, Putnam, Berkley, Signet, Plume and Dutton
- Viacom, which owns Simon & Schuster and Pocket Books (but according to publishing people, not for long)
- Dieter Von Holtzbrinck (Germany), which owns Henry Holt, St. Martin's Press and Farrar, Straus & Giroux

Although not as large as these publishers, Hyperion, which is owned by Disney, is also a major player because of its strength in other media.

The profits from the trade publishing divisions of these conglomerates, four of which are foreign-owned, contribute less than 50 percent of their overall earnings.

Large publishers are prisoners of the system they helped create. They are subservient to Amazon, Barnes & Noble and Borders, the superstore chains who wield more power than publishers. Publishers are also at the mercy of the competitive pressures for which they are partially responsible.

The publicly owned conglomerates also need to placate stockholders with ever-growing dividends, or somebody's head will roll. Business is war by other means. That's why you must be a guerrilla marketer.

The Six Sisters conglomerates are vertically and horizontally "integrated," a six-dollar way of saying that their goal is to create, produce and distribute in as many media and in as many countries as possible.

AOL Time Warner can take an idea and have

- the hardcover published by Little Brown
- the book selected by the Book of the Month Club
- the movie produced and distributed by Warner Bros.
- the soundtrack released by Warner Music
- the mass-market edition published by Warner Books
- the movie shown on HBO
- the book and its subsidiary rights reviewed and promoted in Time magazine and on AOL

An idea can be recycled in all of these media without ever leaving the shelter of AOL Time Warner's corporate umbrella. Because a books' subsidiary rights sales can make the difference between profit and loss on a book, your books' subsidiary-rights potential will affect what publishers offer for it. It's Fat City for best-selling authors like Stephen King, who splits the profits on his books fifty-fifty with Scribner; and Tom Clancy, who inked a $98,000,000 deal with Penguin Putnam.

Consolidation has affected bookselling even more than publishing. An editor at a medium-sized New York house reported that it's easy for his company to track sales because four accounts—Ingram, Amazon, Borders and Barnes & Noble—are responsible for 85 percent of the house's sales. Barnes & Noble alone sells more books than all his independent booksellers combined.

Mass-market sales have stagnated in part because of cover prices but also because of the consolidation of IDs—independent distributors who stock non-bookseller retailers with magazines and mass-market books. In the late sixties, there were 450 IDs; at this writing, fewer than fifty remain. A larger percentage of shelf space is being used for fewer titles by well-known authors. The declining number of independent bookstores is also hurting mass-market sales.

Technology has also affected the two largest book clubs. The clubs arose because millions of readers around the country didn't have local booksellers. Online booksellers solved that problem. The Literary Guild and the Book of the Month Club solved the resulting problem of declining memberships by merging operations.

WAR STORIES

To illustrate how important brand names are for fiction, consider Stephen King. After he became a best-selling author, his publisher raided his closet for other books to sell. The publisher wanted to distinguish between what was unearthed and the new books King was writing, so they resorted to using the pseudonym Richard Bachman. The books failed. It wasn't until the publisher started adding the phrase "Stephen King writing as" in small type on the covers that the older books started to sell.

SCALING THE WALLS OF FORTRESS NEW YORK

Anybody in this business who is right more than 50 percent of the time is a genius.

—FORMER SIMON & SCHUSTER PRESIDENT RICHARD SNYDER

If you haven't yet read Scott Berg's wonderful book, *Max Perkins, Editor of Genius*, you have a treat in store. Back in the twenties, thirties and forties, publishing was small potatoes. In those simpler days when publishing was a "gentleman's profession," Max Perkins fulfilled the traditional role of an editor: nurturing promising new writers.

Few authors make the best-seller list the first or second time out. But back then, Max Perkins could work with writers like F. Scott Fitzgerald, Ernest Hemingway and Thomas Wolfe until they became successful.

Today, the overhead in midtown Manhattan forces publishers to be more selective about the writers they gamble on. The books of the authors they do take on have to improve in quality and sales every time out. If the books don't deliver, the authors will need either a new publisher or maybe a new name.

First-time novelists whose work disappears without a trace may resort to pseudonyms to get a second chance to be a promising first novelist. Nonetheless, selling an author's first novel may be easier than selling the second one, which has to prove that the first book wasn't a fluke.

New writers determined to be published by major publishers must scale the walls of Fortress New York, a confining, provincial, high-pressure environment whose inhabitants share the same mindset. Editors remain eager to find good books; what has escalated is the difficulty of getting books that lack enough commercial appeal past the number crunchers.

Big houses publish fiction and nonfiction on whatever subjects they think will sell. But because of their long lists, the major houses are less able to fulfill their traditional role of nuturing new writers while building an audience for their work. So if the market for your book isn't big enough, or if you feel that your ability to promote it won't excite the behemoths in the Big Apple, choose an alternative.

Small presses can indulge in the luxury of yielding to their passion for books without great sales potential. With their lower overheads, small publishers can make a profit by selling as few as 3,000 copies.

Because they don't publish many books, small presses must make every book count. Your book may fare better as the lead book at a small house than as one of 740 published by St. Martin's Press. A small press will also give you a greater opportunity to be involved in the publishing process.

PUBLISHED ONCE, SOLD FOREVER AFTER

 Successfully articulating the publication of a big book is the test of good publishing, involving the ability to keep in one's head not only the numbers and their daily fluctuation but the harmonious synchronizing of publicity, manufacturing, advertising, and sales—departments often run as independent fiefdoms.

—MICHAEL KORDA

As publishers shepherd books from writers to readers, they face the challenge of sustaining the enthusiasm of the editors who convinced the house to buy the books. Your book will be sold many times as it makes its way to your readers.

- You are the first person to sell your book. First you sell yourself on the idea for it.
- Then you pitch the idea to your professional networks for feedback.
- Then, assuming you want an agent, you send your proposal or manuscript to prospective agents.
- Your agent sells your book to a publisher.
- To buy your book, editors must first sell them to others in the house whose support they need.
- The editors use that support to sell your book at the house's weekly editorial meetings. Depending on the makeup of the editorial board, your editor may need to convince the house's publicity people, sales and marketing staff and executive officers to take a chance on your book.
- Your editor meets with the sales and marketing departments to decide on the size of the first printing and the marketing plan that will be presented at sales conference and in the catalog.
- Your editor presents your book to the publisher's sales rep at a sales conference. This may be done via audio- or videocassette to save the cost of bringing the reps and in-house staff together.
- The sales reps return to their territories and use the publisher's catalogs to sell your book to independent booksellers. Special reps sell to the chains, the two largest wholesalers—Ingram and Baker & Taylor—and other large customers.
- Pre-publication reviews in periodicals such as *Publishers Weekly*, *Library Journal* and the *Kirkus Reviews* sell your book to libraries.
- The art director decides how best to create your book's hardcover jacket or paperback cover to sell your book to bookstore browsers.
- The production department creates or farms out the design of the interior of your book. The goal is to come up with the most effective design, paper stock and typeface for selling your book.
- The subsidiary rights department tries to sell the publisher's subsidiary rights, such as book clubs, first- and second-serial rights, and film and foreign rights. If your agent has retained any of these rights

for you, your agent, usually helped by co-agents, will try to sell them.

- The publicity department decides how they will publicize your book to the media, which helps to sell your book to the public.

- When your book is published, booksellers sell it to their customers. Where your books are stocked in bookstores and whether they're shelved face-out or spine-out makes a big difference. Independent booksellers use shelf-talkers—handwritten notes taped to the shelf below the book—to push the staff's favorite books.

- For literary books, especially novels, the eagerness of independent booksellers to hand-sell books can make the difference between a failure and a best-seller. Competition from the chains and online booksellers is destroying this path to success by putting independents out of business at the rate of three a week.

- The first group of readers reads your book, and if they love it as passionately as you want them to, they sell everyone they know on reading it. Through the comments they write for online booksellers, your readers can also help sell your books online.

The ultimate challenge your book faces is arousing enough passion in your readers that their recommendations cause whoever hears them to buy your book, swelling the size of your unofficial but unstoppable word-of-mouth sales force.

Best-selling authors have an army of such readers. That's why they're best-selling authors. The most clever, heavily financed promotion campaign can't make a book sell if it doesn't provide the benefit—whether it's information or entertainment—that book buyers expect.

If your books don't require revisions, you only have to write them once. But because of the endless book chain between you and your readers, your books will continue to be sold.

Even after books go out of print, libraries continue to lend them, and used bookstores and online booksellers continue sell them. Print-on-demand publishing will continue to make books available around the world until a better technology comes along.

GUERRILLA INTELLIGENCE

An editorial assistant once resigned from Henry Holt & Co. because he found he could make more money as a bicycle messenger. But despite publishing's starvation wages, an endless stream of young people armed with B.A. degrees and a love of books continue to flock to the Big Apple to get jobs at the big houses. One of the reasons publishing is the best business to be in is that it is a labor of love. People work in publishing because they love books. Agents, editors, publicists and bookstore clerks surrender their dreams of becoming rich and famous and dedicate themselves to the next best thing: working with books. Being involved with books out of desire rather than necessity creates a spirit of community that creates a bond between book people.

MINIMIZING RETURNS

To minimize returns and avoid over-printing and inventory taxes on unsold books sitting in warehouses, big houses are minimizing first printings and going back to press if they need more books. Since they can reprint a book in a week or two, they prefer to avoid big initial printings and key future printings to a book's velocity, the rate at which it's selling.

So unless you have a strong track record or publishers have spent so much money on your book that they must go all-out to promote it, they will do a conservative first printing and hope enough momentum for the book develops to justify going back to press.

All authors and media compete for the same prize: owning people's eyeballs. If you can keep your readers' eyes glued to your books instead of focusing on the growing number of alternatives, your future is assured.

Part II

WEAPONS THAT MAKE YOU A GUERRILLA

CHAPTER 3

THE MOST POWERFUL WEAPONS IN YOUR ARSENAL

Hype springs eternal in every publisher's breast.

—COLIN HAYCROFT

Publishing is a people business. That's why the first three guerrilla weapons are about people. As an author, you are the most important person in the process. That's why you come first. You have to assemble an army of allies who will help you launch your book so it blasts through the competitive static that prevents you from connecting with potential readers.

The most valuable way networks can help you is by giving your books irresistible word-of-mouth praise to everyone they know. The more promotion you do, the more opportunities you create for your books and your networks to help you.

This chapter covers the four most powerful weapons in your arsenal:

- The Most Powerful Guerrilla Marketing Weapon: *You*
- Your Books (Expensive)
- Your Networks (Low cost)
- Word of Mouth (Free)

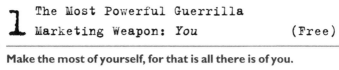

1 The Most Powerful Guerrilla Marketing Weapon: *You* (Free)

Make the most of yourself, for that is all there is of you.

—RALPH WALDO EMERSON

According to *Publishers Weekly* editorial director John Baker, about thirty thousand trade books are published a year—books that are sold through bookstores. Each book is a unique combination of author, text, title, cover, price, format, agent, editor, publisher, publicist, timing, promotion and luck.

Regardless of how much competition you face, your books will have at least one unique advantage: you. You are the most powerful guerrilla marketing weapon in your arsenal. The future of your books and your career depends on

- your ability to write and talk
- your passion for writing and promotion
- your commitment to your career
- your creativity in writing and promoting your books
- your ability to make your books, your promotion and your identity unique
- your ability to create an authentic identity that enables you to present yourself as the embodiment of your ideas
- your capacity for building and maintaining relationships with an ever-growing army of fans, professionals in your field and allies in publishing and the media
- your willingness to spend the rest of your life on sentry duty seeking and seizing opportunities for writing, speaking, promoting your work and creating new products and services
- your tactical flair for integrating your weapons and using as many of them simultaneously as you can
- your ability to overcome problems and bounce back from setbacks

Glancing at the table of contents will show you that most of the weapons in this book are free. You aren't one of them. Guerrillas know that time is more important than money. All but a relatively few lucky writers have to work to support their writing habit.

Even though you may not be able to assign a number to how much income you are giving up to work on your books, it may add up to more than what you earn from them, especially at the beginning of your career.

In any case, you face the never-ending challenge of using your time and talent as productively as you can. The fate of your books and your career is in your hands, which is the best place for it. The goal of this book is to show you how promotion will help you build the career you want, book by book.

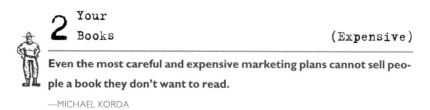

2 Your Books (Expensive)

Even the most careful and expensive marketing plans cannot sell people a book they don't want to read.
—MICHAEL KORDA

Your books are second only to you in importance. Readers will only keep buying your books and tell everyone they know to read them if your books deliver. The most effective and costly campaign imaginable cannot overcome a bad book.

But if your books are as good as you want them to be, they will be excellent calling cards. Only meeting people in person can be more impressive. Books make excellent calling cards. They are an impressive way to introduce yourself to anyone and instantly prove your *author*ity. The more successful your books are, the greater the entree they will create for you.

Your books will help you obtain
- speaking engagements in your field and at writers' conferences
- writing and editing assignments
- trade and consumer publicity in print, broadcast and electronic media
- teaching positions, online and off
- the opportunity to write other books on the subject
- free vacations in exchange for giving talks
- good PR when you use your books for raffle prizes or fundraisers

We will add to this list on our Web site as readers tell us what their books have done for them. Your publisher will have copies of your books sitting in the warehouse, not earning their keep. If you can come up with ideas for using them, try to convince your publisher that the effort will pay off.

3 Your Networks (Free)

The Guerrilla's Golden Rule of Reciprocity:
Ask of others only what you are eager to give in return.

GUERRILLA TACTICS

Unless you or your publisher will make your books available through a print-on-demand system, buy a lifetime supply of your books if you can. Despite assurances in your contract, they may suddenly go out of print without your having the chance to buy copies.

Six Degrees of Separation, a play that became a movie, is based on the premise that we are separated by no more than six people from anyone on the planet.

This was before technology collapsed time and distance. Disintermediation is a fancy way of saying that thanks to the wonders of technology, only E-mail separates you from Bill Gates, any Fortune 500 CEO or the President of the United States.

The relationships between editors, their colleagues and agents; between agents and the editors and writers they work with; between publicists and the media; and between sales reps and booksellers are what keep publishing humming.

Your relationships began the moment you were born. You had a personal network: your family, their friends and your relatives. As you grew up, you added your network of friends and schoolmates and their families.

As an aspiring writer, you need all the help you can get, and there are people around the world who want to help you. They just don't know you yet. So as important as anything you do for your career is making contact with them by building two international networks:

- A publishing network of fans, writers, reviewers, booksellers, sales reps, librarians, members of writers' organizations, writing teachers and the businesses that provide the products and services you need.

    Reading *Publishers Weekly* will keep you informed about what publishers and a small percentage of authors are doing. Write a letter to every author in your field whose work you like telling them why. If their contact information is not in the back of their books and no one in your networks knows their addresses, write to them care of their publishers. Since agents screen their clients' mail, you might find an agent this way.

    Becoming a successful author is not an adventure for the faint-hearted or for introverts content to sit in front of their computers and write. It calls for meeting authors at signings and conferences and attending book fairs, writing classes and writer's conferences. It requires you to join writers' organizations (like those listed in the Resource Directory) that can help you.

- A field network of every opinion-maker in your field in the media, government and academia. This is important whether you're writing about history or writing historical novels. Being an active member of organizations in your field helps prove to agents and editors that you deserve to be taken seriously.

You have direct and indirect networks. Your direct networks are all the people you know; your indirect networks are everyone *they* know. E-mail makes it easier than ever to build and maintain your networks.

GUERRILLA WISDOM
Promotion campaigns for your books are not isolated events but part of a life-long process, the success of which depends on
- the continual development of your knowledge of promotion
- your skill as a promoter, and just as essential
- your relationships with as many allies as you can enlist to help you

How can your networks help you? They can
- be mentors who provide feedback on your ideas, your proposals or manuscripts, and your promotion plans
- tell all the people they know that they must buy your books
- share their knowledge of writing, selling and promoting books with you
- be part of a mastermind group of five to nine knowledgeable professionals who meet regularly by phone or in person to serve as your unofficial board of directors, advising you on how to improve what you're doing
- help you reach media people, experts in your field and other authors
- share information about Web sites and other sources of information online and off

- write introductions and give you cover quotes for your books
- write articles about you and your books
- share or trade their mailing lists with you
- give you tips on how to save money on the products and services you need
- be your eyes and ears for information you need
- sell your books at their talks (Thanks to the zeal of Jack Canfield and Mark Victor Hansen, forty speakers sell *Chicken Soup* books at their talks.)
- give you the lay of the land and a place to lay your head as you travel around the country
- do book tours with you to share expenses, an excellent example of cooperation
- make presentations with you
- have your promotional material at their presentations
- set up reciprocal links between your Web sites
- use their entree to the media to set up joint media appearances
- help you create panels for media appearances, book festivals, writers' organizations and conferences
- collaborate on books
- review your books

Other suggestions are listed under "Cooperation" in chapter thirteen.

If you're writing fiction, a tableful of writers that gets together once a week, online or off, to critique each other's work will help you fine-tune your manuscript.

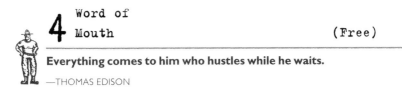

4 Word of Mouth (Free)

Everything comes to him who hustles while he waits.
—THOMAS EDISON

John Gray's *Men Are From Mars, Women Are From Venus: A Practical Guide to Getting What You Want in Your Relationships* did not hit the best-seller list until nine months after it was published. Meanwhile, Gray did

GUERRILLA TACTICS

- The moment you have an idea for a book that you are passionate about writing and promoting, start making a list of people in publishing and in your field who can help you. Begin establishing relationships with them by phone, snail-mail, E-mail and in person. Don't stop adding to this list until you stop promoting your last book.
- When you meet authors you think can help you, recruit them for your networks. Always ask them what they have found to be the most effective ways to promote their books. Learning just one helpful idea will make your conversation time well spent.
- Make a list of everyone around the country you want to be part of your networks. As you travel around the country, invite them to lunch or your talks and give them your latest book. Ask them if they know anyone else in their community whom they think you should invite.
- Create a comp list of key people in your networks who merit receiving copies of your books. Send them to those whom you publisher won't.
- Recruit reviewers. Even if they can't review your books, they may know reviewers who might.
- Enlist booksellers in your cause by establishing relationships with them early on in your career.

For a look at guerrilla networking in action, please see appendix three.

workshops around the country and gave five to ten radio interviews a week. The book went on to sell more than ten million copies and spawned follow-up best-sellers.

Publishing people believe what movie people believe: word of mouth is the most powerful form of promotion, period, amen, end of story. You can read reviews and articles about authors, see the ads and maybe even hear authors speak, but still not be totally convinced. But when someone whose judgment you respect tells you, "You must read this book!" you're a believer.

Andrea Brown, a literary agent who specializes in children's books, finds that this is especially true with children's books. Booksellers who hand-sell their favorite books can create best-sellers, as can parents, librarians, teachers and even kids themselves.

The goal of everything done to promote books by unknown writers is done to generate a critical mass of people who love them. If a book can convince enough people to praise it with enough fervor, the book will succeed. Once that happens, an unstoppable army of fans will keep winning victory after victory for the rest of an author's career.

Convincing people to buy a book is a victory, but a short-sighted one. Sure, the author will receive a royalty check. But we'll bet that you have bought at least one book that, despite your best intentions, you've never read.

If you're like us, your fantasy is that book buyers will take your book home, do nothing else except breathe until they finish it, and tell everyone they know to read it. Is that too much to ask?

Publishers have three approaches to making that happen. The most likely way for a book to reach the best-seller list is if an author's previous book was on it. Once word of mouth elevates sales to that lofty level, a book benefits from the self-fulfilling momentum of appearing on the list. Then future books benefit from the sales momentum of previous books. So as long as the author's books deliver and they are well promoted, an author can stay on the list for a lifetime.

Books by best-selling authors have six- or seven-figure first printings and may have a lay-down date on which booksellers can start selling them. The purpose of a large first printing with a specific on-sale date is to trigger an explosion of sales that will immediately catapult a book onto best-seller lists in as high a position as possible. This is the publishing equivalent of the opening weekend box office sales that enable movie people to gauge the movie's eventual receipts.

Making the list for the first time, however, continues to become more difficult, especially for fiction, which is harder to promote than nonfiction. People are less willing to pay even discounted prices to take a chance on a novel by a new author that may not be worth the money or, even more valuable, the time to read it.

This is one reason it can be easier for novelists to break in by writing genre fiction like mysteries and romances that are published as mass-market originals. When they have enough fans, their publishers will start publishing them in hardcover and promoting their books to their waiting readers.

But even if a publisher goes all out for a new author, the proof of whether their efforts are justified is still in the reading. Despite all of the persuasive hoopla publishers can produce for books, if a book doesn't deliver, it's a lost cause no matter how much money the publisher throws at it. The moment they realize it's hopeless, they'll drop the book in a New York minute and move on to the next likely prospect.

Without an author's previous appearance on the best-seller list, large subsidiary-rights sales, rave pre-publication reviews or an expensive promotional blitz, word of mouth is the easiest, fastest, cheapest and in fact, the only way to create a best-seller by a new writer. In this scenario, the publisher's faith in a book justifies one of the *-ent* words in chapter one: patient.

It took nine months for John Gray's *Men Are From Mars, Women Are From Venus* to hit the best-seller list. It took Diana Gabaldon four books to build enough of a fan base to enable her time-trip historical *Outlander* series to reach best-sellerdom.

That's why it's important for writers and publishers not to give up on a book too soon.

GUERRILLA TACTICS

- Build a list of everyone you can count on to read your book and rave about it to everyone they know. Make sure they receive books ASAP. Treat them like royalty because they are the shock troops of the army you need to recruit to raise the critical mass of devoted readers that will assure the success of all of your future books.

- Here's how to make word of mouth work for you: It's been said that we all know 250 people. If you tell all the people in your direct network about your book, and they tell everyone they know, you will create an indirect network. That's 62,500 people who will hear about your book. That's an army! If all of them buy your book during the same week, your book will make the best-seller list.

  If you can figure out how to get your indirect networks to rave about your book to everyone *they* know, more than fifteen million people will hear about your book! So use E-mail to work those networks!

KEEPING YOUR EARS OPEN FOR THE "BIG MOUTHS"

Every field has what are respectfully called "big mouths," insiders, networkers and opinion-makers who talk to a lot of people and are eager to spread the word about whatever's new and hot. You'll know them when you meet them, and now you'll know enough to make them allies and take special care of them.

BONUS WEAPON

```
Viral
Marketing                                    (Free)
```

Viral marketing—marketing that perpetuates itself—is a fast, easy, effective and economical way to create word of mouth about your books. W.W. Norton used viral marketing with Patrick O'Brian's best-selling nautical novels by including certificates in all copies of his newest novel, offering to send a free copy of the first book in the series to anyone the buyer chooses. The theory is that this will "infect" new readers, who will not only buy all the rest of the books, but will also infect even more new readers.

You can do viral marketing both offline, as W.W. Norton did, or online, by offering information on your Web site that is valuable enough to make your contacts want to read and forward it to everyone they know. Encourage your readers to forward the information and make sure it includes information about your books, products and services, plus a hot link to your Web site and perhaps a special offer to help convince them to visit your site. People who forward your information are, in effect, endorsing it.

CHAPTER 4

THE MOST POWERFUL WEAPONS FOR SELLING YOUR BOOKS

 The first printing of John Steinbeck's *The Wayward Bus* was demolished when the truck carrying the books from the bindery to the warehouse crashed in flames. The truck had been hit by a wayward bus going down the wrong side of the road.

I'm a great believer in luck, and I find the harder I work the more I have of it.

—THOMAS JEFFERSON

eptember 1998: Broadway Books is about to publish *If Life Is a Game, These Are the Rules* by Chérie Carter-Scott. Lightning strikes: a producer from "Oprah" calls. Chérie's going to be on the show!

At the beginning of the show, Oprah tells her viewers to turn off their stoves so they can pay full attention. She also tells them to tape the show so they can share it with their friends.

Oprah sits in the audience, and Chérie has the hour to herself. At commercial breaks, Oprah says wonderful things about the book, telling the audience, "If you buy only one book this year, make it this one."

Chérie is brilliant. Hardened publishing veterans at Broadway Books were in tears watching the show. You could see a best-seller being created right before your eyes. By 4 P.M. New York time, the book had soared from number 22,000 plus on the Amazon.com best-seller list to number one. It went on to become number one on *The New York Times* best-seller list. Nirvana.

Mike and his partner Elizabeth Pomada were the agents for the book, and they were as amazed and delighted at the book's meteoric rise as anyone.

Oprah receives ten thousand books a year. Why was Chérie's book rescued from obscurity and given a first-class ticket on the best-seller express? Many factors affected the book's fate, most of them controllable, some not. Here are pieces of the puzzle that fell into place to explain what happened:

- The book delivers. After all the years Oprah has been doing her show, nobody is a better judge of self-help books, and nobody in or out of television has more credibility.
- Chérie delivers. She's been a professional speaker for more than twenty years and has a smile that can light up a room. She was ready for what could be the biggest publicity opportunity of her life, and she was flawless.
- The timing was perfect: Oprah had just begun a new series of shows about transforming one's life the same month the book was published. The publisher's plan was to publish in September hoping to build sales momentum that would carry the book through the holiday gift-giving season, which is exactly what happened.
- The price was right: fifteen dollars in hardcover, which means that for most book buyers, the book was discounted to the cost of a trade paperback.
- The packaging was right. The jacket had a classy look that made it a beautiful gift for any occasion.
- The length was right. The mega-selling success of *Don't Sweat the Small Stuff* proved to publishers that lower cover prices and shorter reading times were the way to go. At 137 pages, the book didn't require a large time commitment.
- The structure of the book was right. Most of the chapters are two pages long which means that busy readers with only a few minutes to spare could pick up the book anywhere and get something out of it quickly.
- The format of the book was right. At $6'' \times 7''$, the size of the book was not intimidating, so it tempted people who would be put off by a large tome.
- The size of the audience for the book was huge: anyone from teenagers to senior citizens would benefit from its advice.
- The jacket of the book included the names of two of the most potent

names of the century in the self-help/inspirational field, whose books had combined sales of more than ten million copies.

If Life Is a Game is based on Chéri's ten rules for being human that appeared in *Chicken Soup for the Soul.* The list of rules were being photocopied around the country without attribution, so Jack Canfield and Mark Victor Hansen didn't know who wrote the list when they included it in the book.

When the book came out, no writer was mentioned. Chérie contacted Jack and all of the future printings included Chérie's name. Then people kept asking her when she was going to write a book about the rules. Chérie finally succumbed to the request and called Mike. Jack wrote the foreword to the book.

On the jacket above the title appeared these words: "Everyone needs to read these words of wisdom. It's 'simple' yet important stuff." —Richard Carlson, author of *Don't Sweat the Small Stuff*

- The promotion budget was right. Chérie put up thirty-five thousand dollars and Broadway Books matched it. Chérie used part of her budget for satellite tours that Rick Frishman set up for her and for giving talks at Unity churches around the country.

  But even though seventy thousand dollars can launch a book in style, there was no certainty that the book would have made the list without Oprah's magic touch. Large advances have forced publishers to spend much more than that promoting books that die anyway.

- Broadway did an outstanding job on the book. In addition to their contribution to the book's content, design and marketing, they kept the pipeline full to be sure that booksellers had the books they needed to generate the sales that enabled the book to climb to the top of the best-seller list.

September is one of the busiest months of the year for launching new books because of the holiday season. But without Oprah and with all the competing new books on the shelves and their authors vying for time and space in the media, who knows what would have happened?

The lesson from all of this is that the best way to make Lady Luck smile on your endeavors is to do all you can for your books and then hope for the best.

As this story helps prove, publicity is the cheapest yet most effective form of book promotion. Oprah's ability to make Chérie Carter-Scott's book a number one best-seller in one hour is an example of the power of publicity.

When you try to sell your first nonfiction book, large publishers will want you to have a platform high enough to make you and your books visible to all of your potential readers. After discussing your platform, this chapter describes the three most powerful elements of a platform:

- Your Talks (Free or you get paid!)
- Your Grand Tours (Free or you get paid!)
- Your Publicity (Low cost)

5 Your Platform   (Free)

JOHN BARRYMORE: **You should play Hamlet.**

JIMMY DURANTE: **To hell with those small towns, I'll take New York.**

After profit and Oprah, the most important two-syllable word in publishing is "platform." A platform is your continuing national visibility in person or through the media to as many of your potential readers as possible. A platform may be

- a radio or television show that is broadcast nationally
- a syndicated newspaper column or a column in a magazine with a large national circulation
- a seminar or keynote address you give around the country on a continuing basis
- a newsletter you write online and/or offline with a large national subscriber list
- an online presence that offers a daily dose of news or advice to an impressive nationwide audience

The greater the impact in the media that you have on a regular basis, the greater the opportunities you have for promoting and perhaps excerpting your book. Your books will be worth more to publishers because they know that your books will sell to your fans. They also know that arranging speaking engagements and media appearances is easier for writers with visibility.

If you travel the country giving talks as a way of life, you are giving yourself a national tour that enables your publisher's publicist to arrange interviews for you in the cities you travel to.

For new writers, bylines are more valuable than money. Every byline you earn for an article or short story gives you the credibility to approach the next higher rung on the steeply pitched media ladder that rises to the platform you need.

Part of the reason Dave Barry's books are best-sellers is that his column appears in hundreds of newspapers. That kind of exposure generates guaranteed sales regardless of what else Dave or his publisher does to promote his books.

Dave's platform helped him make his first mystery novel a best-seller. So the bigger your platform, the more easily you can switch genres or go from nonfiction to fiction and be confident that your fans will follow you.

When you're ready to jump off your platform into the deep muddy waters of publishing, editors will expect to see the gold medals for past performances that prove that you have the experience to tackle your novel or nonfiction book.

In *100 Things Every Writer Needs to Know*, Scott Edelstein reported that nonfiction accounts for 95 percent of all published material and 95 percent of all the money writers make. That doesn't leave a lot of space or money for fiction writers. No wonder novelists have a harder time getting their short stories published.

To plan your travels, check out the list of the hundred top markets in appendix seven, and keep in mind that a platform isn't something you jump on when you have books to sell, it's something you build plank by plank with

- every talk you give
- every name you add to your networks and your mailing lists
- every bookstore you visit
- every article or short story you have published
- every book you write
- every city you go to
- every media appearance you make

6 Your Talks

(Free or you get paid!)

> Writing and speaking, when carefully performed, may be reciprocally beneficial, as it appears that by writing we speak with great accuracy, and by speaking we write with great ease.
>
> —QUINTILIAN

> When audiences come to see us authors lecture, it is in the hope that we'll be funnier to look at than to read.
>
> —SINCLAIR LEWIS

Without a continuing presence in national media, giving presentations around the country is the most effective weapon for you to use to make the world aware of you and your books.

Winston Churchill found his government salary inadequate so he supplemented it by lecturing. Observed Churchill, "I live from mouth to hand." The benefits you gain from talking may include the chance to

- make money
- publicize you and your books
- sell books and other products and services
- generate sales for booksellers
- make media and publishing contacts and add promotional events for talks in another city
- receive feedback on the content and delivery of your talk
- learn new ideas, anecdotes and humor
- make contact with audience members who can book you for other talks
- add a venue to the list of places where you can talk every time one of your books is published
- get experience customizing your talk for different audiences
- add the event to your speaking resume
- receive a testimonial letter
- ask for names of other individuals and groups who may want to book you for a talk
- add names to your mailing lists
- test the effectiveness of your handouts

Many children's book authors earn a significant part of their income by speaking at schools and libraries for $500 to $1,500 a day.

Ask groups you will speak to how many books you can expect to sell. If the number is high enough and you can afford to forgo the profits from selling them, ask your contact if there's a bookseller who might want to sell books at the event. If it's a group like the Rotary Club, whose members own businesses, a bookseller may be a member.

Another alternative if you don't need the income from book sales: let organizations order the books from your publisher and keep the profits from any sales, a further incentive for groups to invite you. This is especially true for nonprofits, which are in a perpetual fundraising mode, a subject discussed in chapter nine.

If one of the fundraising techniques the group uses is a raffle at their meetings, see if you can supply a promotional copy of your book as a prize.

Concentrate your talks where they create the greatest short-term and long-term benefits for you and your books. In giving slide shows around the country about their books on Victorian homes, Mike Larsen and Elizabeth Pomada found that the smaller the towns, the more attention their talks received.

Chapter fifteen discusses the importance of your ability to talk.

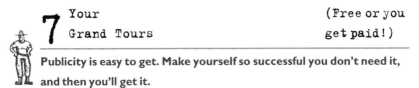

7 Your Grand Tours (Free or you get paid!)

Publicity is easy to get. Make yourself so successful you don't need it, and then you'll get it.
—ANONYMOUS

In the nineteenth century, a grand tour was a European trip that those with the means took to acquire culture. Today, a grand tour is less grand: an endless round of presentations to audiences around the country and abroad that publicize you and your books, and give you opportunities to sell them. Visiting museums is optional.

This is the most common kind of national platform that writers can build for themselves—one you can construct talk by talk. As with writing and publicity, start small.

GUERRILLA TACTICS

- Devise and carry out a plan to increase your visibility through writing and speaking, and to maintain it once it is as strong as you want it to be. You'll see the difference it makes on your bottom line.
- If you can't get your work published online or offline, post it on your Web site or elsewhere online if you don't have one. This will get your writing out there, but it won't count with editors as much as published articles will. However, proudly displaying your published and unpublished work on your Web site will be effective as an audition. You can direct agents and editors there to see the quality of your writing.

Go from small groups to large ones.

Go from small towns to major markets.

Go from your part of the country to the next until you can get yourself around the country giving talks, selling books, cementing relations with booksellers and getting interviewed by the media.

If your books are in the field of spirituality, two national networks are already in place for you:

- The Whole Life Expo, a traveling exhibition of New Age products and services oriented toward health and spirituality. It provides an excellent platform for authors writing on those subjects.
- Unity Churches have authors speak and then sign books at their bookstores.

After you conquer the United States, you're ready to take on the rest of the world.

Because New York publishers keep raising the bar on what they will accept, it will continue to get harder for new writers to be published by the big houses unless they can prove their books will succeed at a level that will satisfy the Six Sisters.

When the promotion plans for your books prove you're a road warrior able and eager to promote your books around the country, you're ready for mounting an assault on the Big Apple.

GUERRILLA TACTICS

- To make free talks pay for themselves, ask for
  — a copy of the group's newsletter with articles about your talk, publicity materials and stories about you in local media for your portfolio. This will help when you approach other groups.
  — a testimonial letter
  — the names and contact information for other groups who may be interested in hearing your talk
  — invitations to your talk be sent to media people and opinion-makers in your field
  — time to sell your books afterward
  — a minimum purchase of copies of your books
  — expenses if the talk will be out of town
  — suggestions from the audience of other organizations that might be interested in your talk
- If you're speaking to a chapter of a national organization, contact other chapters and the group's headquarters (if they have a national convention) about speaking. This might lead to speaking overseas if the organization has chapters abroad.
- If the talk will be in the evening and it's out of town, ask for dinner, a room for the night and local transportation if you won't have a car. If the group is hard-pressed for cash, ask if a member can provide what you need, or if a local establishment might help in exchange for being mentioned at the talk and named as a sponsor of the talk.
- Take advantage of your trip to offer a class or book-signing while you're in town.
- If your talk will be open to the public, help publicize it to increase attendance. Give the organization's reps copies of your news release or press kits, and ask them to mention that you are available for interviews before and after the talk. If the group will only send a news release, make sure the media know your media kit is on your Web site, and that they will receive books and media kits on request.
- If your talk will not be open to the public and the group won't publicize your appearance, ask if anyone in the group has media contacts you can use to publicize your books. If not, research and contact them yourself.

continued

Guerrilla Tactics, continued
- Meet local booksellers and autograph copies of your book if they're in stock. If they aren't, give booksellers an autographed promotional copy if you can. (This worked for Jacqueline Susann.)
- If your book can be used by reading groups, ask booksellers about local groups and see if they would be interested in reading your book and having you present to discuss it. A reading-group guide on your Web site may help them decide. For more on this, see chapter eight.

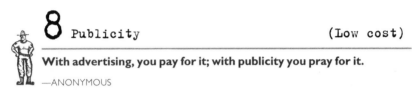

8 Publicity (Low cost)

With advertising, you pay for it; with publicity you pray for it.
—ANONYMOUS

IBM spent $5 million on the chess match between Russian champion Garry Kasparov and their super-computer Big Blue. They estimate that the media exposure generated by the match was worth $100 million.

Despite the fact that 76 percent of what appears in newspapers originates with publicists, free print publicity is considered to be twenty times more powerful than paid advertising.

Publicity can be the great equalizer between authors. Trade and consumer print, broadcast and electronic media need exciting ideas and authors to keep their audiences' attention. If you have what they need, they'll be delighted to hear from you no matter who publishes your books.

The eleven essential keys to gaining publicity are
- books that deliver
- knowing how the media work
- media contacts
- knowing how to approach the media
- knowing how the people you contact prefer to be approached
- skill at being interviewed
- the creativity to make your book newsworthy every time you approach the media
- professional, continually updated publicity materials

GUERRILLA TACTICS

- As soon as you finish your manuscript, sell photocopies of it and let your audiences as well as your networks tell you how to make it better before approaching agents or publishers.
- Always have something to sell. If you're doing talks, there will always be people who want to walk away with a tangible reminder of your presentation. Don't deprive them of what they want or yourself of the profit from giving it to them.

  As soon as you've finished your manuscript, execute the Self-Publishing Maneuver. Even if you have a publisher, sell a single-spaced, back-to-back photocopy of the manuscript until your book is available or you and your publisher agree on a deadline.

  If you don't have a publisher lined up, consider self-publishing the manuscript. Stay with the photocopied version so you can keep asking for suggestions on making it better. Once you're convinced that you have all the feedback you need, you can put it between covers.

  You can hire freelancers to do whatever part of the publishing process you can't or don't want to do. It doesn't make any difference who does the work, but it's vital that it be done professionally or you will undermine the credibility of your book. The books on self-publishing listed in the Resource Directory include the resources you need for producing your books.

- Guerrilla John Kremer recommends giving something away at your talks. Giving your audiences a momento of the occasion at the end of your presentation will make them remember you. It can be as simple as a flier that will help or entertain them enough so they'll put it up on their wall and photocopy it for all their friends (a suggestion you can make on the handout).

  Include your contact information and perhaps the names of your books and the services you offer. But do this unobtrusively, perhaps on the back of the page, or omit it. Your goal is to offer a gift, not a marketing tool.

- As soon as you know your publication date, ask your publisher to print up an order form that you can give out at your talks. If they won't, do it yourself. If you want to fulfill orders, have a space for

continued

Guerilla Tactics, continued
> buyers to request a personalized autograph. If you wish, offer pre-publication and multiple-copy discounts.
> • Try to presell your books to organizations that book you to speak. The better known you are, the more often you will make this happen.
>   Two other ways to use your ability to talk to earn a living are offering telephone evaluations and consultations at an hourly rate. To let callers sample your wares, give them the first five minutes on the house.

- accepting the reality that at least at the beginning of your career, you will receive far more no's than yes's and that the media are not rejecting you, just your book and just for the moment
- follow-ups
- making your contacts glad they helped you by expressing your gratitude

None of these keys is optional. If you are planning to build a career as an author, you must have them all because you will need them all.

WAR STORIES
Terry McMillan gave herself a grand tour booking readings in bookstores in every town where she could find a friend to put her up for the night. When *Waiting to Exhale* was published, her fans helped put her on the best-seller list.

FREE-FOR-ALL

Publicity is a free-for-all in both senses of the phrase. Unlike advertising, it is free, and because it is so effective, everyone wants it. The biggest trade-offs in publicity are:
- Because it is free, you cannot control it.
- Everyone with a product, service, cause or personality to promote competes for it.

- Unless you are appearing on a live show, you may not know when a show you're on will air or when it will be repeated.
- An interview or show may be cancelled at any time because of natural or man-made disasters that erupt suddenly and dominate the media.
- Hosts rarely read the books they discuss, so you have to be prepared to wing it.
- What you say to print interviewers may suffer in translation from your mouth to the printed page.
- Whether they're in print, broadcast or electronic media, the goal of your interviewers is to capture and hold the attention of their audience. If you help them accomplish that, you have it made.

   If your book is controversial, and interviewers think that getting the best story means asking you tricky questions or even discrediting you, they may try to ambush you.

   Antagonistic hosts probably won't be a problem for authors of how-to books, but they may be with an author of a revisionist look at history, or a book about a controversial person or subject.

You and your publisher's publicist will have identical interests but not identical agendas. Staff publicists learn their skills by working on twelve to twenty books simultaneously. That is too many for them to do justice to yours unless it is a potential best-seller.

Media people are also swamped. You both want to create the best possible interview, show or story. Hosts make a living by trading publicity for an informative, entertaining show. Print media want their stories to have the same qualities. Online stories can be either print, audio or video.

Your goal is to promote your book and yourself. Success for a radio host means a multi-phone console filled with blinking white lights from callers waiting to ask you questions. Authors who can light up switchboards may be asked to stay longer than the time allotted for the interview, and they will be paid the compliment that matters most: being asked to return.

The trajectory of author appearances in the media goes from small to large. You don't want Montel Williams to be your first show. You'll need a lot of out-of-town tryouts before you can provide audiotapes and videotapes that prove you're ready for the center ring.

Despite its trials, publicity is the best hope for reaching the greatest number of readers for the smallest expenditure.

TRADE PUBLICITY

The emphasis of this book is on consumer publicity, but don't overlook trade media. *Publishers Weekly* (*PW*) has several departments that you may be able to use to publicize your books. Your publisher may be willing to send publicity info to them if the information is newsworthy enough or your book is important enough. Get to know *PW* well enough to know when you have information they can use. If your publicist is unable to follow through, you can.

Library Journal is published by the same company as *Publishers Weekly* and is the *PW* for libraries. If your book has strong library potential, look at your librarian's edition of *Library Journal* and see if you can come up with an idea for an article for it. Ask your librarian to show you the other publishing trade media.

There are also thousands of online and offline newsletters and magazines in every field that review books and need copies. Investigate them and share the information with your publicist.

WHY SOMETHING FREE COSTS MONEY

Although publicity is free, you still pay for it with

- books after your publisher stops supplying them
- press kits
- a Web site
- travel
- giveaways to listeners

To these costs must be added

- the time spent setting up interviews
- doing them
- sending thank-you notes
- coming up with new ways to approach the media

- updating your publicity materials
- a publicist, if you decide to hire one

But even with its uncertainties and the expenditure of time and money, publicity is still the most cost-effective form of marketing, so make the most of it.

GUERRILLA TACTICS

- As soon as you start developing your book, start a file with names of people in the trade and consumer media who can help publicize your books. Get to know them and make their care and feeding a priority.
- Watch, read and listen to author interviews to see how they're done and how authors respond to questions. This is even more crucial for the media that will interview you. If your budget allows, this justifies a TV satellite system that enables you to see stations around the country.
- Giving great interviews is not a talent you are born with. It's a skill you have to learn if you want to extract maximum value from them.
- The best defense for tough questions is preparation: have someone repeatedly ask you all of the questions you don't want to be asked until you can effortlessly transform them into opportunities for making the points that will sell your book.

  A media coach can help you but if one won't fit into your budget and you can't use guerrilla money (see chapter six) to obtain one, use your networks.

  Have them tape you until you can answer the toughest questions with confidence.
- Make a list of the essential points that you want the audience to know about you and your book. In the list of questions for interviewers in your media kit, include the questions that enable you to make these points.
- Use humor if you can. Other people's is fine.
- Publicists know which hosts may be troublesome. Ask your publicist about it when they book you so you'll be prepared.

continued

Guerrilla Tactics, continued

- Controversy can sell books. So if you need to be combative to make the case for your book, do it. We guarantee it will light up switchboards, enliven audiences and make your hosts happy. The challenge here is to be bold yet avoid offending potential readers.
- One sure way to generate interviews is to make your book newsworthy. Look at hot news stories and figure out a way to tie your book into one of them.

    If, for example, you are the author of a novel of international intrigue about the oil business and there is an oil embargo, your expertise about how the business works will enable you to obtain interviews.

    This is the only way most novelists can get interviews before their books are best-sellers.

CHAPTER 5

THE MOST POWERFUL WEAPONS INSIDE YOU

What's ahead of me and what's behind me are nothing compared to what's inside me.

——JEAN SHAPIRO

s a writer, you are standing on the shoulders of all the writers who came before you and have shown you the path to follow. But you will also have to make your own path. Only you have your goals to keep you motivated. Only you can choose the niche that will enable you to create the career you want. If you're lucky, only you will have your ideas. And only you can bring your creativity to meeting the challenges before you.

To help you gain a perspective on the four most powerful weapons inside you, this chapter takes a look at:

- Your Objectives (Free)
- Nichecraft (Free)
- Your Ideas (Free)
- Your Creativity (Free)

You need literary and financial goals to sustain you. They are expressions of your identity that must motivate you to keep your fingertips tickling the keys every day and to use as many of the weapons in this book as you can to help ensure your success. Your objectives must be compelling enough for you to overcome the obstacles awaiting you.

Nichecraft, or discovering the books that you alone were born to write and promote, will give your talents a laser-sharp focus. It is what will distinguish you and your books from all other authors and their books, and the creativity you bring to whatever you do will guarantee your success.

9 Your Objectives (Free)

Longing performs all things.
—MARY RENAULT

The *Chicken Soup* chefs Jack Canfield and Mark Victor Hansen advise writers to have giant goals. That's part of what motivated them to go from selling more than eight million books in 1995 to selling fifty million books in 2000.

Your books can help you get where you want to go, but only you can decide where that is. You have to set goals that balance desire, necessity and realism, and then go all out to meet them. Put your short-term goals in the service of your long-term goals. Try out your goals on your networks to get feedback on whether they are realistic. Be prepared to change them as often as your situation justifies doing so.

Would you like to eliminate all of the obstacles in your life this instant? It's easy. All you have to do is give up your goals. No objectives, no obstacles. But the greater your goals, the greater the challenges you will face in achieving them.

As a guerrilla, you have a world full of minds and hearts to conquer:

- your own
- your networks
- an agent if you plan to use one
- your editor and everyone at your publisher who can help you
- wholesalers, librarians, and bricks-and-mortar and clicks-and-mortar booksellers
- trade and consumer print, broadcast and electronic media who can review, excerpt and publicize your books
- subsidiary-rights buyers
- audiences who hear you speak
- your readers

After writing and promoting your books as well as you can, your prime objective is creating and maintaining lifelong relationships with the ever-growing army of people on this list. They and the people they know are essential allies in your campaign for success.

Your literary and financial objectives will help determine your future. Choosing what you want to write and for whom, and how much fame and fortune you want to earn from your books will define you as a writer. If you want to make a living writing, you must set goals that balance what you want to write with what book buyers will pay to read.

HEART WORK: YOUR LITERARY GOALS

 Follow your inner moonlight.

—ALLEN GINSBERG

Here are three ways to capture your literary goals so they inspire you every day:

- Write the ideal review of your book.
- Write and design a full-page ad for your book, one that you would like to see in *The New York Times Book Review* or *USA Today*. Include quotes from the people you want to give them.
- Write the front and back cover copy for your books. In *The Self-Publishing Manual,* Dan Poynter recommends authors prepare this to focus their efforts, and he provides a cover design with tips about the kinds of information to highlight.

    Put the review, the ad and the cover copy for your book up on the wall where you write. And whenever fear or doubt assail you, look up and let your literary goals lift your spirits.

MAKING A WISH: YOUR FINANCIAL GOALS

You can establish your financial goals for your books by writing down the publisher and the advance you want, and how many copies you want your books to sell a year. Asking authors and publishing pros about setting goals will give you a sense of what's possible.

Establish annual goals for all of your publishing-related activities. After you determine how many copies you want to sell, figure out how to use marketing to reach that goal. Make sure your networks agree that your publicity goals will enable you to reach your financial goals.

If your goal is to write bestsellers, cut out a bestseller list. Then print the information about your book—title, author, publisher and price—and paste it in the number one position. Add the date. This helped inspire Jack Canfield and Mark Victor Hansen as they rescued *Chicken Soup for the Soul* from oblivion. The more clearly you see your goals, the farther along you will be on the path to achieving them.

Test what you write against your literary and financial goals by including what you have written about your goals with your proposal or manuscript when you send it out for feedback. Ask your readers if they agree with your assessment, and if not, what numbers and literary goals your work does justify.

Including authors and publishing people among your readers will provide you with more knowledgeable responses. Subjecting your objectives to this gauntlet will enable you to be sure you're heading in the right direction. Stick your financial goals on the wall next to your literary goals as a reminder and a source of inspiration.

One of this book's premises is that your goal is to have your books published by a big or medium-sized New York house. Discovering new writers who write well and whose books sell well is the best part of an editor's (and an agent's) job.

Writers who know what they want and how to get it, and who will be professional but relentless in the pursuit of their goals make it easy for editors to buy a book. Armed with the right ammunition, it's a breeze for an editor to

- prepare the computerized P&L (profit and loss) statement they need to justify the acquisition
- build in-house enthusiasm for your book
- make the editorial board salute by presenting an irrefutable case for buying it
- present the book to the toughest audience of all: the reps at sales conferences who have heard it all before and have to relay the house's enthusiasm to booksellers

- excite the subsidiary rights department with the book's potential as a book club selection and other sub-rights sales
- prove to the publicists that the book will attract media attention

The path your books will take from your mind into the minds of your readers begins and ends with a commitment to your goals that must sustain you through the problems, disappointments and challenges you will face. So choose your goals wisely because the purpose of this book is to ensure that if you have the idea, the talent and the persistence, you will reach them.

The English dramatist George Bernard Shaw once observed, "There are two tragedies in life. One is not to get your heart's desire. The other is to get it." Don't look at goals as a final destination, but as a plateau on a never-ending journey, as life's way of telling you you're ready to graduate, to move on to greater things.

That moment of satisfaction when you know you've accomplished what you set out to do is the perfect time to assess what you've learned and set bigger goals for your next book. We hope you will have to do this with every book you write.

10 Nichecraft (Free)

Becoming a successful author requires you to accept the discipline of focus: first the focus of setting goals, and then the focus of developing and using the skills needed to achieve them.

Once you prove you can write a successful novel or nonfiction book, publishers will pay you to write about whatever interests you. The prospect of getting paid to dabble in new fields of knowledge with every book may make you feel like a kid in a candy store.

However, unless one of your literary goals is to be free to write whatever kind of book you fancy, storming the beachhead of a different market with every novel or nonfiction book you write is not the most direct route to becoming a successful author. Synergy isn't possible because different kinds of books won't sell each other.

You may have the desire and ability to write books about history, food and sports, but that doesn't mean readers who enjoy reading about baseball and the history of France will want to read about how to make guacamole. You can't count on readers who garden to buy books about travel or computers. You can't rely on sci-fi fans to buy romance novels.

THE ALCHEMY OF SUCCESS

Nichecraft is the name we use for the literary alchemy of spinning ideas into gold. Pick a niche in a subject that you will remain eager to write about and promote and make nichecraft the heart of your strategy for success.

Every book you can write can help sell every other book you write. Make synergy one of your objectives. The more books you write on the subject, the more copies they will all sell, along with the products and services based on them. Just as you can build a house brick by brick, nichecraft is the easiest, simplest, fastest way we know for you to build a career, book by book.

Nichecraft also makes it easier for you to focus your attention on authors, books, other media and speaking opportunities in the field you want to enter. You have to assess its long-term prospects and convince your networks and yourself that you will enjoy being part of it.

The idea of nichecraft is worth many times the price of this book. It's as logical and powerful as it is simple, and it works as well for Sue Grafton, who is writing her way through the alphabet, as it does for Jay, who laid the foundation for a virtually endless series of books that are needed by more people in more places in more kinds of businesses every day.

Our certainty that practicing nichecraft will make you a successful author can't guarantee that you will be able to sell your books or that they will sell well enough to warrant more books in the series. But the unpredictability of publishing is part of what makes the business exciting and keeps publishing people open to new writers and new ideas.

11 Your Ideas   (Free)

Marketing begins the moment you have an idea, and it never stops.

—GUERRILLA HALL OF FAMERS TOM AND MARILYN ROSS, COAUTHORS OF *Jump Start*

Your Book Sales: A Money-making Guide for Authors, Independent Publishers and Small Presses

GUERRILLA TACTICS

If you have a choice of fields to enter, talk to authors in those fields to learn about the joys and hazards they present. To help you decide, ask yourself the following questions about each field you are considering:

- Is the field growing?
- How much space does the bookshelf occupy in stores?
- Is the field growing enough so you can make a living writing about it?
- What opportunities does it offer for speaking or teaching?
- How much will you enjoy writing about it?
- Does it have enough publicity potential?

The answers to these questions will inevitably lead to other questions. We hope that all of the answers lead you to the career you were born to pursue.

Writing starts with the desire to communicate. Books start with ideas. When choosing ideas for your books, you have to balance passion and profit. Writing and promoting books require passion; making a living at it requires profit.

Here is a checklist of six criteria for choosing ideas for your books:

- Is the idea salable?
- Will the books be promotable?
- Does the idea lend itself to sequels?
- Are you passionate enough about the idea to write and promote a series of books about it?
- Will the books have the potential for subsidiary rights such as film, foreign, book-club and electronic rights?
- Will the books enable you to reach your literary and financial goals?

If you can answer these questions with a resounding YES!, and your networks share your passion, you are ready to go.

Marilyn Ross says aspiring authors always ask: " 'How do I get my books in bookstores?' That's the wrong question. The question is 'How do I get my books out of bookstores?' "

More than half of trade books are not sold in bookstores. If you're writing nonfiction, will it be possible to sell your books in non-book outlets such as gift, gardening or sporting-goods stores? When you are evaluating your ideas, take into consideration the outlets, media and countries in which your books can be sold.

PUBLISHING FOR MAXIMUM IMPACT

If your book is published in hardcover, the sales reps will usually sell the paperback edition of it along with your next book a year later. When the reps reach the page about your book in your publisher's catalog, booksellers will check their computers to see how many copies the hardcover sold and order the paperback edition and the sequel accordingly.

In addition to making your first book profitable for you and your publisher, you have another objective: to establish yourself in the marketplace with maximum impact. If you have a choice of which book to write first, choose the one that will have the greatest impact from a literary or commmercial point of view or, ideally, both.

One day in the not-too-distant future, you will take stock of what you have accomplished, and you will be amazed to see how something as fragile and abstract as an idea was the big bang of an expanding universe of books, products and services that you are proud of and that force you to keep enlarging your goals.

GUERRILLA TACTICS
Start an idea file. Check it while you are deciding which book to write next. Your idea file will grow in value throughout your career, both to yourself and to other writers.

12 Your Creativity   (Free)

The secret of creativity is knowing how to hide your sources.
—ALBERT EINSTEIN

So everyone's an entrepreneur, and everyone has got a book, a media kit and a Web site. What's going to keep you from disappearing in the perpetual onslaught of competing books and media? Your creativity.

The creativity you bring to everything you do will be essential to setting you apart from your ever-growing number of competitors. Your continuing challenge will be to do the same things your competitors do but to do them differently and better.

Among the endless opportunities you have to be creative are
- picking your niche
- how you write and structure your novel or present the information in your nonfiction books
- a small relevant gadget or gimmick to include with your proposal and your media/speaker's kit (You want something that packs small, lays flat and plays big.)
- how you respond to hearing the same questions about your work
- how distinctive, relevant and worthy of publicity you can make your appearance
- figuring out new ways to promote and make money from your ideas
- coming up with ideas for future books

You can be creative in every aspect of your personal and professional life. Few things in life are more satisfying than coming up with ideas and watching them succeed. Think of everything you do to write and promote your books as an opportunity for you to exercise your creativity. This will add a great deal of fun to your life as well as fatten your bank account!

KEEPING IT SIMPLE

 Anybody can make the simple complicated.
Creativity is making the complicated simple.
—CHARLIE MINGUS

One of the qualities common to successful novels or nonfiction books is simplicity. They are based on simple ideas compellingly communicated by their titles, their covers and their marketing. So make your ideas clear, compelling and promotable, but keep them simple.

GUERRILLA TACTICS

- Read books on creativity and talk to your networks for ideas on how you can write and promote your books more creatively. Reward people whose suggestions you use.
- Do one thing differently every day. If you feel too full of yourself, try writing with your other hand. That will settle you down.
- When everyone is looking in one direction, look the other way.

CHAPTER 6

WEAPONS THAT MAKE YOU A GUERRILLA

 When asked by *Esquire* magazine what he would have done if it hadn't been for writing, novelist Richard Ford replied, "Make more money."

Afterter you choose the assortment of weapons you will use in your promotion campaign, integrate them into the first version of your promotion plan. Then cost them out to arrive at a budget.

Next, figure out how much money you can afford to spend to carry out your plan and add to that the guerrilla greenbacks you can mint so you can set a firm figure for your budget. Then do the final version of your promotion plan that fits your budget.

13 Your Promotion Plan: The First Version   (Free)

Follow The 90/10 Rule: spend 90 percent of your time and effort taking a steady, gradual approach, working to establish yourself solidly at one level before trying to move up to the next. But also spend 10 percent of your time and energy on the long shots: the best-known magazines, the biggest book publishers or the major producers. If you succeed, the strategy will pay off handsomely; if you fail, you've only lost a small investment of your time.

—SCOTT EDELSTEIN

Writing a book without a promotion plan is like driving a car with the windows painted over and no brakes. It will only get you as far as the nearest stationary object. But new authors are sometimes intimidated by

the prospect of promoting their first book. It may seem impossible to
- know all you need to know about promotion
- build your nationwide publishing and field networks
- develop a promotion plan
- promote your book from coast to coast

And you must still find the time and energy to write books! But thousands of writers who aren't as smart, creative and determined as you are do it every year. Believe us when we assure you: If they can, you can.

Marketing people are territorial. Your promotion plan will cover everything you will do to market your books. But marketing people don't like writers infringing on their territory, which includes marketing to the book trade as well as the consumer marketing that you will be doing. Since you will need the support of your publisher's marketing department, we recommend calling it a promotion plan.

Although your promotion plan will be flexible enough to change as you learn what works best for you and respond to new opportunities, your plan is the foundation of the campaign you will wage for your book's success.

It will be the blueprint of your plan to transform yourself from an unknown author into one of the top players in your field with an unbroken string of successful books all of which sell each other. Your plan will also be the model for the plans you create for future books.

This approach to promotion is based on the premise that you are either writing novels or nonfiction books such as how-to books, big-idea or big-issue books, or biographies of well-known people, for a large segment of the general public.

If you are writing reference books, serious books about science, or gift or novelty books that will be impulse items; or if you will be happy being published by a small house, niche publisher or university press, you won't need a plan as well developed or as powerful as the one we recommend. After your first book, your publisher will know what you can do, so you won't need as detailed a promotion plan.

All publishers want their books to embody exciting new ideas captured in a fresh, seductive voice. However, if you want to be published by one of the Six Sisters, and you're writing nonfiction books, your promotion plans will be far more important than the content of your books in determining which lucky publisher buys them and for how much.

Although novelists aren't expected to include promotion plans with their manuscripts, having a plan is a necessity. The head of a major mystery imprint reported that for every mystery she buys, there are ten she could have bought. With that kind of competition, a promotion plan that convinces editors about a novelist's commitment to her books can make the difference between acceptance and rejection.

Your promotion plan will show how you will achieve your financial goals for your books, so you must first decide what those are. How big an advance do you want? How many copies do you want your book to sell during its first year and every year after that?

One criterion for the weapons you include in your promotion plan is that they impress New York editors with your ability to promote your books nationwide. You may be planning to walk around high-traffic locations carrying your book so the title is visible, but this is not a weapon that will make New Yorkers swoon.

Your promotion plan, together with your proposal or manuscript must convince your networks, your agent and your publisher that your book will succeed.

HOW SEVEN SENTENCES EQUAL ONE PLAN

Guerrillas can give the essence of their promotion plans in just seven sentences. Here are the seven sentences and how we responded to them for this book:

1. The first sentence tells the purpose of your promotion: The goal of promotion will be to convince all writers they must have this book to become successful authors.

2. The second sentence tells how this purpose will be achieved, focusing upon the benefits of your book: The book will be essential reading for writers because it will

   — help writers understand the importance of promotion and assure them they have the ability to do it

— give writers one hundred proven marketing weapons to use

— guide them through the process of preparing promotion plans that will enable them to sell their books to publishers and readers

— encourage writers to create calendars that enable them to use their most effective weapons at the time when they will yield the greatest returns

— relieve writer's anxiety by assuring them that their networks include us and our guerrilla marketing Web site, which will help them if they need advice, encouragement and a place to share their questions, tactics and victories

3. The third sentence defines your audience: The book is for writers who want to build successful publishing careers.

4. The fourth sentence describes your promotion vehicles: The authors will promote the book with

— review copies to writing and publishing magazines and directors of writer's conferences

— talks to writer's groups and conferences

— classes at which writers can prepare their promotion plans

— speaker's and media kits

— articles in writers' magazines

— online subscriptions to tip-of-the-day nuggets

— serialization of the the weapons at www.gmarketing.com and www.writersdigest.com

— interviews on radio, television and online

— mentions of the book on the authors' print materials, on their Web sites, and in the introductions for their presentations

— a money-back guarantee

— being a book club selection on Oprah (Just kidding! But if you're reading this, Oprah, we're ready when you are.)

5. The fifth sentence describes your niche in the market: The book will provide state-of-the-art information on promoting books based on the biggest selling marketing series and will emphasize maximum clout at minimum cost.

6. The sixth sentence gives your identity: We are three veterans in the field, with almost a century of combined writing and publishing

experience, whose goal is to help writers use promotion to earn the recognition and rewards they deserve.

7. The seventh sentence gives your promotion budget: We will spend five thousand dollars to promote the book.

Finally to capture the essence of your promotion plan, winnow it down to seven words. Here they are for *Guerrilla Marketing for Writers*: Convince all authors to buy the book.

Once you have the essence of your plan, you will be able to write the full-length version, described below, which you will include with your proposal or manuscript. But between here and there comes a reckoning called the promotion budget.

14 Your Promotion Budget (Free)

If you're like most nonfiction writers, you're counting on your advance to live on while you write your book. You can't afford to spend money on promotion. Major publishers will not buy your book because you include a big promotion budget. Nor will they reject your book if it's a small one. Most authors can't afford a large promotion budget, so they just put down what they can afford without compromising their lifestyles or going into debt.

Regardless of how much money you can use for promotion, you still want the greatest value for every dollar. And the goal of this book is to show you how to be penny-wise on any budget.

The first commitment nonfiction writers should include in the promotion plans for their proposals is "On signing the contract, the author will match the publisher's out-of-pocket consumer promotion budget up to $X." If the essence of guerrilla marketing is substituting time, energy and imagination for money, why mention it first?

WHY INVEST IN YOUR PROMOTION?

Here are five reasons to include a budget first:

1 Promoting your book will cost money.

The list of what you will do to promote your book must make sense in relation to your promotion budget. For example, the basic promotional tool for publicity and getting booked for talks is a media/speaker's kit.

Buying folders, printing the news release and other parts of a kit, and mailing them will cost money. For major media, you will also want to include a book. You can economize by just E-mailing or snail-mailing a news release with a return postcard that says a media kit is available at your Web site, and ask recipients to call, E-mail or return the postcard if they want a book and a press kit.

But if you're planning to mail one thousand copies of your book to key people in your field, you can't include a promotion budget of one thousand dollars because editors know it will cost far more than that. That will destroy your credibility as an author who knows what it costs to promote books.

No matter how much you can spend, you have to convince publishers that you know the audience for your books, the best way to convince potential readers to buy them, and how to create a promotion campaign that will be as effective yet as inexpensive as possible. You want to prove that you are a pro who is ready for Big Apple publishers and who knows how to get the biggest bang for the littlest buck.

2 Publishers respect commitment.

Authors and publishers share the same interests but have conflicting agendas. They want all of their books to sell, but they publish too many of them to promote them all.

You, on the other hand, have only one book to promote. Your commitment to promoting your book assures potential publishers that you

- understand your book means more to you than to them
- understand your role in the success of your book
- are committed to doing all you can to make your books succeed
- are willing to put your money where your book is

3 Commitment begets commitment.

The greater the commitment you make to your book, the greater the commitment you have a right to expect from your publisher. You are not giving your money to your publisher. And although you will coordinate your efforts with theirs, they can't dictate what you do with your money.

But unless they spend a fortune for your book or are compelled to promote it for the reasons in the second chapter, the best argument for extracting maximum commitment out of a publisher is to ask them to match yours. If they don't, you are not obligated to spend your budget.

We once heard about an author who had two publishers who were willing to offer a thirty thousand dollar advance for a book. But only one of them was willing to match the author's twenty thousand dollar promotion budget, so the book benefitted from having a forty thousand dollar war chest for promotion.

4 Your competitors are including budgets.

Big publishers are being approached by authors willing to buy forty thousand copies of their books and to spend as much as $1,500,000 to promote them. This is huge ammunition few writers can provide, but if your goal is to sell your books to a large house, you better drum up as much artillery as you can.

Assume that your contract with your publisher will include your promotion budget and the number of books you mention you will sell, so here, as everywhere else in your proposal, never exaggerate. Even if your contract doesn't mention the budget, if your promotion plan does, you're still making the commitment.

Only commit as much money as you can without sacrificing your lifestyle, creating a burdensome obligation, preventing yourself from paying your bills or jeopardizing your future. Publishing is a gamble, so don't bet more than you can afford to lose.

How much money it will take to promote your books will depend on the kind of books you're writing, the size of the audience for them, the campaign you devise, and how large a budget it will take for you achieve the financial goals you set for your books.

Remember that money is not the most important factor in the success of your books—you are. If, like most writers, you can't include a hefty promotion budget, you can still develop a promotion campaign that will make your books fail-proof.

Even if your baby is born without the benefit of a major promotion campaign, if the combination of reviews, word of mouth and your initial promotional efforts generates enough sales momentum for your book, your publisher will step in and promote it to sustain the momentum.

Your bio must convince editors that, based on your experience, you have the ability to carry out your plan. They won't believe that you will deliver fifty talks a year if you haven't done one. Major publishers don't want writers who want to use their books to gain national visibility; they want writers who already have it.

5 You're investing in your future.

How well your first book sells helps determine the fate of succeeding books. If you want your books to attract clients for your business, you're not just promoting your book. You have more at stake than royalties. You're investing in your business. The income you will earn over time from a successful business may justify making a large commitment.

15 Your Guerrilla Greenbacks   (Free)

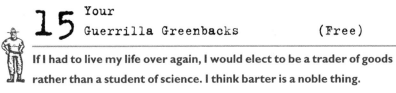

If I had to live my life over again, I would elect to be a trader of goods rather than a student of science. I think barter is a noble thing.

—ALBERT EINSTEIN

This book is introducing the guerrilla greenback. Understanding this new form of currency is as simple as ABC: Anything But Cash!

Being a guerrilla marketer means substituting time, energy and imagination for money. It means being creative in examining all of the alternatives before laying out the long green or the short plastic. The first resource for obtaining anything is your personal and professional networks.

GUERRILLA TACTICS

- It's fine to use all or part of your advance for promotion, if you can. But mentioning that you will use all or X percent of your advance for promotion is not. You can't know what your advance will be, and it may not be enough. If your advance isn't enough to carry out your plan, scale down your plan and your budget when negotiating the contract.
- Including the words "on signing the contract," in the first sentence of your plan forces your publisher to make a commitment. If your publisher won't match your commitment on signing, you are free to spend what you want.
- Ask your agent to include a clause in the contract requiring your publisher to reimburse you for the money if your book hits a national print best-seller list. There are only four slots on *The New York Times* how-to, miscellaneous best-seller list, so if you're writing in that kind of book, you will do better keying the repayment to the *Publishers Weekly* or *USA Today* or another national list.

Do family members, writers or friends have scanners or other equipment you can use?

Do you know people around the country who will give you room and board and help with local transportation while you're doing research or touring in exchange for an acknowledgment?

You can "mint" guerrilla greenbacks in two forms:

- Whatever you use to acquire something you need instead of cash. A hundred years ago, farmers paid their doctor bills with cows and chickens. They were as good as cash. Well, guess what? They still are, if you can find someone who wants to trade what you need for cows and chickens or any other product or service you have to offer.
- The cash you save by being shrewd about how you acquire what you need. Be entrepreneurial and resourceful about obtaining what you need. Make spending money the last option, not the first.

What alternatives do you have to buying something? You can

- borrow it
- barter present or future goods or services for it

- make it yourself
- ask someone to buy it for you, give it to you now and gift-wrap the box for Christmas, your birthday, your wedding anniversary, Valentine's Day or a new holiday that you establish for the day on which you receive the help you need

If you must pay for something, you can
- offer to trade what you need from a business in exchange for help with promotion
- wait until it's on sale
- decrease the cost of what you're buying by arranging with others to buy it in bulk and split the cost
- share the cost and ownership of a product or service
- cut travel expenses by sharing them with another touring writer
- rent or lease what you need
- offer to pay more when your book starts to earn income (Include a fall-back option for payment so if your book doesn't earn out, you will still meet your obligations.)
- pretend you're an agent and negotiate the price (Try this line: "Is there any way to get a better price on this?" If you buy a lot of a product or service at one time or over time, assume the price is negotiable. If they can't better the price, maybe they can forget about the tax or throw in something extra.)
- offer to acknowledge or even dedicate your book to a patron of the arts in exchange for assistance
- pay in the smallest installments you can bargain for until you receive enough income to cover the rest of the bill
- plug a product or service to your networks and in your books, talks, appearances and handouts in exchange for discounts, freebies or loans of equipment
- buy it used at a garage sale, flea market, second-hand store or online (For example, the reconditioned computers that Dell sells will save you a hefty sum of guerrilla greenbacks.)
- buy a damaged copy or a floor model
- borrow money only if you know that you can repay it to avoid

endangering a relationship

- use the papers, your networks and the Web to compare prices, remaining mindful of tax and shipping costs
- get at least three bids for what you need (The cost of printing may be affected by how busy the printer is.)
- find out which is the best hour of the day, the best day of the week, the best week of the month and the best month of the year to shop for what you need
- collect a debt
- sell a collection
- see if a store will defer payments
- sell shares in your book like San Francisco writer Po Bronson did for his first novel, *The First $20 Million is the Hardest*
- do without it long enough to verify that the pain of not having it is greater than the pain of buying it
- find a foundation, business or nonprofit, that will sponsor your book
- use a credit card as a last resort only if you can repay it without affecting your lifestyle, and only after you calculate how much interest you will have to pay

If your budget is minimal, use alternatives whenever you can. Be creative in coming up with ways to avoid paying full price. If you speak about business and you need printing, could you exchange presentations of interest to your printer's business customers for printing? Or can you offer to include your printer's name and address in your handouts for a discount?

To develop a network of businesses you can trade with, join groups like The Rotary Club whose members own businesses. The discount mentality rules commerce. Competition, comparison shopping and buying on the Web make it easier than ever to find and ask for bargains. For a wealth of ideas about saving money, thrifty guerrillas will check out *Guerrilla Cost-Cutting: Secrets for Keeping the Profits in Your Home-Based Business* by Jay Conrad Levinson and Kathryn Tyler.

Most of the weapons in this book are free, many others cost little. The others can only cost as much as you can spend on them, so balance what it costs to use them against what you can afford to spend on them.

GUERRILLA TACTICS

Don't sacrifice quality for price if what you're buying will be seen by the media or professionals in the book trade. Everything you do for your books must be of professional quality. Poor quality, like poor writing, is obvious instantly.

You may not be able to economize with the best, but you are establishing a reputation that will last you a lifetime. So make your promotion plan like your book: impeccable.

16 Your Promotion Plan: The Final Version   (Free)

Measure twice, cut once.

—AN OLD CARPENTER'S SAW

If you want your nonfiction book published by a major house, you will need a promotion plan that is as long and strong as you can make it. To create one, list in descending order of importance what you will do to promote your book during its four-to-six-week launch window and as long after as you can foresee.

For most self-help books and other nonfiction aimed at a national audience, this list will be far more important than the content of your book in determining how salable your book is to a big publisher. But to repeat: no publisher will buy an unsaleable idea or even a good idea if it's poorly presented. Integrate the information in the first version of your plan with the budget you set, using the following list as a template for writing your promotion plans:

- "The author will match the publisher's out-of-pocket consumer promotion budget up to $X."
- "When the book is published, the author will present talks in the following X cities: . . ." Include a list of as many cities as you will go to, starting with the major markets that are listed in appendix seven.
- "After the publication tour, the author will continue to give X talks/classes/seminars/presentations a year." Give the number of presentations that you will continue to make a year.

- "The author will sell **X** copies of the book a year." Give a round number for the books you will sell a year, assuming 25 percent of your listeners buy a book. If you do a concentrated tour on publication and then continue to give as many talks as you can for the rest of the year, your first year's sales will be higher than those in succeeding years.

If you are writing a nonfiction book or any other kind of book with author-driven promotion, and you can't fill in the three previous sentences with significant numbers, you may not yet have a book that will interest the big or medium-sized New York houses. Consider small presses, self-publishing or having the patience to gather the ammo you need. To strengthen your plan:

- Establish a strategic alliance with a business or nonprofit organization that will commit to buying a large quantity of books, sending you around the country as a spokesperson, or lending its name to the book. See chapter nine for more about this.
- Include the line, "The author (or name of publicist) will prepare a media kit containing: . . ." Chapter eight has a list of what to include in a media kit. (If you will hire a publicist, mention who it is and how he or she will help you. Ideally, it should be a publicist who will impress New York editors or one with an impressive track record with books from big houses.)
- Give round numbers for the lists of print, broadcast and electronic media and opinion-makers to whom you (or your publicist) will send the media kit. Indicate which of these people will receive a copy of the book. The publisher will supply a certain number of promotional copies for which you will receive no royalties. If possible, add, "The author will provide the promotional copies the publisher can't." Chapter eleven covers promotional copies.
- Indicate how often you or your publicist will contact the media about interviews. Be sure to say how this will be done.
- Add "The author's goal will be to do **X** phoners a day." Give your goal for the number of "phoners"—radio interviews you can give in your pajamas—that you will do a day and how you will obtain them.

- Mention your Web site and how you will use it. Chapter ten discusses Web sites.
- List people whose names on the cover of your book will give it nationwide credibility and salability two years from now and who will give you cover quotes.
- List trade, consumer and professional conferences and conventions at which you know that you will be able to speak and the number of people who attend. If you will arrange to have your books sold at them, mention how. Estimate your costs for this carefully.
- List media that will impress New York publishers, that you know will publicize the book through interviews, reviews or stories. Local media will only impress editors if they're in major markets. If you want to include them, do it at the end of the plan.
- Consider doing two promotion plans: a plan for the first few years the book is published and a lifetime plan. Elise Babcock's sample proposal at the back of Mike's book *How to Write a Book Proposal* includes a lifetime promotion plan.
- Mention special-interest magazines that will trade stories you write for ads, an idea discussed in chapter fourteen.
- Mention magazines that will do per-order ads (see chapter fourteen).
- Give the name of the periodical, online or print, that has agreed to publish a column of yours that will give your ideas and your books as much exposure as possible. Your compensation for the column will be either money or the publication of a bio you write to promote your book and yourself. Please see chapter twelve for more about this.

This list is only the beginning. You are limited only by your time, energy and imagination. No one will ever criticize you for having a promotion plan that's too long, provided that every idea and every word count. Include only information that will impress the publishers you want to sell to.

In this respect, novelists are luckier than nonfiction writers. Not much is expected from them in the way of promotion. It's a challenge for new writers to have the ammunition that will excite editors in the Big Apple, but big houses are far more demanding than small presses.

If you aren't ready yet to provide a plan that will arouse the interest of

New York publishers, it doesn't mean your book isn't salable. Your book may have best-seller potential. It may just mean that you need a small publisher, who won't need to sell as many copies as a big publisher to make a profit, so they can be more patient in nursing your book along until it reaches its commercial potential.

Self-publishing guru Dan Poynter, the author of the self-published *The Self-Publishing Manual,* believes that if a publisher can't sell four times as many books as you can, you're better off publishing it yourself. This will give you total control over your book and all of the profits from it. If it's successful, you will have the option of saying no to publishers who approach you about republishing it.

There are more ways to promote books than ever. If you find a publisher willing to match your promotion budget, they will figure what to do with their budget. In any case, end your promotion plan like this: "The author's promotional efforts will be coordinated with those of the publisher."

You will be carrying out your promotion plan when your book is published a year to two years from now.

For example, you don't have to know where in Houston you will speak, you just have to commit yourself to going there. Houston is major market, and in major markets, hundreds of social, civic, business, academic, professional and religious organizations meet monthly or even weekly and they need speakers, as do organizations in the field you're writing about.

Most of these opportunities are unpaid, but unless you're speaking in a bookstore, you will usually be able to sell books. Once your book has a pub date, and you and your publisher agree on the order of the cities on your tour, you can start making plans.

The bottom line: The greater the continuing national impact you can give your book, the better the editor, publisher and deal you will get for it.

GUERRILLA TACTICS

- Start immediately to obtain an introduction and cover quotes for your books by developing your publishing and field networks. Go to author events and writer's conferences. Get to know the people who know the people you want to reach. Ask them to intercede on your behalf.

- Write to authors in care of their publishers. Tell them how much you like their books, and if possible, that you're quoting them in your book. The more successful authors are, the more besieged with requests they are. Expect turndowns, but start at the top of the list with the most valuable sources and work your way down. Be professional but relentless. One way to repay the kindness of strangers is to perform the same service for the writers that will one day be contacting you.

- Don't include any introductory remarks at the beginning of your plan. Underneath the subhead "Promotion," begin your plan by writing "To help promote the book, the author will carry out the following promotion campaign:" followed by your list with each new element beginning on a new line.

- Your promotion plan is only about the future. Write about your past and present in your bio.

- How can you go around the country giving talks if you have a full-time job? Do them on weekends.

- Editors do not want to see the words "is eager to" or "is available to." Only two things in promotion plans make publishers' eyes light up: numbers and the word "will." But the words "will contact" no matter who or what organization it is will not impress editors. Who knows if you will get through or if they will give you the help you seek? Because "will contacts" don't count as ammunition, put them at the end of your promotion plan.

The only things that count as ammunition in a promotion plan are things that *will* happen and that you are willing to commit to in a publishing contract. Even if your publisher doesn't add your commitments to the contract, they will be with the proposal or manuscript you submit, so they constitute part of what you are offering to publishers.

Part III

WEAPONS GALORE TO HELP YOU SELL MORE

CHAPTER 7

MORE POWERFUL PUBLICITY WEAPONS

Glory is fleeting but obscurity is forever.

—NAPOLEON BONAPARTE

very day more than four thousand radio and TV shows book more than ten thousand guests. Why shouldn't you be one of them? To help you take advantage of the publicity opportunities waiting for you, this chapter will arm you with more powerful publicity weapons:

- Your Elevator Speech (Free)
- Your Television Interviews (Free)
- Your Radio Interviews (Free)
- Your Print Interviews (Free)
- Your Satellite Tours (Expensive)

17 Your Elevator Speech (Free)

An elevator speech is a newsy, passionate sixty-to-ninety-second pitch to the media that must accomplish two goals: mention three ways your books will change their audience's lives immediately and convey this information with irresistible enthusiasm.

Your elevator speech should last no longer than an elevator ride. Once perfected, it will be your open-sesame for time and space in the media.

The media base their responses to pitches partly on the words and partly on the excitement with which they're delivered. But this pitch, the essence of your book conveyed with passionate conviction, will serve you whenever you need to make anyone excited about your book, including

- other writers
- magazine or newspaper editors
- your publicist
- journalists and talk-show producers
- booksellers
- the people who book you to speak
- the audiences you speak to

Don't share your elevator speech with anyone until your networks tell you that it's dynamite that will explode in the minds of media people, convincing them to book you on the spot. Make sure your elevator speech is equally effective whether it's delivered in person, over the phone, in print or on the net.

GUERRILLA TACTICS

Ask for feedback on your elevator speech from anyone who will be using it on your behalf. Once they agree it's ready for prime time, ask for a commitment on their part to use it.

18 Your Television Interviews (Free)

The biggest revolution in the book business has been brought about by the curious symbiosis that established itself between television's need for free talent and the need of book publishers to reach the public.
—MICHAEL KORDA

Do you want to be the statue or the bird?
—FRANCES WEAVER

The time allotted to authors on television shows at the nation's sixteen hundred television stations is either short or long. It's usually five minutes, a half hour or a one-hour marathon with one author or a panel. This means that you have to rehearse for both short and long interviews.

Visual appeal affects what we buy and what we watch. Television is a visual medium, and interview shows want to get away from talking heads. So one way to enhance your chances for television exposure is to come up with something visual you can do.

Demonstrations that don't require too much space or set-up time are a talk-show standby. Showing how to cook a dish is an obvious choice for cookbook authors. Athletes can bring video clips of themselves in action. Travel writers can bring photos or a video of their adventures. Any author who can do something that's visual, active and fresh has an edge over competitors who can't.

Clothes and props that relate to your books are visual and help establish your identity without saying a word, which is why they're also effective for author photos and print interviews. For more about enthusiasm, see chapter fifteen, and for more about establishing your identity, see chapter seventeen.

Major shows pay for transportation and lodging; small shows don't. If a large show wants you but won't pay the freight, your publisher will be delighted to.

19 Your Radio Interviews (Free)

When Wayne Dyer's first book, *Your Erroneous Zones,* was published, it was on the fast track to oblivion. So Dyer bought out what looked to be the first and last printing, filled his station wagon and headed west, doing as many radio shows and other media appearances as he could wherever he went. There was nothing erroneous about that plan. The book became a best-seller.

One of the ways Scott Peck kept *The Road Less Traveled* on the best-seller list for twelve years was by doing three radio shows a day, anytime anywhere.

When an interview on one of the country's almost 9,700 radio stations is live, your host will gauge the success of the show by how many blinking lights your comments produce on their multiple-line phone.

At night, 50,000-watt radio stations can cover a huge area. KGO, the ABC affiliate in San Francisco, receives calls from Arizona to Alaska!

WAR STORIES

Mike Larsen and Elizabeth Pomada met Frances Weaver, a septuagenarian who calls herself "a recycled housewife," at the Santa Barbara Writer's Conference. Frances had sold 100,000 copies of her self-published book *The Girls With The Grandmother Faces*.

Elizabeth sold it to Hyperion for the same figure. On publication day, Frances appeared on the *Today* show and made Bryant Gumble laugh at the question that introduces this weapon. The next day, the *Today* show offered Frances an eighteen-month contract for appearances as the senior lifestyles editor. The *Today* show later signed her for another eighteen months, giving a boost to her second book *I'm Not As Old As I Used To Be*.

The moral of the story: Every interview is an audition.

GUERRILLA TACTICS

• Unless you and your publicist agree you have a strong shot at being a solo guest on major television shows, give your publicist additional ammo: try to come up with ideas for panels and for panelists. This is an example of how a field network and cooperation, which is discussed in chapter thirteen, can help you. The right idea and panelists can make the difference between indifference and air time.

If you're a romance writer, for instance, you could do a panel on why romances account for more than half of mass-market sales.

• Leave a smile, your business card and, if you can, a copy of your book with the receptionist at every radio and television show.

If your book addresses social concerns, you will probably be able to obtain interviews on radio and television public-affairs shows that run on the weekends when ratings are lowest. The shows may be repeated or syndicated, which will magnify their promotional value.

20 Your Print Interviews (Free)

It's amazing that the amount of news that happens in the world every day always just exactly fits the newspaper.

—JERRY SEINFELD

GUERRILLA TACTICS

- Rick believes there are no small shows, only small authors. Always do your best. Every show builds your skill at interviewing so you'll be ready for Larry King. You never know who's listening.
- There are seven hundred phoners—talk shows that you can do from anywhere—that need guests every day. Use the media directories in the Resource Directory to find them, and give yourself a lead time of four to six weeks.
- Take publicist Jill Lublin's advice: even if you're in your jammies, stand up when you're doing phoners. You'll breathe better and have more energy. Also: smile. The host and your listeners will hear it even though they can't see it.

You have the most time leeway in setting up newspaper interviews. Radio and television shows have to be set up in advance. But editors at America's sixteen hundred daily newspapers assign stories in order of importance on the day that reporters will cover them. You have to approach the preprinted sections of the Sunday paper and the weekly food section, for example, a month to six weeks ahead, longer for supplements in major markets. Large magazines plan their issues six months ahead of publication.

Trade and consumer newspapers and magazines, 'zines and online publications can feature you and your work with

- reviews
- excerpts from your book before or after publication
- articles by you
- articles about you or your subject that quote you
- stories on your special events
- articles about other subjects that include you and your books
- your letters to the editor
- your op-ed pieces

Off-the-book-page publicity is more effective for subjects covered in other parts of the paper such as the sports or food sections.

If they are going to use photos, print and online media will want photos that are more interesting than an author sitting in a hotel room or restaurant.

The demise of *Life* magazine as a weekly publication offers continuing proof of the consumer trend away from general-interest media and toward special interests. The Web is the ultimate enabler of special-interest publishing. This is what accounts for the explosion of 'zines on the Web.

GUERRILLA TACTICS
Take a look at how out-of-town papers handle stories about authors.

21 MDRTs, TPCs and SMTs (Expensive)

Rick Frishman's firm, Planned Television Arts (PTA), invented the Morning Drive Radio Tour® (MDRT®). The MDRT® provides you with live, ten-minute radio interviews in eighteen to twenty cities.

The Satellite Media Tour (SMT) enables you to do live, five-minute television interviews in eighteen to twenty cities.

A teleprint conference (TPC)™ stages a live, one-hour news conference with ten to fifteen news reporters.

MDRTs are a fairly reasonable investment, with their average cost ranging between four- and five-thousand dollars. TPCs cost slightly more—between five- and six-thousand dollars. SMTs, the most expensive option, can cost anywhere from fourteen- to eighteen-thousand dollars.

These specialty tours don't work for every kind of book. Consult your networks and your publicist to see if these tours will help your book enough to justify the expense.

GUERRILLA TACTICS

- If you can come up with half of the cost, ask your publisher if they will spring for the other half. If not, ask if they would be willing to take the funds out of future royalties.
- If you are planning to do broadcast interviews, get a toll-free number when your budget allows so you can mention it during your interview. If this is not possible, mention the toll-free number of a local bookseller who is set up to fill mail orders. Ask TV producers to chiron your title and toll-free number. (Chiron is the electronic lettering that appears at the bottom of the screen.) You want viewers and listeners to buy your book while they are still excited about it.
- To get a 50 percent higher response, create a personalized number. (Do you think 800-BUY-MYBK is still available?)

CHAPTER 8

WEAPONS THAT PROVE YOU'RE A GUERRILLA

he following weapons are essential tools for promoting your books and for proving you're a guerrilla:

- Your Media/Speaker's Kit (Expensive)
- Your Press Release (Free or low cost)
- Your Web Site (Low cost)
- Your Knowledge of Publishing and Promotion (Low cost)
- Your Follow-up (Free)
- Your Evaluation Form (Free or low cost)
- Your Publisher's Publicity Questionnaire (Free)

22 Your Media/ Speaker's Kit (Expensive)

Your book, your media kit and your Web site are the basic weapons you need for approaching the media. Your media kit should give the media all the information you can that will convince them to interview you:

- a one-to-two page news release about your book, which is so effective that it can serve as a low-cost alternative to a press kit

  Keep your book newsworthy by changing your press release periodically to tie into hot news stories or new developments: announcements of related new books, products or services; an award or prize you've won; an anniversary; a milestone you or your books have reached; a holiday; or the birthday of someone well known.

- a list of questions in descending order of importance for which you will rehearse answers, including a few that may have nothing to do with your book but might intrigue interviewers

    Make sure the answers to these questions enable you to give all the essential information you want the public to know. No matter what questions you are asked, your job is still to segue from the questions you are asked to the answers you want to give.

- your bio
- a 5″ × 7″ black-and-white glossy photo of you for print media and television shows
- reviews with praise underlined, which you add to as they appear
- articles that are by or about you or include you
- articles that prove your subject is newsworthy
- a pitch letter explaining why you will make an outstanding subject for an interview
- a fact sheet of the most interesting points in your book
- an impressive audio or videotape of you speaking or being interviewed (A videotape is essential for major shows. Producers are copycats. They don't want to be pioneers; they need proof that you're scintillating.)
- your brochure if you have one
- a small, fun, cheap, eye-catching, easy-to-mail, imaginative gimmick or symbol of your book, perhaps with your name and title on it, that will set your kit off from the others that inundate the media

    When his best-seller *Swim With The Sharks Without Being Eaten*, was published, Harvey Mackay went around the booksellers' convention handing out half-inch brass stick pins of a shark.

- handouts
- your business card
- slides for color photos—they reproduce better than prints
- a Q&A of the most interesting questions you want interviewers to ask you followed by the answers that will best sell you and your books
- quotes from satisfied readers
- letters—or quotes from letters—from journalists who have previously interviewed you
- a list of the cities on your tour

Until your budget enables you to print special folders to hold your press kit, use a glossy Duo-Tang paper folder with two pockets. If printing special folders for the kit is too expensive, arrange with your publisher to have extra copies of your cover printed and affix them to the front of the folder.

Send your "A" list of top media people your media kit and a book, if your publisher doesn't. For the rest, guerrillas economize by E-mailing or snail-mailing just the news release, which asks the media to request the book and the media kit and to visit the author's Web site to see the rest of the kit. If you make the request by mail, include a return postcard, ideally postage-paid.

Appendix four is a sample media kit.

ONE SPEAKER'S KIT TO GO

If you are or will be a speaker, you will find that what goes into your media kit overlaps with what you need for your speaker's kit.

To convert your media kit into a speaker's kit:

- Rewrite your bio to emphasize your speaking experience.
- Put your photo on the cover of the kit, and include another copy in the kit.
- Include a "one sheet": a two-sided page you can fax to bookers interested in inviting you to speak. It should include your photo, information about you as a speaker, laudatory quotes from members of your audiences, a bulleted bio with key points about you, a list of clients, titles and short paragraphs about the programs you offer, and your contact information.
- Also include anything from your media kit that will impress recipients or is relevant to your presentation, such as a postcard-size version of your book cover.
- As soon as you can, have a video demo made. Meeting planners expect to see potential speakers in action. You can include the video and the information in your speaker's kit on your Web site.

Your media kit will be the first impression the media have of you, so it must be impeccably professional. Ask your networks and your publisher's publicist to review it before you print it.

GUERRILLA TACTICS

- Before you prepare your own publicity materials, ask your publisher what they can supply you with. When they stop providing them, ask for a printer-ready disk with the artwork to reproduce.
- Color is the biggest expense in printing. Ask your publisher if there's leftover space on the sheet on which they are printing your cover. If there is, ask to include your business card, bookmark or a postcard-sized version of your cover.

  Cost out the printing expenses before committing to them. Ask if your publisher is willing to absorb them or use the promotion budget for your book to pay for them. Even if you have pay to have the artwork scaled down for your needs and for cutting and trimming the sheets, you will still be "minting" beaucoup guerrilla greenbacks.
- If a magazine runs a story about you that you can use in your media kit, ask about buying enough reprints to last as long as you can use it. Photocopying may be a thrifty alternative.

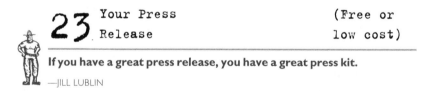

23 Your Press Release   (Free or low cost)

If you have a great press release, you have a great press kit.
—JILL LUBLIN

Your one- or two-page press release can be an economical substitute for a media kit. The goal of your press release is to reveal the essence of your book in a way that shows the media immediately why you will make a great interview.

Here are the keys for an effective news release:

- Come up with an attention-grabbing headline.
- Create a lead paragraph that captures an editor's attention with the five w's and one h: who, what, when, where, why and how.
- Write it in pyramid style, giving information about the book in descending order of importance.
- At the bottom of the last page, include basic information about your

book: title, author, publisher, pub date, price, number of pages, illustrations and International Standard Book Number (ISBN).

- Include one or two bulleted lists of the book's key points or benefits.
- Place the phrase "FOR IMMEDIATE RELEASE" in uppercase letters in the upper left corner.
- In the upper right corner, write "CONTACT:" and give the name and telephone number of the person to contact for more information.
- Avoid sending a head shot or the cover of your book. Instead, use your imagination to come up with an image of you with a caption editors are most likely to use.
- Include all of your contact information: address, fax number, Web site and E-mail address.
- Indicate that a media kit is available on request or at your Web site.
- Update your release when your book is reprinted.
- Include a one-paragraph bio at the end of the release.
- Change the slant of your release every two months to make it newsworthy, and resubmit it.
- Before mailing the release, run it by publicists and your networks for feedback.
- If book reviewers cover books like yours, send them the release. But if, for example, you've written a cookbook, send it to the food editor.
- Use the media directories listed in the Resource Directory to create an up-to-date mailing list.
- At the bottom of the last page of your release, give your book's title, publisher, pub date, format (hardcover, trade paperback, mass market), price and number of pages, and add the book's ISBN (international standard book number).

The ultimate compliment your press release can receive comes from newspapers and magazines that run it unchanged as a story.

THE 9/18 RULE

John Kremer advocates the 9/18 Rule: contact the media nine times in eighteen months. Seize every opportunity to contact the media. Among the opportunities you may have are

- notifying the media and opinion-makers about your events
- winning a prize, grant, award or fellowship
- reaching a milestone for the number of copies your book has sold
- announcing a tour
- announcing a new or revised edition of your book
- a tie-in to a person, event or subject in the news, especially if it's controversial
- a tie-in to the anniversary of a historical event or the birth or death of a well-known person

Here are two reasons to come up with creative mind-catching headlines that make your books newsworthy:

- Like agents and editors, media people only read releases far enough to make a decision about them. So the more effectively a headline captures the media's attention, the more likely it is they will read the release and use it. Five times as many readers read only the headline as those who read beyond it.

    Keep the media reading by

    —presenting the facts behind the headline to convey the essence of your release in the first paragraph (Assume the editor may only print the first paragraph.)

    —using a lively quote from someone else in your second paragraph

    —adding more details to your story in your third paragraph

    —using your last paragraph to cover the basic information about your latest book

- Media people differ in whether they prefer to see faxes, E-mails or hard copy. Until you learn their preferences, use the medium that works best for you.

24 Your Web Site   (Low cost)

The Internet is like a herd of performing elephants with diarrhea— massive, difficult to redirect, awe-inspiring; entertaining and a source of a mind-boggling amount of excrement when you least expect it.

—GENE SPOFFORD

GUERRILLA TACTICS
- Your publisher may be willing to supply you with stationery or let you use their letterhead for your news release. Only use yours if it is more impressive.
- Media people are more likely to open envelopes that are typewritten or, even better, handwritten.
- Surprise recipients by writing or rubber stamping something creative on the envelope to catch their attention and intrigue them.
- If you're snail-mailing releases, use stamps. Better still, use several small denominations that add up to first-class postage. The envelope is more likely to be opened.

Technology is one of your best allies. The possibilities for writing, selling, promoting and communicating about your books with readers around the world put you light years ahead of writers without technology to help them.

Your Web site is the only continuously operating weapon you have for promoting your books. Your site promotes you and your books twenty-four/seven in 180 countries. The continuing rapid growth of the Web makes it an ever more powerful weapon for reaching book buyers and adding them to your online family.

Here is a grab bag of ideas to get you started. Your Web site can include
- your contact information
- your media kit
- a list of your upcoming appearances
- your brochure
- a description of your products and services
- the video of a talk or interview
- the audio of a talk or interview
- a sample chapter or a new chapter every month, a table of contents and/or stand-alone excerpts from your books (check with your publisher for permission)
- updates to your nonfiction books (Information becomes obsolete at the rate of 2 percent a month. That's 24 percent a year. Always mention in your books that your book is being continuously updated at your site.)

- a message board so people can discuss what's going on in your field and their experiences with your books, products and services
- reviews of your books or quotes from them
- quotes from letters about your books
- photos of your book covers
- a place to hold regular forums to discuss your books
- a column, newsletter or a tip of the day, week or month that will bring visitors back to your site (you can also E-mail these to subscribers)
- a forum for classes you teach online
- reciprocal links with other sites, including your publisher's
- surveys and questionnaires
- contests
- a teacher's guide if your books have education potential
- your evaluation form for your talks and your site
- a reading-club guide if your books are potential reading-club selections
- answers to frequently asked questions (FAQs)
- an annotated recommended reading list of books in your field, books about writing and publishing and other books you love (For more on this, see chapter seventeen.)
- the opportunity for visitors to buy your books from you or links to online booksellers (If you want to sell copies yourself, be creative about what value you alone can add to the book such as personalized, autographed, gift-wrapped copies with special papers viewers can choose from on your site.)

What can you do to build relationships with your readers? Encourage them to contact you at your Web site with

- comments, advice, information and discussions that compel visitors to stay and return often
- stories about their lives or businesses that you can use in your talks, on your Web site, in future editions of your book or in new books
- questions, the answers to which you can use the same way you use their stories (Questions may also lead you to ideas for sequels.)
- answers to questions you ask about
  —how to improve the site

—changing and improving your books

—ideas for new books

—opportunities for you to speak

—organizations that might be interested in buying books in quantity for their members

—feedback on new work test-marketed on your site

—creating links from other sites to yours

—names and E-mail addresses of people who might be interested in your books and learning about your site

—other sites that will enable you to improve yours and track what other authors are doing

A WAR STORY

Francesca de Grandis, author of *Be A Goddess! A Guide to Celtic Spells and Wisdom for Self-Healing, Prosperity and Great Sex* developed a Web site that became so popular it appeared in stories in the *New York Times* and the *Wall Street Journal* on Halloween—not the most likely papers to feature a Wiccan Web site. See for yourself at www.well.com/user/zthirdrd/psychic.html.

Your Web site will compete with other Web sites, other media and all other activities your visitors can spend time on. How can you compete with this avalanche of alternatives? Make irresistible offers to bring visitors to your site and then provide them with information, enjoyment and other benefits that make them eager to return and tell their friends about the site.

Developing and maintaining a Web site will continue to become easier. The keys to an effective site are

• being unique and better than the sites of your competitors; otherwise, visitors will have no reason to spend time at your site

• taking what works best for you offline and making it work even better for you online

• continually monitoring other sites, especially those of authors, for ideas on improving the design and increasing the value of yours (Reward those visitors whose ideas you use.)

- continuously update the information on your site and in your books
- planning and executing a promotion plan for making your Web site successful (Create the plan a year in advance as you do for your offline promotion.)
- responding to questions, comments and suggestions as quickly and graciously as you can
- sending out weekly teasers too enticing to ignore about new information on your site
- telling more than selling; don't think store, think resource, making your site the leading source of information and advice in your field
- learning to write for the Web
- seducing visitors to your site with an aesthetically pleasing, effective design that gives visitors what they want ASAP
- making the power of the Web work for you by having links from as many directories, search engines and other sites as possible
- using as many media as you can besides words: images, graphics, audio and video
- defying The 10/40 Law—AOL has found that you have ten seconds to capture the attention of net surfers and forty seconds to keep it before they're off to the next stop
- providing quality content in as few words as possible to prove you understand that wasting your visitors' time is a crime punishable by the click of a mouse
- posting a hassle-free guarantee policy on your books, products and services

Web sites can be just as effective a weapon for novelists as they are for nonfiction writers, and they are even more vital for novelists because it's harder to promote fiction.

Just as the World Wide Web is your window on cyberspace, your Web site is the window that cyberspace opens on you. Your challenge is to open it as wide as you can, to make your site so enticing and enlightening that visitors will always have reasons to return and help you find new visitors by praising it to others.

No matter what kind of books you write, your Web site can be a tremendously powerful weapon. As you use it and explore other sites (www.ronkaufman.com is one of the best author sites on the Web), you will discover more ways to magnify the power of your site.

GUERRILLA TACTICS

- If you have an idea for a fresh, grabby umbrella title with variations that can be titles for a series of books, register it as the domain name for your site ASAP. Otherwise, do it as soon as you and your editor agree on a title for the series.

    Get your Web site up and running as quickly as you can. Use visitors' responses to make sure the look and information it delivers are as effective as you want them to be.
- Investigate your options for designing, launching, marketing and maintaining a Web site. It will cost you either time or money. The more you can do for yourself, the less money it will cost.

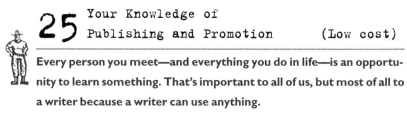

25 Your Knowledge of Publishing and Promotion (Low cost)

Every person you meet—and everything you do in life—is an opportunity to learn something. That's important to all of us, but most of all to a writer because a writer can use anything.

—TOM CLANCY

Understanding publishing and promotion is essential to your success. You have to understand what to do, why you should do it and the best way to go about it.

There are more ways to learn about publishing and promotion than ever:

- your networks
- the trade journal *Publishers Weekly* and other magazines for writers
- the books in the bibliography
- writer's classes and conferences
- online sites for writers, some of which are listed in the Resource Directory
- online discussion groups

- the meetings and newsletters of publishing and writer's organizations
- the cable channel CSPAN2 on weekends
- Book Expo America and regional booksellers' events

Because the industry is changing rapidly, staying on top of what's happening and how it affects you is more important than ever. New media, markets and promotion techniques are filled with promise for writers.

The challenge is using your sources of information to understand what's going on and to figure out how to integrate new opportunities into your writing and promotion.

GUERRILLA TACTICS

Establish a small group that ideally will include writers, a publicist, a sales rep, a bookseller, a reviewer and an agent. The purpose of the group will be to meet periodically online or offline to discuss publishing and promotion.

26 Follow-ups   (Free)

I can give you a six-word formula for success:
"Think things through—then follow through."
—EDWARD RICKENBACKER

Follow-ups are essential to your success. Other writers need the same allies you do, and many of the people you need are busier than you are. Following up with the media, other professionals and your fans is the mark of a guerrilla.

Checking with the media after you have sent them your publicity material is crucial. They're swamped with all forms of communication and need enough repeated nudging to give you a response.

How do you sustain a lifelong relationship with your readers? You use all of the weapons that enable you to stay in touch with and help them whenever and however you can. Think of it as a working marriage. The more you help them, the more repeat and referral business they will be delighted to generate for you.

You can build enduring relationships with your readers by

- realizing that you are the embodiment of your ideas, that how you relate to your readers exerts a strong influence on your success
- E-mailing or snail-mailing postcards to readers around the country about new books and your presentations in their area
- using technology to stay in touch with them (see chapter ten)

This book contains a host of weapons that help you remain a part of your readers' lives. As with promoting your books, the more weapons you use to stay in touch with your fans, the more powerful the weapons become.

If you belong to a book or music club, you have been offered free books and CDs for every new club member you enroll. The clubs know satisfied customers are the best source of new customers.

The people who love your books, products and services do double duty. They are steady customers you can count on, but they are far more valuable as scouts who are delighted to find new readers for you. They feel they are doing their friends a favor by turning them on to you and your work.

Raising an ever-growing army of fans who assist you in reaching your objectives is how guerrillas around the world achieve win-win victories in the endless struggle to own readers' eyeballs.

One essential way to prove the value of your activities is to create a paper trail: make sure that your agent, editor and publicist know about everything you're doing. E-mail is the most efficient way to keep everyone informed,

GUERRILLA TACTICS

Just as you allot time to writing and mailing publicity material to the media, pick a time for follow-up contact. Rick has what he calls "The Rule of Seven." He has found that it takes seven contacts to obtain bookings for authors. The initial one or two contacts may be by E-mail, but they still have to be followed up. The most important verb in promotion is follow up. Without it, you take away the *pro* and end up with just *motion*.

but also forward news and clippings of the media attention that your efforts generate.

27 Your Evaluation Form (Free)

Increase the value of every presentation by using an evaluation form. Guerrillas are savvy enough to understand how potent an evaluation form is. So turn your audiences into focus groups who do free market research for you.

An evaluation form provides you with a scorecard to check on what is and isn't working, and the chance to ask audiences how to improve your presentation. They will also help you discover what to write next and what other talks they want to hear. New talks lead to new articles and books. Your audiences will also be valuable sources of ideas about what to change when you update your books.

The more they enjoy your presentations, the more eager your audiences will be to share their ideas for changes, improvements and additions. Your audiences can be far more valuable to you than whatever you might earn from speaking and back-of-the-room sales.

Here are two ways to add continuing value to your talks:

- You can make the end of your class the beginning of lifelong relationships with your audiences. You accomplish this by staying in touch with them and continuing to add value to their lives. Your evaluation form can ask students if they wish to receive online updates to the information you give them in your class.
- You can also use your evaluation form to ask if your audiences know of others who will benefit from the talk. Ask them to include contact information if they can. Find a way to reward them if someone comes to a class and mentions a friend as the way they found out about it.

Ask for permission to quote praise for your talks. Use it in your promotion materials and as part of an endless and growing list on your Web site.

Limit your questions to one side of a page, but encourage respondents to use the other side of the page if they wish.

Ask whoever is sponsoring your talk if they will provide an evaluation form. If they won't, ask if they will print and distribute yours. Writer's conferences and university extensions often will. If they won't, decide whether it will be less expensive to print them yourself or to go to a print shop.

Appendix eight is a sample evaluation form you can alter as needed.

GUERRILLA TACTICS

- Roger Crawford, a top inspirational speaker and the author of *How High Can You Bounce: Turn Your Setbacks Into Comebacks*, is a true guerrilla. He asks some of his listeners for a photocopy of the notes they take during his talks. This enables Roger to learn what his audiences find of enduring value in his talk.

  You can suggest that if listeners prefer, they can take the form home and fax or E-mail the answers to you, or use the form on your Web site. Include your contact information and the titles of your books.
- If you can, announce at the beginning of your presentation that you have a brochure covering the key points you will make during the session. Offer to exchange it for a filled-out evaluation form after the class.
- Continue to improve your evaluation form as you do your presentations.

28 Your Publisher's Publicity Questionnaire (Free)

Your publisher's publicity questionnaire will help determine what your publisher will do to promote your book, so it's worth all the time you lavish on it.

To help decide how to promote your book, your publisher will send you a questionnaire about six pages long. Like publishing contracts, all publishers' publicity forms are different, but they all cover the same terrain. It includes your media contacts and experience, who might give cover quotes, who should receive a copy of your book, and your ideas for promoting the book.

The publicity questionnaire is your opportunity to describe everything you will do to promote your book. If you have already sent in your promotion plan, your publicist may not have seen it or may have forgotten it if she did.

If you sold your nonfiction book with a proposal, more than a year may have passed. Also, you made more contacts and came up with more promotion ideas while you were writing your book. So either include your plan when you return the questionnaire or integrate your plan into the questionnaire. Respond as fully as you can to every item. Your responses will affect what your publisher does to promote your book. Even if there's no budget for promotion, the creativity, effectiveness and realism of your ideas will affect how your publicist responds to the questionnaire.

Appendix six is Writer's Digest Books' publicity questionnaire.

GUERRILLA TACTICS

- Publicity forms list the kind of information publicists need and leave space for your responses. Typing your information may mean adding information you don't have room for on separate pages. So either scan the form into your computer or just number the answers as you input them into your computer. The information you provide will give you a head start on filling out the forms for future books. If you do type the information, make a copy for yourself.
- Ask your networks for ideas and share your responses with them to help ensure that you've done justice to the questionnaire.

CHAPTER 9

FUSION MARKETING WEAPONS

usion marketing is joining forces with businesses and nonprofits for win-win projects. The weapons that follow are examples of fusion-marketing arrangements:

- Your Strategic Alliances (Free)
- Window and In-store Displays (Free)
- Fundraisers (Free)
- Your Annual Awards (Free)

29 Your Strategic Alliances (Free)

A strategic alliance is so powerful that it alone can yield a national tour and thousands of sales. And the price is right. A strategic alliance requires six elements:

- an excellent book
- the right time
- a benefit for a business or nonprofit organization
- the ability to find an organization willing to collaborate with you
- the patience to negotiate a mutually beneficial arrangement
- maintaining the relationship

A strategic alliance with a major corporation or national nonprofit organization can make a book successful all by itself.

Imagine, for example, that you have written a book on how to fight cancer. The ideal partner for you is a national organization that has chapters around the country and millions of members. How can such an organization help you?

The organization can
- review and excerpt your book
- run an article about you or an interview with you
- buy books to resell or give away; a large enough order can be customized to suit the organization's needs
- have the head of the organization write a forward or give a cover quote
- give you permission to use their logo and say the book is endorsed by, or being published in association with, the organization on the cover
- name you a spokesperson
- arrange and pay for a speaking tour to its chapters around the country
- have its publicity department arrange for media appearances during your tour
- have books for members to buy or receive as gifts and for you to sign at your talks
- arrange for you to speak at conferences
- sponsor conferences on the subject of your books
- sponsor the writing of your books
- connect you with key people in the field who can
  —give you information
  —provide cover quotes
  —do media interviews with you
  —participate in events with you
  —introduce you to other opinion-makers in the field

The organization can repeat this process with all your books. You may be able to forge an alliance with a company that provides a product or service you can mention in your book. They have a bottom-line incentive for helping you: the more exposure they arrange for you, the more sales they make.

The bureaucratic mindset is such that if you want them to help you with a book, they usually want to see the book. You on the other hand, want the alliance to be cooking by pub date. The ideal time for an organization to make at least a tentative arrangement is after they've read your proposal. Even if you have to wait for them to read the accepted manuscript, that still leaves nine months to make arrangements.

The two ways around this are

WAR STORIES

Margaret Brownley's novel, *Wind Song*, got a royal send-off with a little help from a prince of a company. While on the phone with her editor brainstorming title ideas, Margaret spotted the *Wind Song* lotion she kept over the sink. With the title came the idea for a promotional plan. Margaret wrote to the Prince Matchabelli company, telling them about her book and requesting Wind Song perfume samples for promotional purposes.

She got more than she bargained for. A few weeks later, three large cartons of Wind Song products, including full-sized bottles of perfume and lotions, landed on her doorstep. She sent the perfume and lotions with letters and book covers to chain bookstore buyers and distributors. The sample packets were stapled to bookmarks and mailed to bookstores, newsletter editors and reader groups. She also gave them out at conferences and booksignings.

One of her publisher's reps reported that clients receiving Wind Song gift packages increased their orders. Margaret is toying with the idea of calling her next book *Rolls-Royce*.

- having one or more top people in the field intercede on your behalf to raise the organization's comfort level in affiliating themselves with a stranger, especially if the person is a first-time author
- having an idea and a proposal—or better yet a manuscript—so good, a writer whose credentials are so solid, and a personality so persuasive, that the organization will take a plunge into the unknown

30 Window and In-store Displays (Free)

This is an opportunity for a triple play that will benefit you and two merchants. Ask your bookseller if you can arrange for a window display with another merchant in town who sells merchandise that relates to your book, whether it's a how-to garden book, a travel book or a book tied to a holiday.

If you write cookbooks, see if you can use cookware from a local store in your bookseller's window with a sign telling browsers where to buy what they see. Arrange with the store selling kitchenware to use your book in the window with a sign directing window shoppers to the bookstore. You may even be able to do talks and signings in both stores, or maybe the stores can collaborate on an event that will be publicized to both of their mailing lists.

GUERRILLA TACTICS

If you succeed in bringing two merchants together, push your luck and see if a charity, another business or a nonprofit organization is willing to tie in with that event. Using the cookbook example, perhaps the organization will sponsor a fund-raising dinner using recipes from your book and include the cost of the book in the ticket price, or use the book as a raffle prize.

31 Fundraisers (Free)

Act as if what you do makes a difference. It does.
—WILLIAM JAMES

Name one nonprofit organization that doesn't need to raise funds to keep functioning. Give up? We can't either. Suppose you have written *Guilt-Free Desserts You Can Serve in 10 Minutes or Less*, a cookbook on the world's greatest low-calorie desserts modified so they can be made quickly. Have the ultimate dessert party, and make it a fundraiser for the local heart association.

Try to choose a charity with the following strengths:
- Their file of press clippings from previous events proves that their publicist is effective at getting media coverage.
- They have a publicist you will enjoy working with.
- They feel so strongly about your event and its value to them that they will commit all of their resources and contacts to making it successful.
- They have a mailing list big enough and responsive enough to produce the turnout needed to make the event work.
- They are a chapter of a national organization enabling you to use the success of the event to repeat it around the country.

GUERRILLA TACTICS

- Like putting on fundraisers, taking effective publicity photos is both an art and a craft. It takes imagination to think of the photo that the media will run, and it requires skill to capture the moment on film. If a person with these qualities isn't available to work for free, ask the organization to factor in the cost of hiring one into the event budget.
- Ask the photographer to help stage the event in a way that will maximize the opportunities for an irresistible money shot. In addition to using the photo for the organization's newsletter and Web site, the group's publicist can send it to local and national media. Associated Press syndicates material to more than one thousand papers. The right photo will more than pay for the cost of the photographer.

Ask if their publicist can do a mailing to their members, the media and opinion-makers in their field and yours.

Another idea for the same book: have a cooking contest for one of the desserts in the book. Then invite a panel of foodies and media people whose presence will generate the most coverage to be judges. Because the event is for charity, they will feel that they're doing a good deed while they're scarfing down those desserts!

This kind of fun, visual, win-win event can yield major space in the food section of the paper. If you attempt to carry out this or a similar event, mention in your letter to the invitees that calories don't count if they're consumed for charity, and that leftover food will be donated to a worthy cause.

32 Your Annual Awards (Free)

The Academy Awards are the prizes for the winners of the world's most glamorous contest. Adapting the idea for your field will increase your stature and provide publicity for you every year.

When her book *Celebrities and Their Angels* was published, Pat Montandon created a event with the San Francisco Academy of Art at one of their galleries.

The book contains drawings of angels by celebrities, along with their comments. Pat put it together to help fund her "Children as the Peacemakers" project. The academy had students create images of angels for their gallery. At the event, an angelic model posed for art students while celestial harp music and a heavenly choir added to the atmosphere.

The party offered the school the opportunity for publicity, while it provided Pat with an easily accessible space to invite the media and her networks to a signing and an awards ceremony for three celebrity angels, including Sharon Stone.

The television crews had all the visuals they needed for an upbeat story made more timely because the event took place during Christmas season. A local independent bookstore was on hand to sell more than two hundred books.

If there are people in your field who deserve recognition but aren't getting it, why not help them and yourself? You can plan a contest yourself or with colleagues. To find the volunteer help needed to run the contest, give the process credibility and put on the awards ceremony, partner with a nonprofit organization.

The potential to use the event as a fundraiser and a source of publicity will attract needy nonprofits such as academic and charitable organizations. A business, group of businesses or a nonprofit association with business members are also possible sponsors for an awards event, as are chambers of commerce and local governments.

You can be one of the judges, the emcee and the coordinator of the event. The more you're willing to do, the more you'll be able to shape the event.

GUERRILLA TACTICS

- The larger a bureaucracy is, the more difficult it can be to work with. A lucky few seem born with the gift for bending groups to their will. If you aren't one of them, you may need to find someone to run interference.
- In putting together any event that involves other people, use as few people as possible to make the process efficient, yet enough people to benefit from different perspectives and get the work done.

CHAPTER 10

WEAPONS THAT USE TECHNOLOGY TO HELP YOU

We used to have lots of questions to which there were no answers. Now, with the computer, there are lots of answers to which we haven't thought up the questions.

——PETER USTINOV

e've chosen ten weapons that use technology to share with you. *Guerrilla Marketing Online: The Entrepreneur's Guide to Earning Profits on the Internet* and *Guerrilla Marketing Online Weapons: 100 Low-cost, High-impact Weapons for Online Profits and Prosperity,* which has ninety more weapons, were written by Jay Conrad Levinson and Charles Rubin. They provide a wealth of advice on the subject.

As with the other weapons you choose, don't expect miraculous results. Technology is becoming lightning fast; building relationships isn't. We look forward to learning about the weapons you create to add to this list:

- Your Tip of the Day and Weekly Teaser (Expensive but you get paid!)
- Online Booksellers (Free)
- Your Links and Directory Listings (Free)
- Self-writing Sequels (You get paid!)
- Your Webcasts (Low cost)
- Your Giveaways (Free)
- Your Surveys (Free)
- Your Discussion Groups (Free)
- Your E-mail Signature (Free)
- Your E- and Snail-mail Lists (Free)

33 Your Tip of the Day (Expensive but you get paid!)

A tip of the day is a nugget of information that will help readers stay up to date on new information, trends in the field and practical advice that will make them more effective. Since these nuggets are drawn from your book, they attract new readers.

To add variety, consider using the following suggestions to vary the kind of tip you give each day:

- a quote or anecdote that will help, inspire or entertain your readers
- a new piece of advice that will add to your subscribers' bottom line
- something readers have sent in
- a visionary idea subscribers can contemplate over the weekend

Ask your publisher to commit in a letter or in your contract to let you use material from your books in your tips before and after publication. If this is not possible, rewrite what you need to avoid a problem.

At the heart of Net culture is the belief that information yearns to be free, a tradition at odds with aspiring writers who yearn to be paid.

A poet with the soul of a guerrilla found a rewarding way to resolve this dilemma. He offered a limerick a day for a dollar a year. You may think that's a lot of limericks for a buck. But more than one hundred thousand people subscribed to the service. He's our candidate for the best-paid bard on the planet.

Jay embraced this idea, and he now offers three tips a day based on three of his books: the original *Guerrilla Marketing*, *Guerrilla Selling*, and *Guerrilla Marketing Online*. To see examples, visit www.gmarketing.com.

BONUS WEAPON

Your Weekly Teaser (Free)

You must give subscribers reasons to return to your Web site. One way to accomplish this is with a weekly teaser that offers subscribers something

GUERRILLA TACTICS

- Charles Dickens wrote his early novels as they were being serialized in a weekly London magazine. If you write fiction, write short shorts that are perhaps no longer than one screen on a daily basis. Or perhaps you can divide a short story or novel into daily pieces. The more subscribers you attract for your short stories, the more likely it is that they will be collected in book form.
- Sell a tip of the day for all of your books that cover a distinct body of knowledge about which people need advice.
- Once your daily tip is successful, try to extend its reach by getting it syndicated in print media and on radio. Finding a sponsor will guarantee it happens.
- Consider making the tips free, and include an advertisement in each tip.

they need enough to return for. Every week Jay E-mails his tip-of-the-day subscribers a teaser for a new article available at his Web site.

You can also use a giveaway, a survey or the results of a survey. As with every other aspect of your Web site, spend time at what your networks assure you are the latest and greatest, then improve on the best.

34 Online Booksellers (You get paid!)

Online booksellers make your books available to anyone anywhere at any time. The information they provide may include more than just bibliographic information: comments from reviewers, readers and yourself. Enhance their power as a selling tool by making sure they have as much positive, up-to-date information about you and your books as they allow.

Amazon founder Jeff Bezos has predicted that the sales of online books will max out at 15 percent of total book sales. But selling books online involves online publishers. The meteoric sales of Stephen King's novella *Riding the Bullet* proved the potential of online sales directly from publishers or authors.

You can now arrange with online booksellers to notify you or automati-

GUERRILLA TACTICS

- Visit online booksellers regularly to make sure the information about your books is accurate and to add new info that makes your books more enticing.
- When new editions of your books appear, ask booksellers to stop selling the old one.

cally send you novels or books in your field the moment they're available, before you even know you want them.

We predict that by the end of this decade, it will take seconds to download a book, and print-on-demand systems that already spit out books in less than a minute will produce a book in less time than it takes you to open the bag in which they arrive.

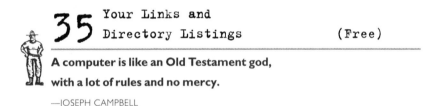

35 Your Links and Directory Listings (Free)

A computer is like an Old Testament god, with a lot of rules and no mercy.

—JOSEPH CAMPBELL

Part of the Web's huge value to authors as a win-win promotional tool is the power of links: your ability to get as many other sites as possible to link to yours. The more links you have to your site, the more visitors you have.

Your links will usually be reciprocal. You will have a link from someone else's site to yours in exchange for a link from your site to theirs. Try to obtain a link from information on your publisher's Web site to yours. Online services, a few of which are free, will place links for you on relevant sites. Directory listings will also give you a link to your site.

36 Your Self-writing Sequels (You get paid!)

How would you like to write your next book at the movies?

By encouraging visitors to your site to discuss their experiences with

GUERRILLA TACTICS

Allot part of your time online for searching for potential new links to your site, especially those that don't have to be reciprocal. Reward anyone in your networks who finds a link for you.

your books and share their ideas and questions, you are giving them the opportunity to collaborate with you on your next book.

If, for instance, it's possible for the sequel to this book to be a collection of war stories—the experiences of authors using the weapons in the book—it can be structured like this book, and the stories collected on www.gmarketing.com would become the material.

Put the information into context, create connective tissue between the stories and you're done.

Here's another approach for us to use online contributions: another book with one hundred more weapons. Because we ask readers to send us information on new weapons they create, we will in time amass enough weapons for another book.

Giving talks and teaching classes is at least as effective as readers posting information online. If an idea excites you, you are eager to share your ideas about it.

And helping authors to write their next book is an incentive, as is being acknowledged in the book and receiving a free autographed copy.

If you're writing a series of novels with reccurring characters, ask your readers to suggest plot ideas or interesting settings or new directions for a character or a sequel to take.

37 Your Webcasts   (Low cost)

Once a week or a month, you can give a talk or have a real-time chat session online.

You can replay radio and television interviews.

You can teach a class, audition new work, and answer questions that will give you ideas for writing and promotion. You can also host a reading group discussing new books in your field and invite the authors to join you.

GUERRILLA TACTICS

- Ask your visitors to set the agenda. Ask them what the most helpful and enjoyable way for them to spend time with you online would be. Do it.
- People will have different ideas. Use as many of them as you can that will deepen your relationship with your visitors and help add to your bottom line.

38 Your Giveaways (Low cost)

Content may be king, but free content is God.
—STEPHEN M. ZEITCHIK, *PUBLISHERS WEEKLY*

Freebies anyone? Getting something for nothing is the consumer's ideal. Why would anyone want to buy something you can get for free?

Offer freebies that relate to your books, products or services. Then promote them through your online and offline communication channels. Use them to generate traffic to your Web site by making them valuable enough to convince people to come to your site to get them.

Among the things you can offer are

- a chapter from a new book
- a helpful handout that you use in your presentations
- an evaluation

GUERRILLA TACTICS

- Time your offer to the pub date of your book to reap the most benefit from your freebies.
- Deliver the giveaway as fast as you can. Use a mailbot which, when someone requests information, responds automatically.
- If you don't hear from recipients of your freebie, follow up shortly after they've received it. Ask about their reaction and if you can be of help to them.
- Make a special follow-up offer to your Web site's first-time visitors to encourage a continuing relationship with you.

- a consultation
- a screensaver with information from one of your books

Always include your contact information, a list of your books and services and a request for feedback. The value of your freebie will rub off on the recipient's perception of the value of your books. Add to your mailing list the E-mail addresses of those who wish to receive notification of future giveaways.

Here's our freebie: to download a screensaver of the *ent* words in chapter one, visit www.gmarketing.com.

39 Your Surveys   (Free)

You can use your Web site as a forum for surveys and questionnaires about anything you want to know: information on your visitors, books in your field that they need but can't find, features they want to see on your site, and their favorite Web sites.

You can offer prizes or a special preview of your next book to randomly selected respondents. You can also give visitors permission to sign up for the prize every time they visit your site. First check other surveys, then run yours by your networks before casting it out into cyberspace.

GUERRILLA TACTICS
The following tips were adapted from *Guerrilla Marketing Online Weapons*:
- Explain the purpose of your survey and set a deadline for responses.
- Promote your site by giving your survey as much visibility as you can: post it in related forums and news and discussion groups.
- Develop relationships with respondents by replying to their comments and questions.
- Give your results maximum exposure by sending them to relevant media.
- Make the questions short, clear and easy to answer. Use yes/no or multiple choice questions.

40 Your Discussion Groups (Free)

Discussion groups or newsgroups are real-time forums, mailing lists that enable members to exchange views. Participating in discussion groups in your field gives you the opportunity to learn, teach and enhance your stature as an authority. Use your comments and your signature to make group members aware of your books. For the best results, do more telling than selling. All major online hosts have discussion groups.

GUERRILLA TACTICS

- Periodically ask your networks about the best discussion groups in your field, and ask them to join you in exchanging information on new ones.
- Monitor two or three discussion groups in your field. E-mail a contribution once a week.
- In the unlikely event that you don't find the discussion group you need, start one.

41 Your E-mail Signature (Free)

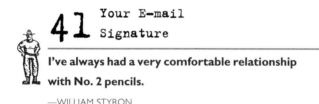

I've always had a very comfortable relationship with No. 2 pencils.

—WILLIAM STYRON

The identification at the bottom of your E-mail is an opportunity to mention the title of your book, your Web site, your theme, and the products and services you have available. Take up to six lines to let readers know about your books and other offerings.

42 Your Snail- and E-mailing Lists (Free)

One way *Guerrilla Selling* coauthor Orvel Ray Wilson builds his mailing list is a raffle of guerrilla goodies at his seminars. He asks participants to

GUERRILLA TACTICS
- Update the information as needed.
- Offer a gift or a discount to those who respond to an offer in your signature or those who come to an event and mention learning about it from your signature.

drop their business cards in a box and has one of them choose the winning card.

Standard Rate and Data Service (SRDS) publishes a directory available at your library. It will convince you that there is a mailing list you can buy for any group of two or more people who share the same interest. Orvel's approach creates a list of people he knows are interested in the guerrilla philosophy.

Selling to people who know you costs one-sixth of what it costs to attract strangers. So building a mailing list of people who have read your book, seen you speak or visited your Web site will create a more potent source of income from new books, presentations and whatever else you sell.

When you talk, ask whoever wishes to know about future talks to give you a business card or write down the information. Make providing this information an option on the evaluation form at your events.

A sign-up sheet is another way to acquire names. Since E-mail is faster and cheaper than snail-mail, ask for both addresses.

Increase your sales while decreasing your marketing costs by building a mailing list of satisfied readers and audiences. The more you have to sell, the more reasons you have to stay in touch with your readers, and the more powerful this formula becomes.

GUERRILLA TACTICS

- Collect people's cards at every opportunity.
- Use the last page of your books to ask your readers to visit your Web site and subscribe to what you offer.
- Prove the value of your list by staying in touch with the people on it with information and news about your books and presentations. Ask about their experiences with your books and use this information in your next communication with them.
- Ask recipients of your E-mail to forward the message to everyone they know who might be interested. You can also use a free or paid newsletter, discussed in chapter twelve, to keep in touch with your readers.
- Express your gratitude to the people on your list. If you're like us, you don't want your name used without your permission. So assure the people on your list that you will not share their names without their permission. You may be able to sell, barter or trade a list of those who don't mind.
- Offer the people on your list an early registration rate for presentations or pre-publication sales of new books. Devise other ways for making their presence on your list valuable to them. Use your imagination, advice from your networks and responses from your mailing list to increase the value of your communications. The more value you can add to the your readers' lives, the more glowing their word-of-mouth recommendations will be.
- Include an option for recipients to unsubscribe from your E-mail list.

CHAPTER 11

WEAPONS THAT INVOLVE YOUR BOOKS

A room without books is like a body without a soul.
—CICERO

 ooks are wonderful. They are compact, portable, reasonably priced, easy to scan and reassuringly low-tech. They encompass all human experience from the sacred to the profane. Your life will be inextricably bound up with your books. We hope they will always be a source of pride to you.

This chapter provides you with weapons that involve your books:

- Excerpts From Your Books (You get paid!)
- New Editions of Your Books (You get paid!)
- Reading Groups (Free)
- Your Promotional Copies (Free)
- Your Titles (Free)
- Your Covers (Expensive)
- Your Illustrations (Low cost)
- Your Acknowledgments (Free)
- Your Bibliographies (Free and you get paid!)
- Merchandising (You get paid!)
- Raffle Prizes (Free or low cost)
- Your Money-back Guarantee (Low cost)

43 Excerpts From Your Books (You get paid!)

Books are where things are explained to you; life is where things aren't. I'm not surprised some people prefer books. Books make sense of life. The only problem is that the lives they make sense of are other people's lives, never your own.

—JULIAN BARNES

Selling first serial rights—slices of your book that run before publication—offers you the opportunity to get paid to publicize your book. If you have been writing articles about your subject for trade or consumer newspapers, magazines, newsletters or Web sites, you may already have the connections you need to sell excerpts.

The best time for first-serial excerpts to appear is on publication, when your book is in stores. This is especially true if your book has newsworthy revelations that you don't want to leak out before publication.

However, there are two reasons to steal your own thunder by selling serial rights before publication:

- You need money to sustain yourself while you write your proposal, or you will need more money to write your book than you can expect in an advance. Selling one or more excerpts from your book or even serializing the whole book as you write it may make the difference in whether you can survive while you write it. In this case, the money you earn will be the meat, and the publicity you generate will be gravy.
- You want to use an article to attract agents and editors. The right article in the right publication at the right time will sell a book. If your idea and your article about it are impressive enough

  —editors and agents will find you (If you have a novel in progress, your short story may enable you to sell it with only a partial manuscript and a synopsis.)

  —you may be able to use the article as a sample chapter in a nonfiction proposal (Your idea and your ability as a writer will have greater credibility if a magazine pays you to write about your topic.)

Can someone else who sees your article write a book based on your idea?

You betcha. You can't protect an idea. However, stating in the brief bio that appears with your article that the piece is from "a forthcoming book" or "a book in progress" will signal agents and editors that a book is in the works and will help deflect potential competitors. For more on articles, see chapter twelve.

Unless they sell articles or first-serial rights on a regular basis, agents won't have the connections, the time or the interest to sell them for you. And unless excerpts from your books will have strong commercial potential or your publisher is giving your book a big push, their subsidiary rights department won't do much, if anything, to sell them.

You want whoever has the most skill and commitment to sell serial rights. Unless you are convinced that someone else will devote more time and energy to selling them than you will, you're better off trying to serialize your book yourself, even if you have to learn how to do it as you go along.

Use your networks, agent, editor and your publisher's subsidiary rights department to advise you on how to go about it. Your goals are to generate as much exposure as you can for your book and pocket as much money as you can.

Serial rights are worth more if
- you are well known
- your previous books were successful
- your excerpts contain newsworthy revelations or juicy dish on a celebrity
- your excerpt appears before rather than after publication when people have access to your book
- you sell them on an exclusive basis
- you sell as many excerpts as you can (or even the same excerpt) to non-competing newspapers or magazines
- you serialize the whole book

The 7,500 trade magazines and newsletters in the U.S. directed to business usually don't pay a lot (medical magazines are an exception), but every industry has at least one magazine. *Publishers Weekly* is the trade magazine for publishing. Trade media can make up in well-targeted exposure what they lack in pay.

They may be willing to trade an excerpt for ad space that may be worth far more than what the magazine pays for excerpts. Another upside: trade media may attract other media.

Trade publications can also be valuable if you want to be a speaker, because executives, speaking bureaus and meeting planners read them. Businesses and nonprofits have conferences and conventions for which they need speakers.

Mailing a printed excerpt to professionals who book speakers, along with a book if the organizations are important, may help propel you from the computer to the podium. The excerpt will also add to the credibility of your media and speaker's kit.

Your publisher will keep second-serial rights, the right to sell excerpts after publication. The contract usually calls for a fifty/fifty split of resulting profits. Even though they rarely command a significant sum, they are still worth selling because they help publicize your books. So if magazine editors express interest in second-serial rights, pass the word on to your editor.

GUERRILLA TACTICS

- Here are two alternatives to selling excerpts:
  —Rewrite sections of a nonfiction book so they won't be excerpts.
  —Write new articles or new short stories.
    Both of these alternatives can mention the title of your book, and it may yield more chances for you to sell short pieces. Everything you do is an audition for the next thing you do.
- Readers can write to you care of the periodical your work appears in, but for faster responses, include your E-mail address in your bio.

Two caveats about excerpting books:
- It's far more likely to happen for nonfiction books than novels. A novel may not lend itself to excerpting as a short story, and few magazines use short stories.
- As we mentioned above, you can't protect your ideas. Magazine editors have been known to take ideas submitted by freelance writers and assign them to a staff writer. This may be cheaper, and they know they'll get an article tailored to their magazine.

44 New Editions of Your Books   (You get paid!)

Publishers set a number for how many copies a book has to sell to warrant keeping it in stock. This number varies depending, among other factors, on the author's other books, whether a book is hardcover or a trade or mass-market paperback and public interest in such books.

When a book's sales dip below a certain number with no apparent hope for them to rise, a publisher has three choices:

- let the book go out of print
- have it available through print-on-demand systems that print books to order
- publish a new edition

For authors, the decision is a no-brainer. Changing just 10 percent of your book will enable it to be considered a new edition. This means your book will be in your publisher's catalog like a new book, the reps will sell it again, and you will get another chance to promote it.

As we mentioned earlier, information becomes out of date at the rate of 2 percent a month, 24 percent a year. Nonfiction authors using information that will become dated must expect to do revisions.

GUERRILLA TACTICS
- Be sure you will have enough time and money to revise your book.
- Publishers don't usually do much to promote revisions, but use what you learned promoting the previous edition to go all out to reignite the sales of the new edition. What happens with the new edition may lead to speaking opportunities and the chance to write more books.

Meanwhile, ask if it's possible to make small changes that won't affect the page length between printings. Updates are one reason to mention your Web site at the back of the book. Ask readers to contact you with new information, perhaps offering a reward for their help.

Depending on the work and time a revision requires, you may be able to get an advance to help you write the revision.

45 Reading Groups You Attend (You get paid!)

A half a million reading groups around the country are reading a book a month. Connecting with them as you travel will do more than sell your present book. You will be laying tracks you can ride to Royalty City every time a new book comes out. This weapon is especially valuable for literary novelists.

GUERRILLA TACTICS

- If you're writing books that have reading-group potential, post a discussion guide on your Web site, along with your travel itinerary. Ask booksellers at the stores where you will be signing to contact local reading groups to see if they will join a discussion of your book. Booksellers will welcome the chance to help you help them sell your books. Consider setting a minimum order to justify your participation.
- Other ways to find reading groups include
  —E-mailing your mailing lists by zip codes
  —searching online
  —asking librarians
  —asking site visitors about their local reading groups—your tour may spark the establishment of new groups

46 Promotional Copies (Free)

SNOOPY **(typing): Joe Greed was born in a small town in Colorado.**
LUCY: **I think your stories are stupid. If they're ever printed in a book, I refuse to waste my money on it. However, if you get some free author's copies, I'll be glad to take one.**
—FROM *PEANUTS* BY CHARLES SCHULZ

When HarperCollins bought *In Search of Excellence* (they were Harper & Row then), they paid only $6,500 for it. When the manuscript finally arrived two years later, it was orphaned because the editor who bought it had left.

The book had a first printing of only ten thousand copies. Six months later, the book had sold 250,000 copies—but not through bookstores. HarperCollins had sent copies of the book to the Fortune 500 CEOs, and word of mouth did the rest. The book went on to spend months on the best-seller list.

Promotion copies in the right hands can start a chain reaction of sales. The time to start this chain reaction is when you write your promotion plan. Publishers are usually willing to provide authors with promotion copies. How many depends on at least four factors:

- how important the book is
- how many are requested
- how they will be used
- who will mail them

Your editor, publicist and networks will help you make sure you have information on all the key people in your field. The media who should receive your book will be taken care of separately. Less important people can receive a letter or news release with an E-mail address, phone number or reply card so they can respond.

Promotional copies should be mailed ASAP so the recipients will start spreading the word and helping to increase the book's velocity.

Publishers are used to hearing round numbers like fifty, one hundred or two hundred. The better use you can make of them, the more likely it is your publisher will oblige you or give you deep discounts for them.

The publisher's willingness to provide you with promotional copies will decrease as time goes by. Since promotional copies are free, you don't receive royalties for them.

47 Your Titles (Free)

A good title should be like a good metaphor; it should intrigue without being too baffling or too obvious.
—WALKER PERCY

Before This Anger
First Impressions
They Don't Build Statues to Businessmen

Do you recognize any of these titles? They are the titles of books that have sold millions of copies and they continue to sell. Perhaps you know them better by their final titles:

Roots
Pride and Prejudice
Valley of the Dolls

The contrast between the initial and final titles for these books demonstrates why the perfect title for a book can make a major difference in its success.

Titles can sell books. Titles for novels should be intriguing and evocative, tempting casual browsers to pick up a book and give it the one-page test to see if it is worth reading.

Titles for reference books or serious nonfiction do not need catchy titles. They can just describe what the book is. This will suffice for those who need or want the information they contain.

But service nonfiction titles must make the biggest promise a book will fulfill. They must tell and sell, convey the book's benefit so compellingly that it forces book buyers who glance at it to pick it up.

We hope you will take our advice to practice nichecraft by creating a series of books that will enable you to become as successful as you wish to be. If you do practice nichecraft, you will need a title that conveys the conceptual unity of your books.

You have to look no farther than the book you're holding in your hands to find an outstanding example of this. *Guerrilla Marketing* communicates the essence of Jay's philosophy in a way that whoever sees or hears the title "gets" it immediately.

The Dummies series, the Complete Idiot's series, Sue Grafton's "Alphabet" mysteries and Lillian Braun's "Cat" mysteries are other well-known examples of titles that have become brands. And you know that any book with Martha Stewart's name on it is about the joys of domesticity.

GUERRILLA TACTICS

- Although you can use both a title and a subtitle, keep your titles as short as they are effective. Brevity helps make them memorable.
- Use your talks, articles and networks to test titles.
- If you're having a hard time coming up with the best title for your books, estimate the value of the right title. Then have a contest to find the title and pay the winner after its toughest critics—the sales reps—accept it at sales conference.
- Take guerrilla Dan Poynter's advice: see if your publisher will print your title vertically on the spine to make it easier to read.

If you're a novelist and you can find a literary framework that excites you and inspires your creativity, you'll be doing yourself a favor. Big publishers will be more inclined to take a chance on new novelists if they like a submission that has series potential. It's a must for new mystery writers. It worked for Arthur Conan Doyle, and it can work for you. The title you choose becomes more important because you have to live with it for the length of the series.

Give high priority to finding a title that can last you a lifetime while it increases the synergy and sales of your work.

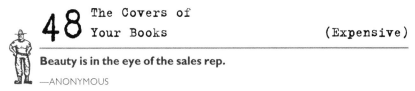

48 The Covers of Your Books (Expensive)

Beauty is in the eye of the sales rep.
—ANONYMOUS

Anyone who says "you can't judge a book by its cover" has never met the category buyer from Barnes & Noble.
—TERRI LONIER

People do judge books by their covers. But judging a cover is as subjective as judging what's inside it. A book cover is a blend of art and commerce; the title, promotional copy, quotes and artwork must captivate bookstore browsers in the two seconds they take to pass judgment on the book.

You've probably noticed that in general, mass-market covers are far more flamboyant than those for more upscale, restrained hardcovers and trade paperbacks. That's because mass-market books are regarded as impulse purchases, so they're expected to pass the Ten-Foot Test: being readable ten feet away.

Over the last decade, owing in part to competitive pressures, publishers have taken far more care in how their books are designed inside and out. The design of books from the major publishers has become far more creative and effective.

Cover design can be extremely important to a book's success. Jacket designers and cover artists (Hardcover books have jackets, paperback books have covers.) spend their lives in the trade but still don't always get it right. One of the industry's clichés is that a good cover is the cover of a successful book. Even more frustrating is that ugly covers can sometimes sell books.

You want the covers of your books to sell them as effectively as possible, especially if you will be writing a series of books, because the basic design of your first book will determine the overall look of the series.

ONE DESIGN FITS ALL

Depending on your promotion budget and how well your covers turn out, you can reproduce them in different sizes for different uses:

- a postcard and a cover for your media/speaker's kit, a giveaway or a promo piece to place inside your other books in stores
- business cards, letterhead and other print materials
- posters, on which guerrilla Laura Lynn Jeffers recommends including the dates of your appearances with a star next to the appearance closest to the poster's location.

BONUS WEAPON

Postcards (Low cost)

You can't tell—but you can sell—a book by its cover.
—THE *WALL STREET JOURNAL*

One use of your cover merits special attention. Because they don't have to

GUERRILLA TACTICS

- Although you can view your publisher's books online and in bookstores, one of the many reasons to visit their office is to see how they design their books, especially books like yours, and discuss your ideas.
- Look at all of the books on your subject in a well-stocked bookstore, making notes about what you love and hate about the covers, and the ideas they inspire. Pay special attention to the covers of best-sellers, especially in your field. Ask booksellers about the covers they find most effective.
- A creative exercise you will find helpful in visualizing how you want your cover to look is to place competing nonfiction books, or similar novels, side by side face out, to establish criteria for
  —design
  —colors
  —typefaces
  —artwork
  —paper
  —matte or glossy finish
  —the relationship in size between the title, artwork, author's name, quotes and the foreword
  —special effects found more often on mass-market paperbacks like silver or copper foil, embossing and die cutouts

  Because beauty is subjective, you will develop your own taste in covers. Your agent may be able to negotiate only the right to be consulted about the cover instead of having the right to approve it. But your publisher should not force you to take a cover you hate.
- Shortcut the process if you can. If you are a graphic artist or have access to one, and you or your artist has a great idea for a cover, have one designed. Make it the same size as the book you envision and no larger than the rest of your submission. However, before taking the trouble to have the final artwork done, give the preliminary sketch two tests:
  —Juxtapose it with competitive covers.
  —Share it with your networks, including booksellers.
- If your cover art passes its tests, include it with your proposal or

continued

Guerrilla Tactics, continued

manuscript. Mention booksellers who have vouched for its effectiveness in your bio or your cover letter.

Even if your publisher doesn't use it, it may spark a better idea, and it will at least give the art director something to improve on.

Publishers don't expect authors to be cover designers. One reason they are reluctant to give authors cover approval is that most authors have neither the artistic judgment nor the publishing experience to judge cover art.

Which is not to say that publishers are always right. Publishers will take all the time needed to get the cover design for a big book right because millions are riding on its success. As with the other aspects of publishing less important books, authors are once again victims of the cookie-cutter syndrome.

Editors may not solicit cover ideas from authors if authors haven't already volunteered their ideas. The book will be one among many books whose artwork will be discussed and decided on quickly. Unless someone has a brilliant idea the group agrees on, the group will be guided by similar books the house or other publishers have done.

- If your book will be heavily illustrated and you have have strong ideas about the interior design:
  —Explain them in your proposal.
  —Do a neat sketch of a sample page.
  —Prepare two sample two-page spreads that show the format you envision and the relationship between text and illustrations.

be opened and can be read quickly, a color postcard of your covers is a small but multi-purpose weapon you can use for

- your stationery and business cards
- invitations to signings, classes and other events
- inside and the front of your media/speaker's kit
- thank-you notes
- handouts at speaking and teaching events
- announcements of your books to your mailing lists
- requests for the media, opinion-makers, speaking bureaus and meeting

GUERRILLA TACTICS

- Always have postcards with you so you're prepared to give them to anyone with whom you discuss your book.
- Print them either in regular postcard size, the standard 6″ × 9″ size of most books or the size of your books. The larger size won't cost much more to print, but anything larger than a standard postcard will require additional postage.
- The only challenge with postcards is their cost. As we mentioned earlier, you may be able to print postcards on unused space on the sheets on which your book cover will be printed.

  If not, print your postcards, bookmarks and business cards at the same time and save a bundle. Check out the possiblity of printing postcards on your computer. You may be able to save money if you ask your printer to do your postcards when they're already printing another four-color job.
- In *1001 Ways to Market Your Books*, John Kremer recommends creating a three-in-one mailer with a postcard, a reply card and your rolodex card.

GUERILLA INTELLIGENCE

Guerrilla Selling coauthor Orvel Ray Wilson laminates his business card, which features the cover of his latest book, and wears it as a lapel pin.

planners to visit your Web site and ask for a book and media or speaker's kit
- your brochure
- your newsletter
- handouts
- buttons
- all of the other uses that you will think of (and share with us)

49 Illustrations   (Low cost)

You can use your illustrations to help you market your books

- in slide shows
- as part of your media kit
- in excerpts of your books
- in advertising
- on your Web site (check with your editor on this)
- for your print materials—stationery, business cards, bookmarks, labels—either with or perhaps instead of the your book covers
- in TV interviews

Merchandising, discussed below, describes still more opportunities for using your illustrations.

GUERRILLA TACTICS

- If doing illustrated books is your goal, research what kinds of illustrations will have the most potential for a book series as well as promotion and merchandising.
- If your illustrations lend themselves to many uses, either create them yourself, buy all rights to them or collaborate with a photographer or illustrator.

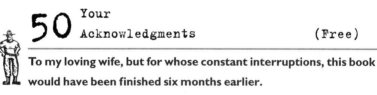

50 Your Acknowledgments (Free)

To my loving wife, but for whose constant interruptions, this book would have been finished six months earlier.

—FRANKLIN P. ADAMS

Most people like to see their names in print, especially in this celebrity-crazed culture. Your acknowledgments are your chance to thank those who have helped you personally and professionally, including those, for instance, who reviewed and marked up your manuscript. Lifetime debts also count. The first thing people who have done you a favor will look for is their name on your acknowledgments page.

No book comes into being without the help of people who deserve to be thanked. A lack of acknowledgments may say more about the writer than the people who helped with the book. Mentioning well-known people will add to your credibility.

Your significant other, editor, others in the publishing house, those who have helped with research, and friends and family who have provided personal support will be delighted to be mentioned. They'll feel like a part of the book and will tell their friends about it.

If you fail to mention them, they may forever resent you and the book. So if only for political reasons, acknowledge the people in your publishing house who helped with the book.

And if only to avoid the silent wrath of those who will be angry for not finding their names in your book, thank everyone who legitimately deserves to be mentioned. Let how you thank them and the order in which you mention them reflect the value of their contribution.

YOUR TURN TO TAKE A BOW

You also deserve acknowledgments, but you may not get them unless you ask. Whenever a bookseller, a talk-show host or an organization is pleased with what you have done, ask them to put it in writing. If a letter seems like it will be too much trouble, ask them just to E-mail you. Besides sending the notes to your agent and publicist, you may be able to use them in your media/speaker's kit and on your Web site.

GUERRILLA TACTICS
Go back as far as you wish in your acknowledgments to thank, for example, teachers who got you interested in reading and writing. Readers appreciate writers who express gratitude to everyone who helped them. Guerrillas understand the value of the attitude of gratitude.

BONUS WEAPON
    Giving Quotes   (Free)

Another group of people worth acknowledging in your books is those who have given you quotes. You can reciprocate and gain publicity by giving quotes to other authors. It will take time to read the book and write the quote, but your quotes publicize your books and help elevate you to the status of opinion-maker.

51 Your Bibliographies (Free and you get paid!)

A bibliography is a literary acknowledgments page. It lets your readers know what books you used to write yours. Authors of other books on the subject will turn rapidly to the back of your book to see if their work is mentioned.

If you wish to make them feel even better, write an annotated bibliography or a recommended reading list of the books that will benefit your readers the most, and briefly tell them why.

Here are six reasons to include bibliographies in your books:

- Competing books have them.
- Librarians, who buy a lot of books, like bibliographies because a bibliography increases the value of a book as a research tool.
- If your books are as good as you want them to be, they will inspire your readers to learn more about the subject. Your bibliographies will point them in the right direction.
- Bibliographies lend credibility to your books. They give the impression that you didn't just make up your information as you went along, but made use of the best work in your field to enrich your books.
- Authors you mention in your bibliographies will be more likely to mention you in theirs.
- Online booksellers have associates programs, in which when someone following a link from your Web site to theirs buys a book, you will receive a small portion of the proceeds. You will benefit whenever your readers buy books in your online bibliograpy. (The bibliography for this book is on our Web site.)

GUERRILLA TACTICS

- Use your bibliography as a handout.
- Put an asterisk before the top ten titles of your favorite books.

52 Raffle Prizes (Free or low cost)

If you belong to or are giving a talk to a group that holds a fundraising raffle at its meetings, donate a copy of your book. If you're not going to be giving a talk about your book, ask if you may speak for a minute about your book just before they raffle it. Then make sure you've mastered your elevator speech.

GUERRILLA TACTICS

- Ask whoever wins your book if he or she would like you to personalize the book when you sign it. Say that if they're planning to give the book to someone else, you'd be glad to personalize it for that person.
- Ask your networks if they know of any raffles that need prizes.

53 Merchandising (You get paid!)

Merchandising—creating products that make use of your book—usually comes into play with best-sellers or well-known commercial franchises.

GUERRILLA TACTICS

- If your books have merchandising potential, start investigating the possibilities and establish the number of books that would have to sell to make merchandising feasible. This way, you'll know what to do and when.
- While you're waiting for your book sales to reach critical mass, consider doing your own merchandising. Sell merchandising products at your presentations, through your Web site, at a store or at a flea market booth. The more successful you are at test-marketing your products, the easier it will be to convince a merchandizing company to sell them.
- Make T-shirts with your book covers, logo or signature for helpful readers, your publisher's staff, people in your networks and members of the media. Sell them to everyone else.

More than a thousand companies made products to take advantage of the arrival of George Lucas's *Star Wars Episode I: The Phantom Menace.*

Products that are based on books, such as notecards, calendars, T-shirts and mugs, are usually based on books consumers already know about. They're most likely to know about them if the books are best-sellers.

Exceptions are subjects of enduring interest like cats, angels or Provence. There are enough consumers enamoured of these subjects to buy related products, whether or not they're connected to books. In such situations, your books will benefit from reverse merchandising. The information on products crediting your book will boost your sales.

Sara Middens' garden books generated a line of products from notebooks to talcum powder. Martha Stewart created everything from TV shows and magazines to a line of sheets, and *Painted Ladies* has spawned puzzles and paint.

54 Your Money-Back Guarantee (Low cost)

To put your money where your book is, offer readers a money-back guarantee. This is a popular and sure-fire way to sell books. It's easy, it's fast, and it works because it makes buying your books risk-free for people unfamiliar with you and your work. You want to know if someone is dissatisfied with your work. At the same time, those who offer money-back guarantees know that most people will not take them up on the offer because it's too much trouble.

OUR NO-RISK GUARANTEE TO YOU

This book will guide you through creating and executing promotion plans that will make your books successful. If this book fails to satisfy your needs, please return it with the receipt to Mike Larsen, 1029 Jones Street, San Francisco, CA 94109, and we will refund your money and book-rate postage, no questions asked. We will also welcome your suggestions for improving the next edition.

CHAPTER 12

WEAPONS MADE POSSIBLE BY YOUR ABILITY TO WRITE

What writers like to write best is their name on the back of a check.
—ANONYMOUS

s an author, you will have to write many things besides books, auto-graphs and your name on the back of checks, although we hope that you will have as many opportunities to write all three as you wish.

In this century, all writers have to do to win fame and fortune is to write wonderful books. The Internet will take it from there. Meanwhile, be glad you have these weapons made possible by your ability to enlist allies:

- Your Brochure (Low cost)
- Your Newsletter or 'Zine (Free or you get paid!)
- Your Articles and Short Stories (You get paid!)
- Your Column (You get paid!)
- Your E-mail Chain Letter (Free)
- Your Book Reviews (You get paid [very little]!)
- Your Op-ed Pieces and Leters to the Editor (Free)
- Your Thank-you Notes (Free)
- Your Handouts (Free or low cost)

55 Your Brochure (Low cost)

Nonfiction writers may be able to provide services in their field. But one opportunity for both novelists and nonfiction authors is to use your writing and publishing experience to offer help to other writers as an editor, ghostwriter or collaborator. Speaking or teaching services you offer can also put food on your plate.

A brochure describing your services can be as simple as one sheet of paper folded twice for a #10 envelope. It's cheaper to make it a self-mailer by folding it in thirds and adding postage, but that may not be the most effective way to impress your recipients. Balance your budget with the expectations of the people you are mailing to.

Your brochure can use an excerpt from your book. You will want to include your bio, photo, Web site and contact information. Look at other people's brochures for ideas on content and design.

Four quick tips:

- Have knowledgeable people review both the copy and the design of the brochure before you print it.
- Include your brochure in your media/speaker's kit.
- In addition to distributing your brochure at your talks, you can include it in your correspondence.
- Mail it to everyone in your field that you want to be aware of you. You can ask in a covering letter for suggestions for speaking opportunities or others who might be interested in receiving the brochure. If you can send them a book, enclose a reply card or ask them to contact you if they want one.

GUERRILLA TACTICS

If you're writing an informational brochure using information from your book, the book will give you the credibility you need to approach sponsors to underwrite your brochure.

If, for example, you've written a book about a health problem, your brochure can list the ten steps that your book prescribes for curing it. If it won't compromise your credibility, ask manufacturers of products and services in the field to sponsor your brochure in exchange for recognition. A sponsor may also be willing to distribute your brochure to hospitals and doctor's offices.

Chapter nine has more suggestions about strategic alliances.

BONUS WEAPON

```
Your Bio                           (Free or low cost)
```

Make your bio a marketing weapon whenever you use it by including in descending order of importance everything you want readers to know about you:

- your name
- your snail-mail address
- your phone number
- your fax number
- your Web site
- your E-mail address
- your books and products
- your services
- the titles of your talks
- prizes and awards you have won
- quotes about you and your work

Include a photo if it will help your cause. Customize your bio depending on how you will use it. The bio on your Web site and in your brochure can be as long as you want as long as it is interesting enough to hold readers' attention.

```
5 6   A Newsletter        (Free or you
      or `Zine            get paid!)
```

Being an authority enables you to start a newsletter or a 'zine in your field, whether it's about romance fiction, writing or health.

Thanks to the wonders of technology, you can E-mail your newsletter to subscribers. 'Zines have illustrations, so publish it on your Web site until it becomes as fast and easy to E-mail illustrations as it is to E-mail text.

Making your newsletter available only at your Web site and promoting it elsewhere on the Net may be preferable to spending the time or money building and maintaining a list.

You also have to decide the most productive way to use your time. That

GUERRILLA TACTICS

- Consider asking for contributions from others. This will force you or someone you choose to edit their work. Assuming that, at least at first, you don't pay contributors, using the work of others will be an opportunity for both of you. It will reduce the amount of your work, and you may find your successor if you need one.
- There's a *New Yorker* cartoon showing an usher in a church passing the collection plate to a churchgoer who says: "I was comped." Have a comp list of key people in your field, the media, and if appropriate, academia and the government.
- Use your newsletter to promote your products, services and upcoming media and speaking appearances, perhaps offering a special discount to subscribers.
- If enough subscribers would rather have hard copy, charge them enough to make producing and mailing it worthwhile.

decision determines whether you will charge for the newsletter. If you see your 'zine or newsletter as an opportunity to promote your services, your books and yourself, and you consider that a sufficient reward for your labors, give it away.

If the information in your newsletter or 'zine is valuable enough and you are convinced people will pay for it, send a few sample issues to your networks with a cutoff date to either subscribe or stop receiving it. Specialized newsletters command three-figure subscription prices. You can get paid for writing material that you can recycle in your articles, books and talks.

Researching what other online publishers are doing and how they do it will help you decide which way to jump. Offering a discount and a money-back guarantee will stimulate subscriptions. Use online and offline media to announce and promote your 'zine or newsletter. You can announce a 'zine in the alt.zines newsgroup.

Encouraging readers to send questions for you to answer in the next newsletter and letters to the editor will make them more responsive. It will also give you ideas for articles and books. You may even ask readers who write you to expand their letters into an article. And you can make use of the information in other ways.

Genre novelists who build a passionate following find quarterly newsletters an effective way to maintain their relationships with their fans. They include reviews, news about their previous and forthcoming books, a list of upcoming appearances and letters from readers.

You can also send your newsletter to booksellers, reviewers, interview media and the rest of your networks. Include the latest edition in your media kit.

Printing newsletters is more costly than E-mailing them. If you can do both, ask your readers to tell you how they want to receive it.

57 Your Articles and Short Stories (You get paid!)

Writing articles gives you the chance to
- test-market your ideas, the style and content of your writing, and titles for chapters and books
- see how well and knowledgeably you write about the subject
- get a feeling for how much you will enjoy writing a book about the subject
- see how readers respond
- gauge how long it will take you to complete the book
- let readers fill in missing pieces
- find new sources of information
- correct mistakes
- mention them in your bio
- have your work seen by agents and book, magazine and newspaper editors as well as pros in the broadcast and electronic media

Who publishes the story, how much you are paid for it, and whether your editor asks you for more are all signs of the commercial potential of your idea.

Best case: An editor at a big house reads your work and calls brimming with excitement wanting to buy a book.

Worst case: You can't sell the article, which may be fate's kindest way of telling you that you may not have any more success selling a book on the

GUERRILLA TACTICS
- If you can afford it, you may be better off bartering articles or short stories, online or offline, for ad space and/or a bio. Chapter fourteen includes a discussion of trading words for ads.
- Be warned: Freelancers endure indignities including being underpaid (Is *that* why they're called freelancers?), being paid late, being paid in copies, and having editors maul their work.

  To help protect yourself, mine your networks for advice and join the National Writer's Union and the American Society of Journalists and Authors. The ASJA helps members with problems and its excellent monthly magazine keeps tabs on how magazines treat writers. If you plan to sell articles as a way of life, join the NWU and ASJA.

subject. You will suffer a great deal less pain having query letters rejected than you will going to the trouble of writing a proposal only to find that you can't sell it.

Being unable to sell a slice of your novel may have no relationship to the fate of your book. What may not work as a short story may be irresistible when expanded into a novel.

For more on articles, see "Excerpts from Your Books" in chapter ten.

Once your short pieces start earning you four-figure sums for articles or short stories, you will find them a good way to keep your name before potential book buyers and publishers. If you become successful enough, your publisher will give your articles or short stories a second life by issuing a collection of them.

Guerrillas recycle their ideas and their writing in as many media as possible by reformatting or rearranging their work:
- Short tips can be expanded into articles.
- Answers to commonly asked questions can be collected and used as an article and/or as a FAQ (frequently asked questions) feature on your Web Site.
- A response to a question may contain the seeds of an article or book or provide information you can use in a brochure or press release.
- Guerrilla Fire Captain Robert "Captain Bob" Smith, a professional

speaker, recommends writing a 750-word article you can customize and reuse for trade and consumer magazines and association newsletters.

Articles in newsletters of small associations do double duty: the editors also book speakers. You can put the articles on your Web site and invite print media to use them with your bio and contact info for free.

If you are giving talks, you can recycle a series of articles as both a "special report" you sell in the back of the room and as material for your next book.

Maximize the value of everything you create. Save your outgoing E-mail and snail-mail and rummage through them periodically for ideas and copy you can reuse.

New Web sites continue to appear that can use your articles and promote you and your books. Dedicate time every week to looking for them.

58 Your column (You get paid!)

Chapter four discusses the importance of having a national platform—a continuing national visibility with potential book buyers around the country. A column that appears in a national magazine or is nationally syndicated in newspapers is an effective way of staying in touch with your readers. It will also convince publishers that your books will sell.

Being an author gives you the credibility to approach magazines and newspaper syndicates with a proposal for a column. Double-space your proposal for a column and include

- six sample columns suitable in length and content to the media you're approaching
- a page about your concept for the column
- a page of titles or ideas for future columns
- a bio

If you plan to answer reader's questions in your column, make your sample columns reflect that approach.

What makes selling a column challenging is that magazines and newspapers are already full. Using your work means that they would have to get rid of something they're already running. It usually takes a super idea or enough visibility to convince syndicates that enough people will read your column to justify handling it.

GUERRILLA TACTICS

- Jay self-syndicated a Guerrilla Marketing column for twenty small papers in exchange for a bio that includes mentions of his latest book, Web site, 800 number and newsletter.
- For a newspaper column, start by syndicating your own work to non-competing papers in your area. If it succeeds in your area, syndicates will be more likely to give it a try. If they won't, keep doing it yourself until they will. E-mail makes the process faster, easier and less expensive.
- To test-market a magazine column, write articles for the target magazine on the subject you want to write about. If you can sell articles on the subject, you develop a good working relationship with your editor, and if the reader response is fervent enough, it's time to mention a column if your editor doesn't mention it first.

59 Your E-mail Chain Letter (Free)

E-mail makes it possible to use your networks to announce the publication of your books. Create an enticing letter about your book including the basic bibliographic information and why you feel it will interest your networks. Use quotes from reviews or opinion-makers and mention impressive subsidiary rights sales.

Add that while you would be delighted if your networks bought your book, you're writing just to let them know it exists. Ask them to forward your E-mail to their networks. Ask them to contact you if they have questions or want to discuss the book, or if there's a way you can repay their kindness.

Once you've gotten feedback on the letter, send it to all your networks: personal and professional, direct and indirect, publishing and field.

GUERRILLA TACTICS

- Keep the letter to one page. One screen will be still better. Always remember: time is more important than money.
- Tell your recipients that you will be very grateful if they will tell their friends about your books.

60 Your Book Reviews (You Get Paid [Very Little]!)

We can't all be heroes because somebody has to sit on the curb and clap as they go by.

—WILL ROGERS

Book reviews are another opportunity for you to be underpaid. But as you write more of them, you will become proficient at turning out the best review you can write in the shortest amount of time.

The reason to write reviews is not for the teeny weeny fee, but because they will help you

- keep your name and the title of your books before book buyers
- build your stature as a writer and an authority in the field
- earn you the gratitude of a writer who may one day want to give you a quote or review your books
- establish a friendship with book review editors who have much helpful information you need and whose friendship will increase the likelihood of your own books being reviewed
- understand the reviewing process that your books will be subjected to and to learn the discipline of quickly writing a brief but balanced review
- show potential readers how discerning you are and how well you write
- obtain speaking and writing opportunities, if only for more reviews
- build your library with free books
- gain the attention of the editors and agents of the books you review
- stay on top of new work in your field

REVIEWS OF YOUR BOOKS

Publishers Weekly receives thirty thousand trade books a year, so as of this writing, that is as official a number as the industry has of the number of books published a year. Most magazines and newspapers review less than 10 percent. Learn enough about review media to judge whether books like yours get reviewed. If they don't, skip what follows and go on to the next weapon.

If your books have review potential, ask your publisher to send—or let you send—autographed copies of them to opinion-makers, reviewers and writers you know who may be able to review them. Include covering letters for the local and national media your publisher isn't mailing to. If the house publicist is mailing review copies, ask if it will help to send autographed and personalized copies along with a letter from you to at least the most important reviewers and opinion-makers.

Publishers Weekly reviews only 20 percent of the trade books that are published. *The New York Times Book Review* reviews 10 percent, and other papers that have pullout review sections cover fewer.

Why include a letter? The *San Francisco Chronicle* receives fifteen thousand books a year. A personal letter will help separate your books from the rest of the deluge. This is essential if you're a local author, which increases your book's chances of being reviewed. To help personalize the mailing, address the mailing label by hand.

In addition to local review media, send a book and a personal letter to the editors of *The New York Times Book Review* section, the *Los Angeles Times Book Review, Chicago Tribune Books,* the *San Francisco Chronicle Book Review* and *The Washington Post Book World,* even if it means duplicating your publisher's efforts. Mailing a copy to *USA Today* and *The Wall Street Journal* might also be worthwhile.

If your book is appropriate for reviewers in special-interest media, include them in your publisher's questionnaire to be sure your publicist knows about them.

If you luck into reviews, underline the good parts and add them to your media kit and Web site. If they're laudatory enough, make sure your publisher adds them to the cover or first page of your book.

GUERRILLA TACTICS

- Try to sell only first North American serial rights to the reviews you write.
- If the person who assigns the review doesn't mind, try to resell the review to non-competing media.
- Add reviews you write to your media kit if they relate to your books.
- Put them on your Web site.
- Use them in your newsletter.
- Use information from the books you review in any way you legally can, noting sources. This is a win-win situation that adds to your credibility and publicizes the books you cite.
- Don't wait until a book editor asks you to write a review; take the initiative any time you see a book reviewed in *Publishers Weekly* that you want to review.
- Get to know as many book reviewers as you can. They may review your books, a possibility enhanced by sending them a copy with a personal note.
- When you are considering what to write, factor in how likely it is your books will be reviewed. If it's not likely, figure out a way to use promotion to compensate for the lack of reviews.

61 Op-ed Pieces and Letters to the Editor (Free)

One of the perks of being an author is that it gives you the authority to comment in print on subjects you write about. This is true whether you're writing fiction or nonfiction.

If there's a news angle to your novel, use it to get media exposure for your books and yourself.

The letters to the editor and the articles that appear on the page opposite a newspaper's editorials can be your chance to give the world a piece of your mind and to publicize your books.

Op-ed pieces are responses to articles that have appeared in the paper or subjects in the news. They are usually serious, but they can also be humorous. Magazines may also present opportunities for freelance articles on hot topics or a reaction to material in the magazine.

The differences between letters and op-ed pieces are

- op-ed pieces are bigger and therefore more visible than letters
- magazines and newspapers use more letters than op-ed pieces so a letter is more likely to be used
- the title of your book is more likely to be included with your bio for an article than a letter

GUERRILLA TACTICS

- Syndicate your letter or article to non-competing print media. Print media like to run letters from around the country to vouch for the breadth of their readership.
- Put it on your Web site, and if it's relevant and impressive enough, in your media kit.

62 Thank-you Notes (Free)

Appreciative words are the most powerful forces for good on Earth.

—GEORGE W. CRANE

When someone does something you are thankful for or has given above the call of duty, send them a small Jiffy envelope with a roll of Lifesavers candy and a note that says "Thanks! You were a life saver!"

—NANETTE MINER, AUTHOR

The two most important words in promotion are "thank you." Everyone likes to receive thank-you notes, so use every opportunity to thank the people who help you. Assume that your paths will cross again, and they will remember your thoughtfulness.

Guerrillas know thank-you notes are a marketing weapon, an opportunity to make a lasting impression on fans, booksellers, media people, and their publisher's staff.

In the age of E-mail, handwritten notes are the most personal and therefore the most welcome form of communication. Handwritten notes command attention just because they stand out from all the printed material that assaults people every day.

GUERRILLA INTELLIGENCE

Shelf-talkers are the short handwritten notes attached to bookshelves explaining why a bookstore's staff like certain books. Booksellers have found that handwritten notes sell more books than those that are typed.

Like thank-you notes and the surge of coffee houses and reading groups, this proves that John Naisbitt's assertion is right: the more technology we have in our lives, the more we crave human contact—a major advantage guerrillas exploit every chance they get.

GUERRILLA TACTICS

- P.S. Although you are writing to thank someone, use a P.S. to mention a talk, class, media appearance, future book, a piece of information he may enjoy or find helpful, or a piece of good news about your book.
- Make your response suit the situation. Send flowers or another gift (ideally relating to your book or the recipient's interests) if the service merits it.
- People who merit gifts and thank-you notes are worth adding to your snail-mailing and E-mailing lists.

You can use a postcard with your book cover on it. But using a pretty note card on colored paper—perhaps one with an illustration from your book—will also make a thank-you note stand out because it will look different from a business letter, especially if the address is handwritten.

Businesspeople spend a growing chunk of their lives responding to mail and E-mail. Just knowing that your thank-you note won't require a response will raise their spirits.

Make your note a pleasure to read by

- keeping it short
- thanking the reader for helping and mentioning the difference her help made
- personalizing it by adding something that relates to the reader
- welcoming the opportunity to be of service
- offering to get together if the reader comes to your area
- naming a staff person who was especially helpful

If your handwriting is illegible, use your computer, but mention that you're only doing it so they can read your note. For another way to say thank you, see "Acknowledgments" in chapter eleven.

63 Handouts (Free or low-cost)

Audiences like handouts. They are visual aids that reinforce your words. They give listeners something to make notes on, as well as something tangible that helps them recall what they learned.

Use handouts printed on your letterhead so they will include your contact information and the titles of your books.

Your audiences may share them with other people, which will help promote your books and increase attendance at future talks.

Handouts also add value to your presentations and enhance your stature as an authority. Use what works best for you and is right for the kind of presentations you do. But make sure your audiences leave with something that includes information about your books and how to contact you. If it is helpful enough, they will share it with their networks.

Number and collate your handouts in the order you will refer to them, and paperclip them together unless your budget or your sponsor's budget allows you to use a folder or a binder.

GUERRILLA TACTICS
- Use different colored pages for each handout. Color makes them pretty to look at, and audiences find it easier to look for "the blue sheet about X topic."
- Using material from your books promotes them by showing the value of the information they provide.
- If people are inviting you to speak, ask if they will print and distribute your handouts.
- Save surplus handouts for your next event.

CHAPTER 13

WEAPONS MADE POSSIBLE BY YOUR ABILITY TO ENLIST ALLIES

fter the quality of your books and your ability to promote them, your allies are your most important assets. That's why the third most powerful weapon in your arsenal is your networks.

Building and maintaining your networks requires the ability to communicate effectively with the wide range of people you come into contact with during your career.

The effectiveness of the weapons in this chapter will depend on your ability to do two things: imbue others with your passion for your books and persuade them to help you. All of these weapons are made possible by your ability to enlist allies:

- Your Book Signings (Free)
- Book Festivals (Free)
- Your Special Events (Free)
- Your Contests (Free)
- Your Cooperation (Free)
- Your Promotion Potlucks (Low cost)
- Your Broken-in Walking Shoes (Low cost)

64 Book Signings   (Free)

If you and your publisher agree on the value of book signings, your publisher will usually be willing to arrange for book signings at least in your area. If you're giving yourself a national tour, your publisher may be willing to set up book signings for you in the cities you travel to. But the day will come when you have to arrange bookstore events yourself. So your ability to work with booksellers will help sustain the sales momentum needed for booksellers to keep stocking your books.

Book signings can promote your books while providing a valuable opportunity to build relationships with booksellers and readers. Once you figure out how to make bookstore events productive and you establish a network of stores around the country anxious to book you, you can integrate signings into your travels whether or not you have a book coming out. For example, authors of children's books can hold storytelling events and parties. Stores specializing in children's books are eager to put on events.

As part of their efforts to reinvent themselves as community centers, chain and independent booksellers have embraced events as a means of attracting new and old customers. Novelists give readings, nonfiction writers do demonstrations or discuss their books, and then they respond to questions.

In addition to talks or readings followed by signings, bookstores may offer classes you can teach. They will be sources of income as well as publicity, and they give you the opportunity to support the booksellers you want to support you.

However, let's be frank about two brutal, inescapable realities you have to contend with:

- The average number of books sold at a book signing is four. We give you this frightening statistic not to dissuade you from doing bookstores' events but to help make you determined to keep this from happening to you.
- Unexpected things over which you have no control can screw up booksignings: natural or man-made disasters, weather, a sports event—anything that rivets public and media attention.

The authors you know who have given book signings have war stories to share. So mine your networks for information about what does and doesn't work.

Publishers choose the most promising books on each list to be eligible for co-op money. If booksellers order enough copies of your books, they can take advantage of this co-op money to advertise your books and to help with out-of-pocket book-signing expenses: signs, refreshments and space in their calendars, which are mailed to the media and to customers. Signings also require time from everyone involved.

If your publisher can't help you with book signings, or after they have stopped helping, you will be on your own. They may be willing to provide you with information about bookstores that are best for signings.

You have a head start on successful book signings where you live. Go to signings, especially for books like yours. Ask events coordinators how many books they must sell to make a signing worthwhile.

Then go through your little black book, Rolodex or database and convince yourself that your personal and professional networks will buy at least that many. Then sales that the booksellers' promotion generates will be icing on the cake.

Ask booksellers:

- What days of the week and weeks of the month generate the largest turnouts, particularly for books like yours?
- What kinds of books attract the most listeners?
- What kinds of promotion are most effective in reaching listeners?
- What do audiences most enjoy: readings, how-to information, slide shows or talks about how authors wrote and sold their books?

Be sure to ask booksellers what brings buyers into their stores. This is part of the fundamental question, "What can I do to make your job easier?"

What you learn from reps, booksellers and the rest of your networks will tell you what you need to know to help ensure successful signings. Booksellers will benefit if your event draws new customers, people buying books other than yours or people who can't make the signing but come at another time to buy the book.

Take the long view about bookstore events. As your books and sales get better and your readerships grows, so will the royalties you earn doing events in bookstores.

Bookstore event coordinators are swamped with details, so here are nine quick tips about how to help your signings come off without a hitch:

- Request copies of the stores's promotional materials.

GUERRILLA TACTICS

- Put the information about your local signings either on a postcard (perhaps with the cover on the front) or on a sheet of paper folded twice to be used as a self-mailer. Send it to your networks. Include all the events and media appearances in your area, subsidiary rights sales, quotes from reviews and any other ammo you have.
- Ask your publisher to make a poster or flyer, even $8\frac{1}{2}'' \times 11''$ with room at the bottom to list the bookstore and other events where you will appear in each area. If your publisher won't print one, perhaps you can make one on your computer. Ask people in your networks to put up the posters for you.
- If your photo will help attendance, use it in your promotional materials.
- Ask your editor and publicist for the names of the sales reps. If that doesn't work, here are four other sources for finding reps:
  —your networks
  —the house's other authors
  —regional associations of booksellers who have lists of the reps in their area
  —independent booksellers (The chains order books at their head-quarters, but you can ask independents who sell your publisher's books to them.)
- If you have no other resource for finding bookstores, use your local library's copy of *The American Book Trade Directory*, an annual listing of bookstores by state.

continued

- Contact bookstores a week ahead of the event to be sure your books have arrived and ask how many copies they have.
- Bring books, in case more are needed.
- Ask to sign unsold books. They will usually want you to sign at least as many copies as they believe they will sell.
- Bring stickers with the word "Autographed" on them in case book-sellers are out of them. (Ask your publisher for them.) Booksellers usually give autographed books a better location, and the autograph is an incentive to buy the book, especially if it's a gift.
- If it's true, ask booksellers to announce after your talk that your book

Guerrilla Tactics, continued

- Here are suggestions for warming the seats at your bookstore events:
  —Look at your calendar or have your publicist check the calendar and ask booksellers if they are aware of any conflicts before agreeing to a date. Granted, if you will only be in Chicago for one day, you're stuck with that day.
  —If you have an effective publicity photo instead of the usual head shot, use it with the news release about the signing. A local calendar of events may print it.
  —Big cities have suburbs that may also be worth visiting for signings. For example, the San Francisco-area signings you can do include stores in Marin County, Berkeley, Oakland, the Peninsula between San Francisco and San Jose and San Jose.
  Events for a gardening book might pull better outside of San Francisco than in the city itself.
  —Raffle off one or more free books at the event and announce this in the promotional materials. Collect business cards so you can add names to your mailing list or have the audience sign up in note pads or guest books.
  —Offer a free book to people who bring five or ten people with them. One free for ten is a promotional technique publishers use to encourage booksellers to take more copies than they would otherwise.
- Ask if your publisher will supply you with promotional or at-cost copies for the following ideas.
  —Attend bookstore events and sound out your networks and readers for suggestions about your talk. Whatever you do will, in effect, be a sales pitch for your books, so your primary goal is to excite potential buyers with whatever will most effectively convince them to flock to the cash register with copies of your books.
  —A happy surprise: you don't need a book to talk in a bookstore. Booksellers want bodies in seats who may buy books even if they can't buy yours. If they think your topic will interest their customers, and particularly if you can recommend books about your subject, they'll book you.

will make a great gift, and that the staff will be happy to gift wrap it. This will spur sales if your appearance occurs before a holiday such as Christmas or Valentine's Day, or in the Spring for a book about gardening or baseball. You might even bring special wrapping paper for the bookseller to hold up.

- Travel with bookplates. You can sign them for people who have left your book at home or whose friends have them.
- Write thank-you notes to the owner or manager of the store and the staff person directly involved with the event.
- Hand deliver window display materials, posters and bookmarks to local stores and libraries. Personal contact is always the best way to promote your books.

BONUS WEAPON

Sales Reps   (Low cost)

If you are going to be traveling the country as a way of life, you will need to know the best bookstores in cities around the country. Your publisher may be willing to provide that information if they're not going to arrange for the signings. Their sales reps certainly can, but unless you're important to the house, your publisher probably will not want you to contact reps.

Reps spend their lives covering their territories and may not return phone calls, or they may respond faster to E-mail. When you do make contact, ask reps how they work, what the most effective weapons for promoting your books are and how you can excite booksellers about signings.

GUERRILLA TACTICS

As soon as your book has a pub date, invite the reps—major markets require more than one—for a drink (if you're on a guerrilla budget) or as nice a lunch or dinner as your budget allows. Repeat the process when you travel. Reps are dedicated people who like their work. Treat them like royalty; they're worth thousands of dollars a year in royalties.

65 Book Festivals (Free)

A growing number of book festivals around the country provide you with the opportunity to connect with your readers, potential readers and the publishing people who organize the events.

Festivals are always looking for writers to speak, especially local ones who they hope will attract their friends and fans but won't incur travel and hotel expenses that aren't in the festival's budget. They also present talks and panels about writing and publishing.

The Los Angeles festival takes place in April, "New York is Book Country" closes a stretch of midtown Fifth Avenue in September, and the Miami festival in November attracts 800,000 visitors. They all differ in ways that reflect the visions of the people who started them.

The San Francisco Book Festival, for example, usually takes place in November and hopes to attract book-lovers shopping for Christmas. Publishers and booksellers take booths, and after each talk the speaker's books are sold. This means that the authors committee prefers authors who have fall books or at least books published that year.

The authors committee starts rounding up speakers in the spring. As with talk shows, if you can suggest ideas and speakers for a panel, you are enhancing your chances of speaking.

In addition to benefitting from book sales at the festival, authors are listed in the program and may attract media coverage.

If your town is large enough to support a festival but doesn't have one, see if you can stir up enough interest to make one a reality. It was the vision of one man, marketing pro David Cole—author of *The Complete Guide to Book Marketing*—that brought the San Francisco Book Festival to life. Maybe you can be the David Cole in your community. The LMP lists book festivals.

66 Your Special Events (Free)

If you are writing a book about saving the environment and you quote leading environmentalists around the country, ask university extensions to

GUERRILLA TACTICS

- Book festivals need contributions and volunteers to keep going. The book festival nearest you needs your time and money. Contributing what you can is an excellent way of making your community aware of you and your books, as well as expanding your professional networks.
- Serving on the committee that is responsible for putting the program together will help you understand the committee's needs and boost your chances for speaking when the time comes.

let you create one-day symposia featuring top environmentalists and of course you, perhaps serving as emcee as well as a speaker. Who knows? Maybe the Sierra Club will be willing to participate and even help sponsor the events. Maybe CSPAN2 will tape it.

Media people like positive news stories because they provide relief from all the bad news they report. Adding a public-service aspect to the story by having a business or a nonprofit organization sponsor the event will give the media another reason to cover it.

This is one idea out of the endless possibilities for promoting books. The better your idea for a special event, the more likely it is that your publisher and local organizations will pitch in and help. If an idea has national potential, test market it in your area first.

Because fresh, creative ideas are rare in publishing, publishers and the media respond to them eagerly. As long as you can convince them they will benefit enough from an event, they will help you make it happen.

HAPPY BOOKDAY

If you do nothing else, at least throw a birthday party to celebrate the birth of your book. Where you hold it, who you invite, the look of your invitation, how your guests dress and what they bring with them, what happens at the party, and the refereshments you serve are all open to use your imagination.

If your soiree will be creative and visual enough to interest the media, invite them. But unless you can tie your party into a hot news story, the media is more likely to cover it on a slow news day.

GUERRILLA TACTICS
Look at the chance to create special events as an opportunity for the businesses and nonprofits you collaborate with. Think about what their goals are and the best way for you and your books to help them achieve their goals. Once you know that, you will be able to create an event that will benefit both of you. We look forward to hearing about them.

67 Your Contests (Free)

Contests can be another way to help worthy causes. Let's say your book is about the history of television sitcoms. You can have a contest to see who in town knows the most about the subject.

You can encourage colleges, businesses and nonprofits to have their own in-house contests using your book for the questions and answers. The winners of these contests would participate in the town championship.

A repository of knowledge, a bookstore, school or library will be a logical site for the contest. If the contest can be a fundraiser, local media may cover it. The paper and local radio and TV personalities may be willing to ask their audiences questions and give prizes—your book?—for the first right answers. A local media outlet may also be willing to host the event.

Maybe a local cable channel will televise the event. Perhaps you can ask the questions, referring to your book for the answers. If not you, then the mayor, a representative of a sponsor, or whichever local personality will draw the biggest audience.

To help generate excitement for the contest, find sponsors who will benefit from the exposure your contest will give them. Try to find

- sponsors who will provide prizes—a trip, a car, cash, an autographed copy of your book (If all the prizes can relate to the contest, such as all of the "I Love Lucy" videos for a sitcom contest, so much the better.)
- a sponsor who can furnish a place to hold the championship, unless the organization that will benefit from the event has one or can arrange for one
- a media sponsor who will publicize the event and may donate a prize

(This idea may seem too complex, but it can also be as simple as a bookstore event with, ideally, your publisher providing books as prizes.)

GUERRILLA TACTICS
Sell your books at special events and announce that part or all of the profits will go to a worthy cause.

68 Cooperation With Your Peers   (Free)

Cooperation has replaced competition in the lexicon of guerrillas. If you're writing mysteries, you and other mystery writers have far more in common that unites you than writing the same kind of book divides you. That's why the Mystery Writers of America (MWA) was formed, an organization which has chapters around the country. Contact information is in the Resource Directory.

Mystery writers depend on the same audience and the same small group of publishers, and they have the same hurdles to surmount. The MWA gives them a forum to share information, discuss complaints and celebrate victories. Indeed, the MWA's annual awarding of "Edgars," named for Edgar Allen Poe, is one of the industry's most popular events. Romance writers and science fiction/fantasy writers also have national organizations and newsletters.

Make a list of ways that you and other writers can help each other. Cooperation is another example of how guerrillas are limited only by their time, energy and imagination.

69 Your Promotion Potlucks   (Low cost)

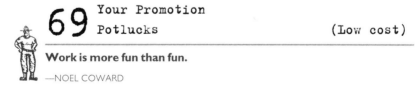

Work is more fun than fun.
—NOEL COWARD

First-time authors share the challenge of promotion. So one form of cooperation deserves special attention: promotion potlucks. You will need all the

GUERRILLA TACTICS
- If there are enough writers writing the same kind of books you are, but no group exists yet for them, start one.
- Share the costs of
  —touring
  —attending regional and national trade and consumer events
  —supplies, media directories, the latest and greatest technology or a subscription to *Publisher's Weekly*
- Create panels for book festivals, writers' organizations and conferences.
- Collaborate on a book.
- Create an event built around books on your subject. Example: Team up with other authors writing about tennis to put on a tennis clinic. Invite tennis organizations and equipment manufacturers who can sponsor a national tour of the clinic. If this works, use the videotape of the event and press coverage to snare more sponsors.
- Distribute each other's promotional material.
- Have reciprocal Web site links.

GUERRILLA TACTICS
Make the most creative contributors at your potluck the core of a mastermind group that meets over the phone or in person to help each other. For more on mastermind groups, see "Your Networks" in chapter three.

help you can find, so why not spend time with other authors and see what you can learn from each other?

Since you share the desire to be successful writers, breaking bread together at a promotion potluck will be a valuable learning experience for all of you.

70 Your Broken-in Walking Shoes   (Low cost)

This is the simplest weapon of all. If you're proud of your book, don't hide it under a bushel. Carry it on the bus. Take it to restaurants. Get your exercise by walking in high-traffic locations with it so everyone you pass can read the title.

Wearing a pin, T-shirt or sweatshirt with the cover on it will make you a walking billboard for your book. Also helpful, as discussed in chapter nineteen, make your appearance evoke your books so it becomes a part of your identity.

WAR STORIES

Kurt Eichenwald, a *New York Times* reporter and author of *Serpent on the Rock: Crime, Betrayal, and the Terrible Secrets of Prudential-Bache*, had the book in plain sight on a flight and happened to sit next to a producer for *60 Minutes*. Guess who got Sunday evening TV coverage?

The moral of this story: Never leave home without your book.

Suggested exercise venues: the busiest streets in town, airports, book festivals, shopping malls, multiplex theaters, antique fairs, events in your field, universities, classes, concerts and sporting events. Fit the place to your books, and choose a day and time when the most people will be out. If you write books about football, football games are a must. Carrying your book around gives new meaning to the proverb "Put your best foot forward."

Bring copies of your print materials with you to hand out to interested passersby.

GUERRILLA TACTICS

- Alert local media about your strolls, including, if you can, a publicity photo with strong visual interest of how you look. Think costume and sandwich boards. Think slow news days like weekends and holidays.
- If there's a bookstore where you will be walking, see if they're willing to tie into your presence with a sign or by discounting your books and telling buyers you will be happy to autograph them.
- Wear eye-catching sandwich boards made of light-weight fiberboard over your chest and back.

CHAPTER 14

WEAPONS THAT DELIVER FREE ADVERTISING

P ublishers believe that advertising doesn't produce sales that justify its cost. But when ads are free, they're all for them. Among the weapons that deliver free advertising for your books are

- The Last Page of Your Book (Free)
- Bartering Stories for Space (Free)
- Per-Order Ads (Free)
- Catalogs (Free)

71 The Last Pages of Your Books   (Free)

A list of your other books will be part of your books' front matter. Your bio may go either in the front or the back of your books.

If the last pages of your nonfiction book are not needed for the text, it is usually possible for the author to use them as an ad. Usually they don't include graphics, just text. Make sure your last page includes

- your name
- your E-mail and snail-mail addresses
- your phone number
- your Web site
- the services and products you offer
- your logo
- your theme

- the offer to have your readers contact you with questions, problems or suggestions for the next edition

GUERRILLA TACTICS

- Let examples of how other authors use their last pages serve as models.
- Offer a reward for suggestions for your next book, perhaps a copy of the book or something readers can download from your Web site.
- Your publisher will probably consider using space in their books to tout the offerings of other houses a breach of etiquette. Your books by other publishers will be mentioned in the front of the book and in your bio so readers will know what they are. Don't mention that your books are for sale on your Web site, as this might cause bad feelings with the bookstores you want to stock your books, who will see it as competition.
- Once you know if your books will have a blank page, ask your editor if you can provide a drawing of how you would like the page to look. They won't want to spend a lot a time on it, so keep it simple, especially if your book is a classy, upmarket hardcover.

72 Bartering Stories for Space (Free)

Magazines may be willing to trade unused advertising pages for articles or short stories. The space they offer may sell for more than the going rate they pay for material.

If the response to your work is strong enough, one piece may lead to calls from other magazines and assignments for articles. If you're trading short stories, trading them for ads may lead to the publication of a collection.

73 Per-order Ads (Free)

Your publisher has copies of your books sitting in the warehouse. Magazines have blank pages that they would like to see ads on. Per-order (PO) ads solve both of these problems.

GUERRILLA TACTICS

The ease of buying books online and in stores has, with the exception of book clubs, ended the era of direct-mail ads in print media. But guerrillas will dream up ways to make it happen.

- Could a local bookstore handle the fulfillment?
- Could you handle the fulfillment? Being able to include your Web site and a toll-free number will help.
- Could you autograph and even personalize the books?
- What about gift-wrapping?
- Overnight delivery?
- What about including something extra with the book like a short, photocopied special report, a short story or a sneak preview of the first chapter of your next book?
- What about offering to visit reading groups in your area to discuss the book?
- What about offering a Webcast discussion about the book for any reading group around the country that buys X copies?

Try to get magazines to trade ad space for your books in exchange for sharing the profits from the ad with your publisher. The magazine supplies the space and prepares the ad. Your publisher supplies the copy, provides the books, handles the fulfillment and sends the magazine their 50 percent of the profit.

If the first ad brings in enough orders, the magazine will keep running the ad when space is available. This is a win-win-win situation.

PO ads are more likely found in special-interest rather than general magazines, although you can try the regional editions of national magazines.

Guerrillas will also tackle radio, television and cable stations and the Web. We're sure you can come up with more creative ways to stimulate PO

GUERRILLA TACTICS

Ask your editor if the house is willing to trade excerpts from your books before or after publication for ads. If not, rewrite parts of your books so the text will be different.

sales than those that you are about to read, and we look forward to learning about them.

74 Catalogs   (Free)

Ask your publisher about their plans for getting your books into catalogs.

Agree on a time limit after which you will be free to arrange catalog deals and then let the catalog and your publisher crunch the numbers. Ask for a commission on deals you set up. Better still: let your agent negotiate the best way to handle selling to catalogs as part of your contract with your publisher.

Guerrilla Tom Ross reports that catalogs pay on time, don't return books, and buy thousands of copies at a time. Have we gotten your attention?

GUERRILLA TACTICS

Despite the Internet, direct-mail catalogs remain a billion-dollar business. The moment you start to develop the ideas for your books, start a file of catalogs that may sell your books right next to your file of promotion ideas.

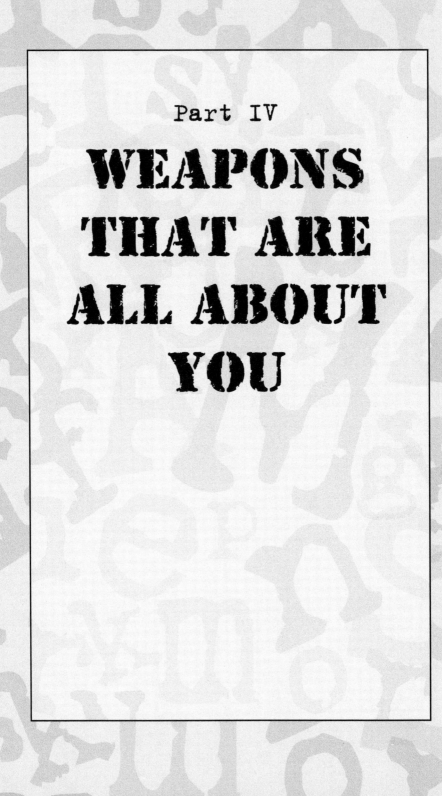

Part IV

WEAPONS THAT ARE ALL ABOUT YOU

CHAPTER 15

WEAPONS THAT PROVE YOU'RE A PRO

verything you do that is connected with your livelihood is an expression of your professionalism, so make one of your goals to be regarded by your peers as a consummate professional.

The following five weapons will prove you're a pro:

- Your Professionalism (Free)
- Trade Shows (Expensive)
- Professional Conferences (Expensive)
- Your Memberships in Professional Organizations (Low cost)
- Your Memberships in Community-service Organizations (Free or low cost)

75 Your Professionalism   (Free)

Your networks and the media can tell instantly if you are an amateur or a professional. Here are ten ways to impress them with your professionalism:

- Make your printed materials impeccable.
- Dress, talk and act like the professional you want people to believe you are.
- Answer questions in as few words as it takes to do justice to the question and prove you know what you're talking about.
- If you don't know something, admit it and learn it.
- Accept all suggestions with gratitude and use those that make sense to you.
- When you make a promise, keep it.
- Make your knowledge of publishing and promotion apparent in

everything you do and say.

- Be cyber-savvy.
- Put everything you do into the service of your immediate and long-term personal and professional goals.
- Embody your determination to succeed.

This long list is a short way of telling you that everything you do is a clue to your professionalism. So another way to make use of your networks is to help you learn how to be the professional author and promoter you aspire to be.

GUERRILLA TACTICS
Find the mentors you need, people in your field and other fields whose professionlism you admire and want to emulate.

76 Trade Shows (Expensive)

Trade shows are conventions for the "trade," not for consumers. The most important one in the publishing field is the annual Book Expo America (BEA) held Friday through Sunday in May or early June. *Literary Market Place* has the yearly BEA dates.

The primary purpose of the show has traditionally been to make booksellers aware of publishers' fall lists. However, between the decreasing number of independent booksellers who now generate less than 20 percent of book sales and the fact that sales reps have already sold the fall list by the time BEA takes place, the convention is in the process of reinventing itself. But your understanding of publishing will not be complete until you have been to BEA. It's the only opportunity to see almost all of trade publishing in one place. Observing how publishers promote their books to the trade will be an eye-opening experience.

Going to the breakfasts will enable you to watch authors sell themselves to booksellers. It will also offer you the chance to tell a table of booksellers about your book. There are state-of-the-art sessions about industry trends and realities that will help you understand what you to have to do to create the career you want.

The BEA offers an unparalelled opportunity to meet other authors, publicists, people in the media, subsidiary rights buyers and your publisher's sales and marketing staff.

You will also have the chance to shake hands with as many "blue badges" as you can find. They are worn by booksellers who, as their numbers decline, are treated like royalty. Until the industry started losing 150 booksellers a year, the number of booksellers in attendance was a litmus test of how successful the convention was.

The BEA will enable you to place your books in the context of the thousands of others that will be published in the fall. Going to BEA is one of the best ways to keep tabs on what's happening in the business, especially if you're living outside of New York.

It will be most worth your while to attend BEA when you have a book coming out in the fall. Then you will want to talk up your opus to as many blue badges as you can buttonhole. They will be valuable sources of information about local media and about what kind of promotion generates sales. The booksellers you meet may be willing to host book signings in their cities. The BEA is a superb opportunity both to learn about how publishing works and to forge friendships that may last a lifetime.

All you need to join the family is a passion for writing and books and a bemused fascination with the industry's perpetual gyrations. The more you attend BEA, the larger your family will grow.

Attending BEA will also give the sales and marketing staff in your publisher's booth the opportunity to make you books stand out from the hundreds of others they sell by matching your books with the author behind them. BEA may also create speaking opportunities for you. The four most likely opportunities are:

- If your book is important enough or if it will help booksellers, your publishers may be able to get you the opportunity to speak at the convention by yourself or as part of a panel.

    Suggest this to your editor. If your publisher is interested in making it happen, providing ideas for panels and possible participants will help.

- Just being listed in the program for the convention will bring you and your book to the attention of booksellers, the media, subsidiary rights buyers and foreign publishers attending the convention. Being listed in the issue of *PW* devoted to BEA will make those not attending aware of you.
- Press conferences take place at the convention, and if your book will be newsworthy enough, this may be a possibility for you to present it to the media and field questions.
- Another opportunity for you to talk to booksellers at BEA is while autographing advance copies. More than one hundred authors attend BEA just to sign books for booksellers who wait patiently in long lines for the privilege of meeting them. This is more likely to happen after your books have sold well enough to make booksellers fans of your work.

WAR STORIES

If your book is newsworthy enough, you may want to keep it under wraps at least until it's in stores. Robert Stinnett spent seventeen years researching *Day of Deceit: The Truth About FDR and Pearl Harbor*. He and Bruce Nichols, his editor at The Free Press, wanted to keep a lid on the book's explosive revelations until the logical publication date for it: December 7.

Books arrive in stores about a month before the pub date. But before pub date and before Rick and The Free Press could start publicizing it, the book created an instant buzz as soon as it was available. This forced Bob and The Free Press to respond to questions sooner than they anticipated. But the early attention enabled the book to go back to press before publication, a harbinger of good things to come.

TAKE TEA AND SEE

The Northern California Book Publicity and Marketing Association (NCBPMA) has a "tea" at the end of the day on Saturday. Tea is never served, but publicists and local media people are. Because BEA will be in

New York, Chicago or Los Angeles—the three biggest book markets—until at least 2005, local media can be sources of national publicity.

The tea gives staff and freelance publicists the chance to meet and chat in person with talk-show producers and other media people they may have known only by mail or telephone. For tickets and information on the tea, use NCBPMA's listing in the Resource Directory.

The tea is only one of the many parties at BEA. Many are closed affairs requiring tickets. For others you need only show up. Ingram, the nation's largest wholesaler, hosts an extravaganza for all badge holders.

Parties provide excellent opportunities for networking and for one of the major delights of the show: accidentally bumping into people who turn out to be valuable connections. Like everyone else, publishing people are more open to meeting new people and sharing information at the end of the day while they're relaxing at a party.

KNOCK KNOCK: GETTING INTO BEA

Publishers bring only a few authors to BEA, if any. Their first choices will be the authors who need the exposure least but whom booksellers most want to hear and meet: celebrities and best-selling writers.

Your publisher may not want other authors in their booth distracting the staff, whose job is to justify their travel expenses by helping as many blue badges as they can.

That said, if yours is a fall book, your publisher may be willing to provide a badge for you for at least one of the three days the show runs. If not, you can register as an author. Register in advance or the day before the show opens. Opening day generates a line that may take you hours to get through.

If your agent is attending, he or she may be willing to add your name to the registration form, especially if you pay for the ticket.

BEA is a valuable source of contacts and knowledge, making it an essential learning tool for authors. For many of the more than twenty-five thousand people who attend it, BEA is also like a family reunion at which they meet friends from around the country they see only at the show.

The excitement of being at the convention, the parties, learning about the business, being inspired by the speakers, catching up with old friends and making new ones make BEA an extremely enjoyable way to combine business and pleasure. You will also enjoy picking up complimentary galleys of upcoming books and other freebies.

Although what the BEA offers is worth more than the cost of attending, traveling costs will add up. So guerrillas make it a goal to find people with whom they can stay or share the cost of a room. Ditto for the cost of driving to the convention if that's an option.

An alternative to attending BEA is going to regional booksellers' meetings which are mini-BEAs. *LMP* has contact information for regional booksellers' groups.

GUERRILLA TACTICS
- When you're at BEA, check out the press room to see if any media people are around and do a reconnaissance of the publicity materials set out for the media.
- Also attend trade shows in your field. Thousands of regional and national trade shows take place a year. Whether you're writing about interior design or gifts, there is a trade show that can help you understand how to make your books as salable as possible and reach the gatekeepers between you and your readers.

77 Professional Conferences (Expensive)

The nonprofit version of trade shows is the professional conference. It offers the same opportunities as a trade show: networking, keeping up with new ideas in the field and learning about new products and services.

Academic fields such as history and psychology have associations that sponsor conferences. If your book will interest scholars or has adaption potential for classes on the subject, investigate the possibilities for speaking at the conferences in your field.

If your book has strong library potential, ask your editor if it will be worth your while to attend (on your dime) the annual convention of the American Library Association.

GUERRILLA TACTICS
Presenting papers at professional conferences will help you gain recognition and stature in your field.

78 Your Memberships in Business Organizations (Low cost)

One way to convince agents and publishers that you are serious about being part of your field is by joining professional organizations in your field.

If you're writing mysteries, join Mystery Writers of America. If you're a travel writer, join the Society of American Travel Writers. Serving as a high-ranking officer or on a committee will convey your acceptance as a valued member of the group and your ability to make use of that connection to promote your books.

So be a joiner. Memberships in groups in your field and in writer's organizations will make people aware of you and your books. One way to benefit from this weapon is to be thought of as a giver, not a taker.

GUERRILLA TACTICS
Because these organizations depend on help from volunteers, you can make a name for yourself by being as helpful and therefore as visible as your time allows.

79 Your Memberships in Community-Service Groups (Free)

Welcome the chance to help the groups in which you are genuinely interested. Look at joining community organizations as an opportunity to hone your skills and learn new ones you can use to write and promote your books, and maybe even earn a living. The more you help the groups you join to achieve their goals, the more willing they will be to sing your praises and help you achieve yours.

Here are eight ways to get you started:

- Go to meetings.
- Volunteer to help with committees and special events.
- Serve as an officer.
- Give copies of your books as raffle prizes.
- Become a spokesperson and help with publicity to develop your promotional skills and media contacts.
- Encourage members to contact you if they have questions you can answer.
- Give talks to interested groups, sell books afterward and donate profits to the organizations.
- Tithe yourself: devote a percentage of your time and income to worthy causes. People like to support those who are doing something for the community.

WAR STORIES

Mike and his wife Elizabeth Pomada have written six books about Painted Ladies, Victorian houses that are painted in three or more contrasting colors.

When one of their books is being published, they call preservation groups and historical societies around the country and ask to give slide-show presentations. They use a car for transportation whenever possible and integrate their talks into business trips. Their publisher provides plane fares, so they have been able to give talks in more than thirty cities.

Groups are delighted to invite them to speak. Mike and Elizabeth don't charge for the talks. Their presence increases the publicity for the meeting and the attendance, and the groups keep the profits from the sales. In the course of writing the books, they have spoken to the same groups as often as three times.

The hidden benefit: creating Painted Ladies is contagious. After home-owners see the slides of houses and the books, many of them go home and transform their homes into Painted Ladies—creating houses for future books.

GUERRILLA TACTICS

When talking to community groups, consider these tactics:

- Offer to write the announcement of your talk for the organization's newsletter.
- Write your intro, as well as your "outro"—what the person who introduces you will say after you finish your talk.
- Try to present your talk just before the holidays if your book has gift potential. Ask whoever is introducing you to announce after your talk that your books will make good presents and, if you wish, share part of the profits with the organization.
- Here are three ways to have books on hand:

   —Supply them yourself.

   —Have a local bookseller take care of sales if you want booksellers to smile at the sound of your name. However, as we mentioned earlier, before arranging a signing, ask a bookseller how many books must sell to make a signing worthwhile. Ask the organization if the event will generate enough sales to make it worth their while. Booksellers may even be willing to donate a portion of the proceeds to the group.

   Part of the value of signings to booksellers is to entice new customers into the stores where they may buy books other than the one being discussed. They will be more willing to help if your talk is held in the store.

   Another benefit of holding talks for groups in bookstores: they have mailing lists to which they send lists of events. Your talk will benefit from the attendance of people who are not members of the group you are speaking to and who may even become members afterward.

   —The third way for organizations to obtain books is to buy them from the publisher (see the next tactic). A credit card may be needed for the sale, and whether the group can return unsold books may affect how many they buy.

- Arrange with your publisher to give discounts to groups that order enough copies. You may be able to get groups a higher discount if they buy books on a nonreturnable basis. Suggest to groups that

c o n t i n u e d

Guerrilla Tactics, continued

they order enough copies for both the meeting and for members who can't come but will buy the unsold autographed copies later. Have the group compare the publisher's price with that offered by online booksellers.

- Writing and promoting books are both full-time jobs, so weigh the desire to help and the visibility of getting involved against the most productive way to use your time.

CHAPTER 16

WEAPONS TO MAKE PART OF YOUR IDENTITY

 It's your attitude not your aptitude that determines your altitude.
—ZIG ZIGLAR

People will sense your attitude the moment they meet you, read your E-mail or talk to you on the phone. Your attitude toward your work and the people you work with will affect how others feel about you.

So beyond the essential *ent* words in chapter one, there are personal qualities that will affect your career and your bottom line. There's nothing mysterious about them. They will serve you equally well in any endeavor. But even though they are really only common sense in action, guerrillas understand how important they are for obtaining and sustaining the support of all the people needed for success.

You need to exemplify the following virtues every day to inspire your allies as well as yourself. Weapons to make part of your identity are

- Your Passion for Books (Free and you get paid!)
- Your Enthusiasm (Free)
- Your Sense of Humor (Free)
- Your Sense of Balance (Free)
- Your Courage (Free)
- Your Competitiveness (Free)
- Your Speed (Free)
- Your Flexibility (Free)

- Your Smiles (Free)
- Your Optimism (Free)

80 Your Passion for Books (Free and you get paid!)

Loving books is what makes readers become writers. Your recommended reading lists in the back of your books and your Web site give you the chance to share your favorite books with the world.

Create lists of the books you love and sell those books on your Web site through an associate's program with an online bookseller. An annotated reading list of your favorite books that tells visitors why you love them will

- generate more sales than just using your bibliographies (see weapon 51 in chapter eleven)
- gladden the beating hearts and enrich the pocketbooks of authors whose books you recommend
- add to your credibility as an expert
- endear you to those who believe you are what you read and who love the same books you do
- tempt visitors to read your books to trace the influence of your favorite authors on your work
- and best of all, encourage people to start lists of their own favorite books

If you're a novelist, you can have two lists:
- a list of the best novels like yours
- a list of all your other favorite books

Fiction and nonfiction authors can also help other writers by creating lists of their favorite books about writing, publishing and promotion. But while you're at it, why not just include all the books you love?

The greatest compliment your fans will pay your virtual library is that whenever they want to read a book, they will visit your site to find one. Happy reading!

GUERRILLA TACTICS

- Add new books to the top of the lists to give ardent readers reasons to return.
- Find other ways to use the lists, such as part of your media kit, your handouts, or as the basis for a Webcast book club or book-of-the-month club, and in your E-mail signature.

81 Your Enthusiasm (Free)

If you're not fired with enthusiam,
you'll be fired with enthusiasm!

—VINCE LOMBARDI

My feeling about technique in art is that it has about the same value as technique in lovemaking. Heartfelt ineptitude has its appeal and so does heartless skill; but what you want is passionate virtuosity.

—JOHN BARTH

Your enthusiasm for your ideas and your books, and your ability to communicate your passion is essential to your success.

It's been said that no man is a hero to his biographer. So regardless of how enthusiastic you are when you start to write a book, remaining passionate for as long as you want your book and the talks based on it to keep generating income may become a challenge.

The one and a half or two years from now that it will take your book idea to reach the bookstores is a long time, yet it's only the beginning of the life of your book. It's easy to get caught up in the excitement of publication and promotion. As difficult as it may be to guess how long your enthusiasm for a book will last, make a careful judgment before committing yourself to living with the book.

This is another reason to test-market your ideas by giving talks and writing articles. Novelists may be able to give readings or have excerpts published of works in progress. This will help you decide how much you enjoy writing and talking about your book, gauge the response your books will get, and establish your credentials with agents, editors and book buyers.

The late Ken McCormick, who was editor in chief at Doubleday, had this advice to offer: "It is up to you to be enthusiastic about your work, your book, when 'selling' it to others. You must convey inordinate enthusiasm for your book to your editor—so much so that the editor becomes 'infected' with your enthusiasm . . . and then your editor is able to convey genuine enthusiasm to editorial peers and marketing people. If they too become infected, they will share that enthusiasm with copywriters, sales reps, artists . . . and so on, and through the ranks of the entire house . . . ultimately 'infecting' the retail and wholesale buyers with enthusiasm sufficent to buy your book. It works."

GUERRILLA TACTICS
- Read about how people like Helen Keller and Nelson Mandela over-came obstacles in their lives. Let their courage inspire you.
- Use exercise and high-energy music to rev you up in the morning and whenever you're down.
- Let the good your books will do and the pleasure they will give your readers around the world inspire you.
- Fantasize about what your life will be like as a successful author.

82 Your Sense of Humor   (Free)

Laughter is the shortest distance between two people.

—COMEDIAN VICTOR BORGE

Having fun has always been an integral part of the book-publishing business.

—MICHAEL KORDA

People like to laugh. It's good for them. Having a sense of humor will help you write and sell your books. Humor increases your audience's enjoyment of your books and talks. It inspires people and makes them remember you and your ideas.

But don't feel that you have to be the next Dave Barry. There are more sources of humor now than ever: books, magazines, online joke sites and networks, comedy clubs and CDs.

If you're giving a talk, look for humor in local media beforehand. Stay alert for observational humor that arises before or during your talk, such as something an audience member says or the lights going out. Creating humor and taking advantage of opportunities to use it is a skill you can develop.

You will need a sense of humor to cope with problems that arise in writing, publishing and promoting books. Looking for humor in tough situations will lead to material you can use in your talks, articles and books.

GUERRILLA TACTICS
- Learn from what makes children laugh.
- Look for the humorous possibilities in every situation, especially the serious ones.
- Watch humorous videos, listen to humor on audiocassettes and read humor books and books on writing humor.
- Take classes on writing humor.
- Start using humor in your writing and your talks now.

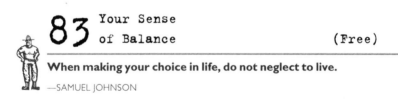

83 Your Sense of Balance   (Free)

When making your choice in life, do not neglect to live.
—SAMUEL JOHNSON

Decide on the balance that you want between writing your books and promoting them. Somewhere along the way to selling a million copies of his self-published book *1001 Ways to Be Romantic*, Greg Godek realized he was not a writer who promoted but a promoter who wrote. What are you?

Jack Canfield believes there is a yin and yang to being an author. The yin is when you're in your cave massaging your keyboard to create your books. Ensconced in the comfort of your home, you're in your creative mode and have complete control of your book.

The yang is when you leave your cave to market your books. In the real world, you share control over promoting your books with your publisher, the booksellers you want to stock your books, the media you want to help you promote them and your growing legions of fans.

Meeting your fans will help you sustain your energy and sense of mission about your books. You have to be dedicated to reach your goals. But you also have to find and maintain the right balance between the conflicting obligations in your life: writing and promoting, your family and the demands of being a writer, your personal and professional goals.

One of life's lessons is that we learn what having enough is by having too little and too much. Maintaining the balance between the yin and yang in your life may be as great a challenge as becoming a successful writer.

During the heady days of the success of *The Joy Luck Club*, Amy Tan was torn between the rigors of promotion and the joy of writing. She loves to write, but the endless demands of being a successful author prevented her from doing it.

When you're young and living alone, you have the freedom of living to work instead of working to live. You can live whatever way works best for you. This can be especially important at the beginning of your career when you are establishing yourself as an author. But having a family and a mortgage creates obligations, including the need to balance work, home and leisure. Time away from work and away from thinking about work will refresh you, help put your career into perspective, and give your subconscious mind time to solve your problems.

You also have the obligation to take care of yourself to maintain optimal health, because writing and promoting your books will demand all the effort you can muster. Another challenge is that we yearn for stability, but at a time of rapidly accelerating change, we must keep anticipating and responding to it. We need to balance the old and the new. The miracles of technology make us crave the values and the cultural legacy that we have inherited.

Satisfying all your needs will enable you to return to work refreshed and with a renewed sense of purpose. Maintaining a balanced perspective will help you survive the inevitable uncertainties of writing and promoting books. Communicating with a sense of balance will enable you to present yourself, both in person and in your books, not as a single-minded zealot but as a well-balanced embodiment of your ideas.

GUERRILLA TACTICS

- Maintain balance in your professional life by taking breaks and listening to music you love.
- Maintain balance in your personal life by giving yourself down time to enjoy life at as slow a pace as you wish. Meditate. Take walks. Do yoga. The good will pass, and the bad will pass. And in the context of the universe, the Earth is not even a grain of sand.

84 Your Courage (Free)

If we had to say what writing is, we would have to define it essentially as an act of courage.

—CYNTHIA OZICK

If you wait until you're really sure, you'll never take off the training wheels.

—CYNTHIA COPELAND LEWIS

Writing a book takes courage, but your belief in your future and the value of your books will sustain you. When fear makes you question your ability to write your books, get them published or promote them, think about the readers who will benefit most from your books. Pick one of them, real or imagined, and write for that reader.

Always remember that thousands of writers who don't have your ideas, talent, persistence, and ability to write and promote your work have become successful. If they can do it, you can. Uncertainty about the quality or commerciality of one's work is an occupational hazard, so find kindred spirits with whom you can share your fears and bolster your faith in yourself and your future.

Accept Eleanor Roosevelt's advice to "do the thing you cannot do." Once you accept your mission and commit yourself to building the career only you can create, your life will take on a sense of purpose. You will experience the certainty that you are living the life only you were born to live. Then courage will become as integral a part of you as breathing.

Two things worth remembering about courage:

- It's contagious. You can get it from the role models who inspire you, and you can pass it on to those who need it.
- Courage is like a muscle. The more you use it, the more of it you'll have when you need it.

GUERRILLA TACTICS
Make a habit of reading about people who performed courageous acts. Keep a file of stories about them. Read as many as it takes to restore your courage.

85 Your Competitiveness   (Free)

At a restaurant, the French playwright Georges Feydeau was once served a lobster with only one claw. When he protested, the waiter explained that lobsters can lose claws because they fight in the tank. "Then take this one away," instructed Feydeau, "and bring me the victor."

We don't advocate clawing your way to the top, even if the obstacles you encounter sometimes make you feel it's the only way to get there.

To get a sense of the environment into which your books will be delivered, consider the competition they will face:
- all the books produced by your publisher that are mentioned on the same list as yours
- all your publisher's past and future books
- all the books coming out from other publishers at the same time as yours
- all the books on the same subject (This is easy thanks to the ease of finding out-of-print books online.)
- all the books that have ever been written like yours (A beginner's book on French cooking will face more direct competition than a mystery that has the author's unique style, story and characters. However, no matter what kind of mystery you're writing, yours won't be the only one on the shelves.)

- all your previous books
- all the media that compete with books including television, radio, films, CDs, newspapers, trade and consumer magazines, newsletters, computer games, the World Wide Web, 'zines, E-mail, e-books and online publishing
- all the ways people can spend their money and time after satisfying their other obligations

Only 5 percent of new businesses survive longer than five years. So only your passionate belief in your work and your competitive spirit will enable you to sustain your efforts to break through the forces of competition that separate your books from your readers (and your royalties!).

No matter what bookshelf your books will be stocked on, it is full now and will be when your books arrive. But if you can summon the strength to campaign for your books, a bonanza awaits you.

Media that compete with books may become sources of promotion and royalties. Thanks to the emergence of new media and new ways for readers to buy and read literature, your books can earn far more income than ever before. So fight as hard as you can for them.

The novelist Jane Smiley once said, "There is something I have noticed about desire, that it opens the eyes and strikes them blind at the same time." To maintain your competitive edge, you must remain blind to distractions and more single-minded about reaching your goals than your competitors are.

86 Your Speed (Free)

If you don't run, you won't trip but you may never get there.
—CYNTHIA COPELAND LEWIS

We say that there are two successful books on a subject: The first one and the best one.
——A PUBLISHING EXECUTIVE

Technology breeds impatience. E-mail creates the expectation of a speedy response. You've probably heard it said that businesses can offer speed,

GUERRILLA TACTICS

Read biographies of business titans. Then try to combine their genius for innovation, organization and marketing and their competitive spirit with guerrilla values. (This will make promotion look easy!)

quality and economy, but customers can only have two of them. Now consumers want all three, and they have cyberspace at their fingertips to help find them.

How can you use speed to serve your customers better and faster?

- Respond to requests in order of importance.
- Make it possible for key people to reach you instantly during business hours and anytime in an emergency.
- Respond to E-mail as soon as possible after it arrives.
- Respond to all other communications the day they are received. Michael Korda, the editor-in-chief of Simon & Schuster and a best-selling author, answers all of his calls the day he receives them. If he can, you can.
- Let people know in advance how soon they can expect you to respond to them, and keep your word.
- If you can't respond to a request, notify the person immediately and if possible, find someone who can.
- If you can, promote the speed of your responses as a reason to do business with you.
- Reward ideas for serving your networks better and faster, and the ideas will keep coming.
- Imbue those who work for you with your concern for speed.
- Never stop asking yourself about everything you do: is there any way I can do this better and faster?

87 Your Flexibility (Free)

Part of the reason established companies fail in the age of e-commerce is that they don't want to cannibalize the traditional "legacy channels" that

WAR STORIES

Andy Ross, the owner of the famous Cody's Bookstore in Berkeley, California uses a bicycle messenger to provide same-day delivery service. It saves money and symbolizes his commitment to serving his customers as well and as quickly as possible. This is an example of how small businesses can use creativity, speed and flexibility to their advantage. It's such a good idea that the chains have started providing same-day service.

GUERRILLA TACTICS

- Make yourself available quickly to the media. Talk-show producers keep a file of local guests they can call on at the last minute when a scheduled guest can't make it. But when they're caught in a last-minute scramble, they can't wait for a response. If they can't reach you immediately, they'll go on to the next author on the list.
- Structure your books so they start delivering the benefit readers expect as soon as you can. In the first edition of Mike's book on finding and working with a literary agent, how to find an agent wasn't discussed until chapter five. When his assistant Antonia Anderson read the draft of the revised edition, she asked why. In the second edition, it's in chapter one.
- Provide the products and services you offer faster than your competitors without sacrificing quality, and you can stress this advantage in your marketing.

made them successful. This partly accounts for how Amazon.com got a big head start on their bricks-and-mortar competitors: by creating a new business model instead of grafting online bookselling onto an already existing company. This confirms the Silicon Valley maxim: if you don't eat your lunch, someone else will.

In business, you have to keep bending over backward to please your readers and everyone else who needs your help or whose help you want. To do that, you have to be flexible. One of the huge advantages you have as an entrepreneur is flexibility: your ability to adapt to rapidly changing business conditions so you can take advantage of new opportunities the moment they arise.

In an age of unprecedented change, flexibility is essential. When new writing and marketing opportunities arise, jump on them as soon as you feel reasonably confident you're doing the right thing and your networks agree with you. One good thing about bending over backward to serve your readers and your audiences: it gives you a fresh perspective.

GUERRILLA TACTICS

- Keep your body flexible. It will help keep your mind flexible.
- Look at every piece of information you absorb with the understanding that it may contain a new idea for doing something better. Great ideas can come at any time. Be prepared to make use of them as soon as you figure out how.

88 Your Smiles　　　　　　　　　　　　　(Free)

A smile is a kiss bestowed with your lips open.
—ANONYMOUS

How many free things are more beautiful and easier to give than a smile? Raise your hand if there are too many smiles in your life. That's why smiling in your first contact with someone can make a lasting impression. For some people, your smile will be the most valuable freebie you can offer.

Fascinating facts about smiles:

- A smile produces automatic physiological responses in both the smiler and the smilee. It makes both of them feel better about themselves and each other.
- Callers can tell if the person at the other of a telephone line is smiling.
- One of the hazards of living in cloudy northern climes is that you may become smile-challenged. There really is such a thing as a sunny disposition. That's why you will find more smiling faces on the Mediterranean than the Baltic.

Your smile may be the only thing a new acquaintace remembers. Because of the importance of first impressions, it may become the enduring image someone has of you. So if people are worth meeting, do it with a smile on your face. If you don't know whether they are, pretend they are, and they will usually justify your expectations.

The more successful you become, the more calls you will receive. So make the warmth of your hello and goodbye capture your pleasure in spending time with your callers.

GUERRILLA TACTICS
If you're not giving or receiving enough smiles, change now. If someone smiles at you, smile back. If someone doesn't, smile anyway and watch what happens.

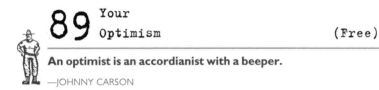

89 Your Optimism   (Free)

An optimist is an accordianist with a beeper.
—JOHNNY CARSON

If you are doing all you can to achieve your goals, you have a right to be optimistic. Assume that your career, like that of most writers, will continue to flourish over time. Assume every book you write will be better than the last, bringing you closer to reaching the critical mass of readers you need to break out and become as successful as you want to be.

To keep your publisher happy, you have to keep
- giving presentations around the country based on your books
- using your speaking schedule to increase your national visibility in the media
- building your stature in your field
- making sure there is an uptick in the sales of every book you write
- ensuring your past books continue to sell

To keep yourself happy, you need optimism to help sustain your enthusiasm and determination to bounce back from setbacks. You can't allow the problems you will confront throughout your career to affect your positive outlook.

Optimism is contagious, and you want to infect everyone you meet with it. It's been said that when we talk, only 7 percent of what we communicate is words. The other 93 percent is everything else about us, including tone of voice, facial expression, gestures and clothing.

You want to exude optimism, so that when people think of you, they think of someone who loves life and lives it with hope and gusto. People would rather be around an optimist than a pessimist. That's one of the reasons talk-show hosts will invite you back, and why the people in your networks will always be glad to hear from you. A bonus: optimism is better for your health.

GUERRILLA TACTICS

Make a list of all the reasons you have to be optimistic and put it on the wall where you write. On bad days, look at the list. It will convince you that you are one of the luckiest people on the planet. Welcome to the club.

CHAPTER 17

WEAPONS FOR COMMUNICATING YOUR IDENTITY

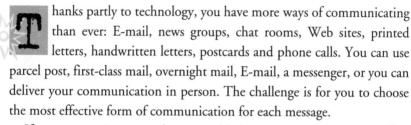hanks partly to technology, you have more ways of communicating than ever: E-mail, news groups, chat rooms, Web sites, printed letters, handwritten letters, postcards and phone calls. You can use parcel post, first-class mail, overnight mail, E-mail, a messenger, or you can deliver your communication in person. The challenge is for you to choose the most effective form of communication for each message.

If you create print materials you would like to share with other guerrillas, please mail them to Mike at 1029 Jones Street, San Francisco, CA 94109, or scan and E-mail them to us at www.gmarketing.com. Please let us know how they helped you. If they will inspire other guerrillas, we'll post them on the Web site. How's that for guerrilla marketing?

This chapter contains five weapons for communicating your identity:
- Your Audiocassettes (You get paid!)
- Your Videocassettes (You get paid!)
- Your Stationery (Low cost)
- Your Business Cards (Low cost)
- Your Bookmarks (Low cost)

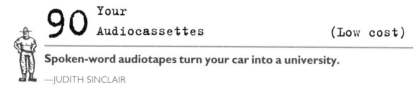

90 Your Audiocassettes   (Low cost)

Spoken-word audiotapes turn your car into a university.
—JUDITH SINCLAIR

Audiocassette versions of books, abridged and unabridged, are a two-billion-dollar business. Tens of millions of Americans spend enough road time, exercise time and hospital time to make them customers for audiocassettes.

If you are giving talks as a way of life, you have a built-in market for selling audiocassettes and videocassettes as well as books. Agents usually try to either keep audio rights for their authors or make a separate deal for them. If your publisher has an audio division, let them integrate the timing, packaging and marketing of your books and cassettes.

However, Simon & Schuster expects audiocassette sales to be 10 percent of print sales. The lowest number of potential sales that makes it worth their while to invest in an audiocassette is ten thousand copies. This means they are looking for books with the potential to sell at least 100,000 copies: a safe bet with best-selling authors, a risk with almost all first books.

You may be able to get involved with the abridging of your book or the reading of it. Producing cassettes is not expensive. So if you self-publish a tape and make it first rate, you may be able to find a distributor. If you sell enough copies, you'll be able to sell it to one of the audio publishers listed in LMP.

However you make them happen, audiocassettes can mean thousands of dollars a year in back-of-the-room sales. They can also trigger other sales and make new fans of your work. There are one thousand new audio books published every month. Why shouldn't yours be one of them?

GUERRILLA TACTICS

- If you don't have a videocassette of yourself speaking, an audiocassette is the next best weapon to send to the media and groups you want to speak to. A tape of you before an audience will show how well audiences respond to you.
- According to speaker Larry Winget, people think in twenty-dollar bills, so develop products that you can sell or combine to sell for twenty dollars or multiples of that amount. This is especially helpful if you don't accept plastic.
- At the end of your cassette, add whatever information about yourself you want your listeners to know.
- If you produce your own audiocassettes, enclose a business card or a folded bookmark.
- At the end of your cassette, offer a giveaway to listeners who contact you with their reactions, questions and suggestions.

Something to look forward to: as soon as your books sell enough, cassette publishers will be knocking at your door.

91 Your Videocassettes (Low cost)

Except for their feature film versions, not many books are made into videocassettes. They're expensive to produce unless

- you know someone who can videotape and edit one of your presentations
- you can find a video class willing to make your video a project

They're not expensive to reproduce, however, so if you can get one made, you will be able to make copies of it to send to the media as a demo tape and sell at your events with a large markup.

GUERRILLA TACTICS
- Use the beginning and end of your video cassette for promotion.
- Include a bookmark, postcard or brochure.

92 Your Stationery (Free or low cost)

Your letterhead may be your first contact with agents, editors, the media, opinion-makers and people who book speakers. Media people especially are so inundated with mail that, like the rest of us, they toss envelopes that don't look promising into their circular file.

Your envelopes and labels will include less information than your other printed materials. But they may be the only thing on which the recipients of your mail base their response to it.

So the biggest challenge you may face in creating your letterhead, envelope and mailing label isn't deciding the information to include but finding the best design for it.

A well-designed letterhead will not redeem a poorly written letter, but it will convey with silent eloquence a sense of your identity, character, professionalism and, ultimately, your books. So make that lasting first impression impressive.

The contact information on your letterhead should give readers as many options as possible to respond to you. Like your business cards, brochures and bookmarks, your letterhead may include

- your name
- an advanced degree (anything above a Master's degree)
- a professional degree such as M.D.
- the name of your business
- the year you started your business if it's long ago enough to be impressive
- your snail-mail and E-mail addresses (If you use a box, also include a street address to lend a sense of substance to your enterprise.)
- your phone number
- your Web site
- your memberships in professional organizations
- your book covers
- a photo of you if it will help
- an illustration from one of your books
- a list of other products and services you offer
- a quote from one of your books or from a review
- sales worth bragging about
- office hours
- the title and pub date of an upcoming book, if you are certain of both the date and your ability to use the printed materials on which it appears before your next book comes out
- prizes you've won
- your theme
- your logo

You can't use all this information without creating an impossibly busy design. If the top of your letterhead is too busy with information, move some of it to the bottom of the page.

After you decide what information to include, a number of creative decisions await you including

- the typeface
- the size of the lettering
- what color(s) of ink to use
- the paper stock
- the best way to integrate the information into a unified, aesthetically pleasing design that communicates your identity as effectively as possible

You may want to use the typeface or colors on the covers of your books for your name or the list of book titles, especially if you're doing a series of books with the same basic look. If you want to try your hand at design, experiment with the typefaces available on your computer and with clip art you can download. Clip art is also available on CD-ROMs.

Your printed materials, even your address, will have a subtle but certain effect on people's perception of you. You want them to convey a positive sense of your identity as a writer and a person.

In designing your letterhead, keep the following concerns in mind:

- Computers make it possible for you to design your letterhead. But whether you design it yourself or you have someone help you, find a design that you will be proud to be represented by.
- Look at your printer's portfolio of letterheads. They may have a designer who can create one for you or work with you on your design. It probably won't be very expensive because your printer expects to profit from printing what you need.
- Check out online sources for ideas.
- Make sure that the design will look good and read well in black and white as well as color.
- Experiment to ensure that your name and logo will look good and be readable if they're blown up or reduced in size.
- Choose a design that will be equally effective for all of the other uses you will make of it: business cards, bookmarks, mailing labels, newsletters, promotion materials, news releases, brochures, postcards, audiocassettes, videocassettes, handouts, evaluation forms, and per-

GUERRILLA STRATEGIES

- Use your mail and networks to build a collection of print materials you love and hate. You may be able to learn more from failures than successes. Make a list of the reasons why you feel as you do about them. Then, as with your writing, emulate the best book.

- If you can't afford a graphic designer, find one online or offline to give you feedback on yours for a reasonable fee.

- Ask teachers of graphic design if you can make the design of your letterhead their class project.

- Plan on using your design for at least ten years. Since you want to get it right the first time, before you make any final desisions, take the design out for a test spin. Try it out on your printer, your networks, design pros and the people whose letterheads you looked at.

  Keep in mind that like the design for the cover of your book, the reactions to the design for your stationery will be subjective and fallible. Your publisher's art director will be willing to give you feedback on it and perhaps even design it for you on the side.

- Take advantage of the free advertising space on your return label; use an icon from your book's artwork or the title of your book.

- Print as many forms in as great a quantity as you can at the same time. The more you print, the lower the unit cost. At the same time, you will want to add the titles of new books to your materials, so don't print more than you expect to use before the next book.

- Unless you relish the taste of glue, use self-adhesive envelopes with peel-off strips. They're faster and easier to use.

- Consider printing at least your letterhead on your own printer.

- People like to patronize and work with those who share their values. One value people share today is protecting the environment. Use recycled paper when you can, and unobtrusively include the symbol for it (your printer will have it).

haps invoices, questionnaires, receipts and purchase orders.

- Make your typeface distinctive and evocative, yet easy to read and reproduce.

- Get three printing estimates before deciding on a printer.

WAR STORIES

Because of a paperwork mix-up, one writer unexpectedly received a letter from a stranger. She wrote back complimenting him on his stationery. Then he wrote back. It turned out that the reason he had beautiful stationery was that he owned a printing company. Then she wrote back, and although they lived two thousand miles apart, they met and married. They're still living happily ever after. There's no telling how your stationery will change your life!

GUERRILLA TACTICS

- Double the width of your card and fold it in half, so you have four sides for information. And if you leave it flat—voila!—it's a bookmark.
- If you are not planning to use any folds, here's a way to make your card memorable. Use different cards for different occasions: a solid brass card (if your budget allows) for the contacts you want to impress most; a color card for most contacts; and a black on white version for putting in bowls at conventions for drawings or to receive information.
- A mind- and card-expanding idea: don't limit yourself to one fold. Add as many folds as you wish and your budget allows so you can include more information. John Kremer reported that Robert Conklin, the author of *Be Whole!*, uses a folded eight-page brochure the size of a business card that includes excerpts from his book.

  The two tradeoffs: The more folds you add, the more costly the design, printing and folding will be. The thicker the card, the more likely it is that the recipient will make a conversation piece out of it, but the less likely it is that the card will remain in a wallet or cardholder.
- Card etiquette: when you're exchanging cards, smile, examine the one you receive respectfully and compliment it if you can.
- If you offer services to the general public, carry push pins and your cards with you and, if it's appropriate for what you're offering, put them on bulletin boards in print shops and laundromats.
- Guerrillas investigate the possibility of printing promotional materials on their own printers and check online sources for printing.

93 Your Business Cards (Low cost)

Like stationery, business cards used to include only basic contact information. But guerrillas use business cards as mini-brochures.

There are more ways than ever to be creative with your business cards: color, see-through paper, mylar, die-cuts and embossing. The challenge is to balance cost and creativity while making your card a potent guerrilla weapon.

The following reminders about business cards will help:
- Be unique without letting cleverness overshadow what you're promoting.
- Include as much information as you can without sacrificing an effective design.
- Use a standard-sized card so it will fit into a card storage file, wallet and Rolodex.
- Since business people are using scanners to capture the information on business cards for their databases, check to ensure a scanner will be able to read your card.
- The more important your card is to your book and your business, the more you should invest in it.
- When you give somebody a card, ask, "Would you like a second card?" or "Do you know anyone who would like a card?"

94 Your Bookmarks (Low cost)

The discussions of stationery and business cards above also apply to the content and design of bookmarks.

GUERRILLA TACTICS

- Booksellers are usually willing to insert bookmarks in books as they bag them for customers. If you can afford to supply booksellers with bookmarks, at least in your hometown, do it. If you have enough for other cities, bring them to bookstores as you travel.
- Insert bookmarks (or business cards) into the copies of your books on store shelves.
- Ask booksellers if you can insert your bookmarks in the books most likely to attract buyers for your books. The sales this may generate will help ensure that booksellers keep your books in stock.
- Heighten the surprise of browsers by adding a handwritten note asking the reader to call you with questions or to discuss the book. Browsers may make use of the card even if they don't buy the book.
- Use bookmarks as giveaways at your speaking appearances.
- Include bookmarks in your media/speaker's kit.
- Have bookmarks inserted in videos based on your books.
- Stick a bookmark or flyer into every personal and business envelope you mail. At least some of them will become conversation pieces and find their way into the right people's hands.

CHAPTER 18

WEAPONS FOR BUILDING YOUR INVINCIBLE MARKETING MACHINE

In order to succeed, you must know what you are doing, like what you are doing, and believe in what you are doing.

—WILL ROGERS

our theme, logo and package are expressions of your identity. These weapons will assist you in branding yourself to give all of your marketing efforts maximum impact. We hope that over time your efforts generate enough synergy to make your brand the *Guerrilla Marketing* of your field. These weapons for building your invincible marketing machine will help you shape

- Your Identity (Free)
- Your Theme (Free)
- Your Logo (Free or low cost)
- Your Package (Free)
- Branding Your Books (Free)
- Your Promotion Calendar (Free)
- The Ultimate Weapon: You to the Fourth Power (Free)

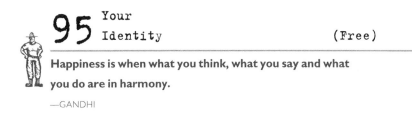

95 Your Identity (Free)

Happiness is when what you think, what you say and what you do are in harmony.

—GANDHI

Increasing the profits of a small business by using unconventional weapons and tactics and substituting time, energy and imagination for money is the essence of guerrilla marketing. And guerrilla marketing is the essence of Jay's identity as an author and speaker.

What's the essence of yours?

One of the ways Workman established and maintains its identity as the most creative publisher in New York is their covers. They don't look alike, but Workman has a distinctive approach to design that communicates and reinforces the company's identity.

There once was a cartoon in *The New Yorker* showing two sharks swimming next to each other, and one of them is saying, "I have a spiritual side, but basically I'm an eating machine."

The six conglomerates that dominate trade publishing may have a spiritual side, but they're basically profit machines. Because conglomerates have to focus more on profits than people, consumers yearn for warm one-on-one relationships with the businesses they patronize.

WRITERS FOUND IN AMAZON

A major factor in Amazon.com's meteoric rise is mass customization. Amazon.com's identity is based on its one-on-one relationships with customers that enable the company, for example, to suggest new books for customers based on their previous purchases.

Amazon.com's goal is to make shopping so personal and pleasurable that customers want to return and won't be tempted to start new relationships from scratch with other online vendors. Ploughing profits back into marketing is part of Amazon.com's strategy to make the company a brand synonymous with online shopping, no matter what customers want or need.

One of the opportunities you have as an author is creating, establishing and maintaining your identity as the living personification of the ideas in your books.

An identity is not an image that may conceal a different reality. Your identity must be the essence of you and your books. Come up with a list of qualities that conveys who you are, use your networks to verify it, and then make sure that everything you write and do communicates your identity.

WAR STORIES

Randall Reeder is a speaker who decided to become the reincarnation of Will Rogers. He has an easy smile. He looks and sounds like Will Rogers, and when he gives talks, he uses a hat, a lariat and saddlebags as props, and he quotes Rogers in his presentations.

Randall has assumed the identity of someone else, but he makes it an authentic expression of who he is as a speaker. It is so effective that his business card features photos of himself and Will Rogers striking the same pose. Randall's Web site is www.WillRogersToday.com.

Your identity has to be

- an authentic expression of who you are as a person and a writer. As in all other things, you must trust your instincts. Your identity must feel right and be a comfortable fit with your personality.
- unique. Randall Reeder, for example, is the only speaker impersonating Will Rogers (see above). If there was another speaker imitating Will Rogers, why would anyone want to be the second? What can you be the only embodiment of?
- marketable. It has to help sell you to your agent, your publisher, booksellers, potential readers, the media and to people who can book you to speak.
- durable. If you're using nichecraft to build your career, you have to be able to convince yourself and your networks that your identity will last you for the duration.
- flexible. The ideal identity enables you to write and speak about as broad a range of topics as possible. Guerrilla marketing is Jay's identity. However, it's adaptable enough to encompass a virtually endless range

of subjects that can make use of guerrilla techniques. These include *Guerrilla Selling, Guerrilla Negotiating* and *Guerrilla Cost-cutting.* The guerrilla approach to business is broad enough to take in all of the subjects that small businesses need to know about.

CLOTHES MAKE THE PHOTO

Your writing and speaking style, your sense of humor, the creativity of your novels or your ideas, your ability to move your readers and listeners—any of these may be the basis for forging your identity.

If you want to write a series of books about gardening, you could wear overalls with flowers or vegetables embroidered on the front, a well-worn straw hat with a flower sticking out of it and a pair of old gardening gloves sticking out of a back pocket. You could even make appearances with gardening tools in hand. Doing interviews, book signings, talks and appearances at gardening shows in your outfit will help establish your identity as a knowledgeable, hands-on gardener.

Another take on the same idea: suppose your goal is to show city dwellers living in apartments how easy and creative it is to grow flowers and use them in different ways. You might want to call yourself "The Elegant City Gardener." Instead of wearing overalls, you don a tux or an evening gown.

The media want to avoid headshots from book covers. A creative shot of you in costume practicing what you teach will yield publicity. You can use the photo and variations of it for your stationery, postcards, business cards, Web site, coffee mugs, gardening tools and seed packets.

Establishing an identity gives you the opportunity to think carefully about who you are and how you want to spend your career. Making that decision will stimulate your creativity. You will come up with ideas for using your identity to reach your goals, such as creating an elegant gardening series for the home and garden cable channel and fusion marketing arrangements with gardening product manufacturers.

Giving talks and writing articles give you the chance to test-market your identity. So figure out who you want to be, try it out on your networks and if they approve, tell the world about it.

Once you are comfortable with your identity, you can integrate it into everything you do, say and write, including

- how you talk
- how you dress
- how you respond to people online, on the phone and in person
- the tone, wording and design of your letters and printed materials
- the other elements of your package

GUERRILLA TACTICS
Think about all of the virtues you want to incorporate into your identity, then create it as an inspiration for yourself as well as others.

BONUS WEAPON
Start an Organization   (Low cost)

If your book takes off because it excites an underserved group, consider starting an organization. Thanks to technology, this is easier to do than ever. Being president or publicist will help you publicize your books. Early warning: learn how to delegate or you may be buried in commitments and immobilized by clinging vines.

96 Your Slogan   (Free)

When you care enough to send the very best.

Fly the friendly skies of . . .

Good to the last drop

If you don't know which companies* use these slogans, you must be new to these shores. These slogans are three of the best-known phrases in America, and it costs the companies that use them millions of dollars a year to make sure you remember them.

A slogan is a phrase or sentence that captures the essence of your identity,

---

*Hallmark, United Airlines and Maxwell House Coffee, respectively

of what you aspire to be—of your mission—and how you want your readers to feel about you.

The slogan for Mike's agency is "Helping writers launch careers since 1972." Using the year his agency started conveys experience, ability and the sense that his is an established company that has proven itself over time. It also suggests that his agency is willing to work with new, unpublished writers, which is not true of all agencies that have been in business for more than a quarter of a century.

One criterion for an effective theme and logo is that they will remain effective as long as you need them. So think through what you want in your theme—the best of who you are and the benefit you provide. Then try it out on your networks before you commit yourself to it.

GUERRILLA TACTICS

To establish a criterion for how effective your theme is, search for all the themes you and your networks can find in print and broadcast media, and judge yours next to theirs.

97 Your Logo (Free)

The Pillsbury Doughboy. The Jolly Green Giant. The rainbow-striped apple with a bite taken out if it. These are three enduring logos that have held up well over time.

A logo is the visual counterpart of your slogan. They are often used together. Like your slogan, your logo symbolizes your character, what you have to offer and the benefit it provides. A theme or a book title in a distinctive typeface can serve as logo. It may use color, a typeface, an object or an abstract design to create a positive impression on consumers and the media. Logos are so important that the Fortune 500 companies pay the top pros in the field seven figures to design them. You can trademark a logo.

GUERRILLA TACTICS

- See if there's a design element or typeface on your covers that you can use as a logo.
- If you want to design your logo yourself, try this: Step back far enough from your work so you can look creatively and objectively at your books and yourself. What captures the essence of you, your books and the rest of what your business offers?

Chefs who write cookbooks can use the tools of their trade either to create a logo or integrate the tools into the letters of the titles of their books or business. If possible, use the same design for both, so every time you promote one, you promote the other. If you can't use your logo as part of the title, ask your publisher to include it at the bottom of the back cover.

Gardeners can use garden tools, shades like green and brown, or the colors of their fruits or flowers. They can also choose a typeface that evokes gardening.

98 Your Package   (Free)

The primary physical manifestations of your business are your "package." They include

- your books
- your business card
- your stationery
- your brochure
- your media kit
- your Web site
- the colors you use
- your clothes
- your office, if it's open to the public

Media people, your networks and the public will at least subconsciously take the elements of your package into consideration in forming an impression of you. So make sure the components of your package

- make your name and the title of your books easy to read
- convey your identity
- are consistent with each other as well as with your other weapons
- use words, colors and designs that inspire confidence (Use research and your networks to verify your choices.)
- contain enough information about you, your book and your services to enable prospects to make a decision
- differentiate your books from your competitor's books
- include your slogan
- show your logo
- make people remember the other marketing you do
- are effective for all the uses you will make of it: publicity, speaking, teaching, online marketing, using speaking bureaus and creating strategic alliances
- will remain effective throughout your career

How you package your products, your services and yourself are among the most important decisions you make. If people know all about what you have to offer but are still undecided, your package may tilt the scales in your favor.

GUERRILLA TACTICS
- Go to the your library and page through the books on design and packaging for ideas.
- Balance the aesthetics of design with practical considerations.

99 Branding Your Books (Free)

You are the brand.
—TOM PETERS

Branding yourself and your work means using every opportunity to make a positive impression on everyone who sees any part of your package. Branding requires endless repetition in as many forms and media venues as possible.

The more impressions the elements of your package make on people, the more powerful your brand becomes. This is a simple, subtle weapon, but its cumulative effect is unstoppable if you use it consistently.

Your logo and your slogan are weapons you can use to unifty everything you create into a brand known worldwide like the Dummies books, the Chicken Soup books and Sue Grafton's "Alphabet" mystery series. Besides being a title, a brand can also be a character like James Bond or an author like Fodor's, Martha Stewart and Tom Clancy.

A brand can even be the name of an institution like the Mayo Clinic or Berlitz, or a name that has no relationship to publishing. Should we be surprised that MacDonald's is leveraging its brand by launching a series of books?

Building your brand requires you to coordinate the look of everything you produce, including your Web site, with all of your print materials.

In addition to print materials, you can use your slogan and logo for T-shirts, sweatshirts, coffee mugs, the door or window of your office, on your briefcase and on your car. Children's books are rich with opportunities for merchandising products such as toys, games and stuffed animals.

We draw the line at using a slogan for tattoos or to decorate your roof, but as you can see, you're only limited by your time, energy and imagination—and fortunately, your good taste.

WAR STORIES
In 1934, Irving Stone's *Lust for Life* was such a successful best-seller that it created a Van Gogh fever, with Van Gogh-colored gloves and dresses, Van Gogh windows in 5th Avenue stores, sunflower hats and more. Stone even received a letter asking permission to market a *Lust for Life* negligee.

At Mike's classes, the writers he teaches don't recognize the name Jay Conrad Levinson, but they always recognize guerrilla marketing. That's the power of branding. You know you're a brand when someone thinks about your field and the first thing that leaps to mind is you or your books. So start branding yourself now and prepare for the recognition and rewards your efforts will yield.

GUERRILLA TACTICS

Stay on the lookout for all of the ways that the Fortune 500 use branding to communicate their identity and whenever possible, adapt them for your use.

BONUS WEAPON

Test-marketing   (Low cost)

You can use test-marketing to guarantee the success of your books from the moment you concieve the ideas for them.

- Test-market your idea with your networks to see how excited they are about it.
- Test-market your ideas and titles in your talks: Try out your ideas with your audiences until they have the eloquence and the impact you desire.
- Test-market your ideas with articles: Who publishes them, how much they pay and the feedback they generate will give you a sense of how marketable your idea is. An article may be able to serve as a sample chapter in a nonfiction proposal and may attract agents and editors. Novelists can do the same thing if their novels lend themselves to being excerpted.
- Test-market your identity: Make everything you do an authentic expression of who you are and observe how people respond.
- Test your goals: Establish literary and financial goals for your book that motivate you to write and promote it. Write the ideal review of your book and note the advance you want for it. Include them when you send out your proposal or manuscript for feedback. Ask your networks if your work justifies your goals.
- Test-market your promotion plan: Sharing your promotion plan with published authors, especially those writing the same kind of books, will help you make sure you're on the right track. Your plan has to enable you to achieve your financial goals, or you must revise your plan or your goals.

- Test-market your work: Once you finish your proposal or manuscript, test it with Jack and Mark's recipe for chicken soup. Send it out to forty or more readers. The more specific you are about the feedback you want, the more it will help you. The more readers who review it, the fewer problems you will have selling it.
- Test-market your manuscript: If you're giving talks, make every audience a focus group. Whether you've sold your book to a publisher or not, as soon as you integrate feedback into your manuscript, have it photocopied (single-spaced, double-sided) and bound. Sell copies at your talks and offer to acknowledge those who make suggestions in the published version. Make changes before you reprint.
- Test-market your self-published book: If you want to sell your book to a big publisher and you have enough promotional ammunition, now's the time. If you don't have enough promotional firepower but you will be happy with a small publisher, you're ready now because small publishers aren't as concerned about promotion.

  If you need more ammo, maximize the value of your book: Self-publish it, sell it at your presentations and get feedback on the text and the design. Sell enough copies of your book, and you'll trigger a stampede of agents and editors beating a path to your door.
- Test-market your cover: Whether you design your cover, hire an artist to do it or your publisher does it, use your networks for feedback on a sketch of the design. The key question: Will the design and the copy sell your book as effectively as possible?
- Test-market your final promotion plan: If you sell your book with a proposal, more than a year will elapse between when you write your plan and when your book will be published. Add new information to your final promotion plan and test it again with your networks.
- Test-market your plan on a small scale: Pick a city to test-market your promotion plan. See if you can generate publicity and if the publicity generates sales.
- Test-market your plan on a larger scale: Integrate what you learn from your first city into your promotion plan and materials. Then do a publicity mailing to the other cities on your tour. However, book only

GUERRILLA TACTICS
If you can't find an event or anniversary to tie your book into, create a day of your own.

half of the cities initially. After you tour those, use what you learn to book the other half.

If you test-market your books every step of the way between you to your readers, they will be fail-proof and success will be inevitable.

100 Your Promotion Calendar (Free)

Every day of the year is a special day, week or month for saluting a person, event, cause or activity. February, for instance, is Black History Month, so publishers release books to take advantage of media interest. In addition to holidays like Christmas and seasonal interests like June weddings and the start of baseball season, there are thousands of opportunities into which you can tie the promotion of your book.

People may be more responsive to your books at certain times of the year. Look at a calendar and decide what times during the year will work best for promoting your books and what kind of promotion will be most effective. Create a promotion plan that concentrates your efforts during the most productive times of the year for your books, adjusting it every year in response to its effectiveness. By the end of the third year, you will have a year's worth of what we call "slam dunks."

Then all you have to do is stay alert for ways to fine-tune what you're doing and to add new opportunities. This is the best way we know of to take the stress out of wondering what to do next.

BONUS WEAPON
The Ultimate Weapon: *You*[4] (Free)

Being a guerrilla enables you to create four overlapping activities that will generate a whirlwind of synergy:

- Practicing nichecraft—doing a series of related books—produces synergy by creating more value for your readers and yourself than stringing together disparate books.
- Selling books, articles, short stories, and related products and services. For novelists, this may mean teaching writing, writing about fiction or merchandising a line of products.
- Using as many weapons as you can. The effect of all of them will be greater than the sum of their parts.
- Developing as many as ten ways of earning a living that create synergy with each other and with your other activities. For example, besides writing books, Jay:
  —gives thirty keynotes a year
  —writes a column for AOL
  —publishes a newsletter
  —sells books and services on his Web site
  —publishes three daily guerrilla tips
  —acts as a marketing consultant

In addition to protecting you in case one or more of your revenue streams temporarily dries up, developing diverse but synergistic sources of income will help compensate for the small royalties and advances that are the lot of most authors.

The best way to begin making a living with your ideas is to start producing them in as many media and countries as possible as soon as possible.

The moment you align nichecraft

- the growing number of books, products and services you have to sell
- the growing assortment of weapons you are using
- the varied but related income streams you integrate to make a living

If you follow these guidelines you will have an invincible marketing machine, the key to unlocking all of the treasures of your calling. As long as you base your life on the synergy described above, this marketing machine will grow stronger with every book you write.

CHAPTER 19

THE GREAT ADVENTURE: GIVING YOURSELF A PROMOTION

Predictions are hard, especially about the future.

—YOGI BERRA

 n *Copyright's Highway*, Paul Goldstein wrote:

> *The metaphor that best expresses the possibilities of the future is the celestial jukebox, a technology-packed satellite orbiting thousands of miles above Earth, awaiting a subscriber's order—like a nickel in the old jukebox, and the punch of a button—to connect him to any number of selections from a vast storehouse via a home or office receiver that combines the power of a television set, radio, CD player, VCR, telephone, fax, and personal computer.*

The potential to earn acceptance for your books and a living from your ideas is greater than ever. But first you need
- ideas
- craft or editorial assistance
- an agent
- a publisher, unless you plan to self-publish
- promotion

Promotion is tooting your own horn. But rather than thinking about yourself as a horn player, think of yourself as a conductor leading a symphony orchestra or a general leading an army of volunteers.

Your army consists of your personal and professional direct and indirect publishing and field networks. You will continue to swell its ranks with every new relationship you create as long as you continue to write, speak and travel.

You want your army to help you recruit everyone in the world who will enjoy and benefit from reading your books. Your army faces a lifelong campaign in which every book you write wins another victory in the battle for the hearts and minds of your readers.

How successful you are at building and maintaining your army depends on how its members feel about themselves and about you. You are the heart and soul of the identity you create through everything you do. So no matter what you write, make sure your books have a lasting impact on your readers—make them eager to recommend them and eager to read your future work. Mystery writer Mickey Spillane once said, "The first page sells the book." To which he added, "The last page sells the next book."

Whether you write your books primarily to enlighten or entertain your readers, always strive to do both. This is the surest way for your books to benefit from the gift that keeps on giving: word of mouth.

POWER BEYOND MEASURE

There's a poster showing a catepillar on a branch and butterfly hovering in the air above it saying, "You can fly but that coccoon has to go."

You should be perpetually breathless from the opportunities for writing, promoting and profiting from your books. So starting from the moment you finish reading these words, stop thinking of yourself as a writer with something to say. Start thinking of yourself as an author with a lifetime's worth of books to sell to the millions of people around the world who want to read your work.

If you believe you can become a successful author—however you define the word successful—you can. The right ideas pursued with relentless determination will enable you to become a one-person-Bertalsmann—a multimedia, multinational conglomerate all by yourself.

This is not a challenge for the faint-hearted. Only a total commitment to your literary and financial objectives will motivate you to hit the keys and the streets and enable you to overcome the challenges you will encounter.

At his inauguration as president of South Africa, Nelson Mandela immortalized the words of Marianne Williamson in her best-seller *A Return to Love*:

> *'Our deepest fear is not that we are inadequate. Our deepest fear is that we are powerful beyond measure. It is our light, not our darkness, that most frightens us.' We ask ourselves, Who am I to be brilliant, gorgeous, talented, fabulous? Actually, who are you not to be? . . . Your playing small doesn't serve the world. There's nothing enlightened about shrinking so that other people won't feel insecure around you. We are all meant to shine, as children do. . . . And as we let our own light shine, we unconsciously give other people permission to do the same. As we're liberated from our own fear, our presence automatically liberates others.*

You are needed. Millions of readers around the world hunger for the entertainment novels provide and the empowering information and inspiration in nonfiction books. They want to be moved and enlightened by ideas that transcend time and space. They need only learn about your books. In promoting your work, you are doing them a service as well as yourself.

You are lucky to be writing in the international language of the Internet, business and the emerging global culture. Potential readers who are online and read English can order your books as soon as they appear in your publisher's catalog.

So think nationally, write globally. The faster the globalization of business, culture and technology transforms people's lives, the more they need the understanding that only well-conceived, well-written books can provide.

No soul gives itself more work to do than it is fully equipped to accomplish.
—EMMANUEL

None of this diminishes the challenge you face of making a living and building a career as an author. So for you, this book will have lasting value only if it helps you achieve your goals. Promoting a book, like writing it, is not an event; it's part of the publishing cycle that we hope you will continue to repeat for the rest of your life.

If you have questions, problems, opportunities or successes you want to share with us, please write to us at www.gmarketing.com. In addition to posting readers' success stories, the site will also provide advice from readers and updates on the book.

PLANTING A FUTURE

 The two best times to plant a tree are twenty years ago and tomorrow.
—CHINESE PROVERB

The Columbian novelist Gabriel Garcia Marquez once said, "In the end, the best thing a writer can do for his society is to write as well as he can." There is truth in this statement but not the whole truth. Herman Melville wrote as well as he could, but in the four decades between when *Moby Dick* was published and when Melville died, the book sold less than five hundred copies.

We're not suggesting that anything Melville could have done would have altered the fate of his book, just that writing a good book doesn't guarantee recognition or royalties.

Ideas are worth nothing unless they're used. So we hope that we have inspired you to take action, if not today, then tomorrow. Learning what to do is relatively easy; doing it is the challenge. This book can help make you a successful author, but for that to happen, you have to follow its advice. Remember: promoting your books is performing a service for your potential readers as well as yourself.

TESTING ONE, TWO, THREE

Despite the challenges you face in becoming a successful author, it's still easier than becoming a successful actor, artist, dancer or musician. People who want to build a career in the arts have to pay their dues. Look at running the gauntlet of mistakes and rejection you must run as tests of your commitment:

TEST #1: Coming up with an idea for a series of books that you are passionate about writing and promoting.

TEST #2: Assembling publishing and field networks to help you.

TEST #3: Doing the research for your books.

TEST #4: Summoning the courage to write your novels or nonfiction books.

TEST #5: Finding an agent, selling your books yourself or self-publishing.

TEST #6: Promoting your books.

TEST #7: Extracting the greatest value out of your books through sales and subsidiary rights.

TEST #8: Using all the creativity you have to pass these tests.

TEST #9: Repeating this process for as long as your books continue to sell.

TEST #10: Starting again at Test #1 if your passion or the sales of your books diminishes.

ANSWERING THE SIREN'S CALL

For most authors, writing is a hobby. They have to keep earning a salary from a day job until their writing income enables them to quit and concentrate on writing. Unless a working spouse supports them, most writers begin their careers by working a full-time job and writing nights and weekends. Writing while you work at a job that pays the rent is relatively easy. Promoting your books isn't.

It's been said there are only two kinds of writing: writing that works and writing that doesn't. Well, you can look at the obstacles you face in becoming a successful author as commitment tests with two grades: pass and fail.

If you feel overwhelmed by the challenges facing you in your quest to become a successful author with a New York publisher, maybe you're not ready to take that plunge yet.

If so, start small. Don't waste time trying to succeed until you are ready to make the commitment required for success. Scale down your initial goals. Until you are ready for the Big Apple, consider

- being published by a small house
- self-publishing
- publishing or self-publishing online
- using print-on-demand technology

Don't let yourself be seduced by the siren call of fame and fortune until you're ready to meet the demands of major publishers and major media. Show your colors only when you have a sense of mission about your work and are unshakably committed to your success.

JUMPING WRITE IN

 Jump right in or you may change your mind about swimming.
—CYNTHIA COPELAND LEWIS

We have given you the weapons you need to succeed, but this book can help only you if you use it. Whether you haven't started to write your book or it is already out, start using this book immediately.

FULFILLING YOUR POTENTIAL FOR TRANSCENDENCE

You were born to make your life count by creating something for posterity as well as the present. So make transcendence your mission. Creating something of enduring value to your community, the rest of the human family and yourself is a goal worthy of your potential as a human being and worth making a total commitment to. Authors do it day by day word by word, book by book, and they do it for all of us.

BORN TO DO WHAT YOU LOVE

 Life hasn't always smiled on me, but I have always smiled on life.
—RAOUL DUFY

You can't grow by doing what you already do nor will it enable you to fulfill your creative potential. Ray Bradbury urges writers to jump off a cliff and make their parachutes on the way down. The great adventure of writing and promoting your books begins by trusting yourself enough to meet the challenge of doing more than what you have already done.

Cervantes believed that there are no limits but the sky. You can't know what your limitations are, so don't believe that you have any. Avoid encountering them by keeping busy writing and promoting your books. Have indomitable faith in yourself. Believe that you are an instrument of the universe born to share the light you have with those who are eager to see it. We promise that you are capable of doing far more than you can imagine, and that every goal you achieve will increase your ability and confidence to do more.

Face the challenges you confront with a willing heart and an open mind. Always remember how lucky you are to be alive at this remarkable moment in history and to have your talent for writing and speaking. Never has the written word been able to reach as many people in as many places as quickly as now.

Look at the obstacles you meet as stepping stones on the path that only you were born to tread. They're there to help you grow, and they will deepen the satisfaction and serenity you will experience when you achieve your goals.

Susan Taylor, editor-in-chief of *Essence* magazine once said, "What you love to do is what you were born to do." So whatever you set out to do, strive to be a happy warrior, to live a life that marries truth to charity and capitalism to compassion. Approach your daily efforts inspired by the words of St. Catherine of Siena: "All the way to heaven is heaven."

RESOURCE DIRECTORY

BOOKS

Literary Market Place (LMP)

This directory of the publishing industry includes lists of publicists, publishers, agents, lecture agents, organizations, media and writer's conferences.

RR Bowker, 121 Chalon Rd., New Providence, NJ 07974

Tel: (888) 269-5372   E-mail: info@bowker.com   www.bowker.com

Speak and Grow Rich by Dottie and Lilly Walters, Prentice-Hall.

The authors also do seminars, publish a magazine for speakers called *Sharing Ideas* and run Walters International Speakers Bureau.

PO Box 1120, Glendora, CA 91740

Tel: (626) 335-8069, (800) 438-1242   Fax: (626) 335-6127

www.walters-intl.com

Speaking Successfully: 1001 Tips for Thriving in the Speaking Business edited and compiled by Ken Braly and Rebecca Morgan, members of the National Speakers Association. For a free twenty-page sample or to order, go to www.speakernetnews.com.

EVENTS

How to Build a Speaking and Writing Empire, a seminar put on by Mark Victor Hansen and Jack Canfield. For a brochure, call (714) 759-9304.

Literary Market Place and the May issues of *Writer's Digest* and *The Writer* magazines list writer's conferences.

PMA Publishing University, held the two days before BEA begins.

Publishers Marketing Association, 627 Aviation Way

Manhattan Beach, CA 90266

Tel: (310) 372-2732   Fax: (310) 374-3342

E-mail: info@pma-online.org

LEARNING AND TEACHING OPPORTUNITIES

Adult learning centers around the country offer free magazines that list the seminars they sponsor.

You don't have to publish a book to teach at them, and they need copy about classes for their catalogs. The following list is a starting point for your inquiries:

- Boston Center of Adult Education
- Colorado Free University—Denver and Colorado Springs
- Discover U—Seattle
- Discovery Center—Chicago
- First Class Seminars—Washington, D.C.
- Knowledge Shope—Orlando
- Learning Annex—Los Angeles, New York, Sacramento, San Diego, San Francisco, Toronto
- Learning Connection—Providence
- Learning Exchange—Hartford
- Leisure Learning Unlimited—Houston
- Open Exchange—Kensington, CA
- Open University—Minneapolis

University extensions sponsor one-day to semester-long classes. Adult learning centers and university extensions may have courses on book promotion. *LMP* lists universities that have publishing programs lasting from one week to two years.

MEDIA DIRECTORIES

LMP has lists of book reviewers and talk shows as well as publicists. The first place to check out media directories is at your library. You can see what they offer and how much they cost, and then decide how to get what you need.

Bacon's media directories

Newspapers, magazines, radio, TV

Bacon's Media Calendar Directory

Lists the lead editorial calendars of two-hundred daily papers and 1,100 magazines. Important if your book's sales are keyed to a season or holiday. Includes a free bi-monthly newsletter.

Bacon's Information, 332 S. Michigan Ave., Ste. 900, Chicago, IL 60604
   Tel: (800) 621-0561

Broadcasting & Cable Yearbook
   121 Chalon Rd., New Providence, NJ 07974
   Tel: (888) 269-5372   Fax: (908) 771-7704
   E-mail: info@bowker.com   Web site: www.bowker.com

Burrelle's Media Directory
   Burrelle's Information Systems,
   75 E. Northfield Rd., Livingston, NJ 07039
   Tel: (800) 631-1160

Marketer's Guide to Media
   Adweek Directories, 1515 Broadway, New York, NY 10036

The Yellow Book Leadership Directories
   Directories of media, associations, law firms.
   104 Fifth Ave., New York, NY 10011
   Tel: (212) 627-4140
   www.leadershipdirectories.com has media and industry news.

PUBLICITY SERVICES

Media Distribution Services

Has lists for all media. Will blast-fax or do printing and mailing.
   307 W. 36th St., New York, NY 10018
   Tel: (800) MDS-3282

MediaPro

Lists for different categories.
   Infocom Group, 1250 45th St., #200, Emeryville, CA 94608
   Tel: (800) 959-4331   Fax: (510) 879-4331
   E-mail: info@infocomgroup.com

Metro Publicity Services

Prepares and sends a feature news story to more than seven thousand newspapers monthly. Also sends out themed material to targeted audiences.

22 W. 34th St., Fourth Floor, New York, NY 10001

Tel: (212) 947-5100

PR Newswire

Sends news releases to targeted or all media nationally and internationally.

Harborside Financial Center, 806 Plaza 3, Jersey City, NJ 07311

Tel: (800) 832-5522

Radio/TV Interview Report

Sends a description of your expertise and a media pitch to more than four thousand media outlets.

Tel: (800) 989-1400, ext. 411

Publicity Blitz Media Directory-on-Disk

More than twenty thousand print and broadcast contacts in more than seventy-three categories on disk or labels or in a report. Free catalog of lists, databases and publicity resources.

Tel: (610) 259-1070, (800) 784-4359   Fax: (610) 283-3704

QuickSilver Database

Seventeen thousand publicity contacts

Jenkins Group, 400 W. Front St., Traverse City, MI 49684

Tel: (231) 933-0445, (800) 706-4636   Fax: (231) 933-0448

E-mail: jenkinsgroup@bookpublishing.com www.bookpublishing.com

NEWSLETTERS

Advance

A free newsletter about publishing from BookZonePro.

www.bookzone.com

BookFlash Bulletin

A free publishing newsletter from www.bookflash.com

Book Marketing Update

A twice-monthly newsletter about promotion. Editor-in-Chief: John Kremer, author of *1001 Ways to Market Your Books.* Provides news, marketing tips, Internet sources, media contacts and marketing techniques.

Open Horizons
   P.O. Box 205, Fairfield, IA 52556
   Tel: (515) 472-6130, (800) 796-6130   Fax: (515) 472-1560
   E-mail: info@bookmarket.com   www.bookmarket.com
Bulldog Reporter's Book Marketing & Publicity
   Infocom Group, 5900 Hollis St., Ste. R2, Emeryville, CA 94608-2008
   Tel: (800) 959-1059
   E-mail: Bulldog@infocomgroup.com   www.infocomgroup.com
Partyline
   New media, interview opportunities
   35 Sutton Pl., New York, NY 10022
   Tel: (212) 755-3487
   E-mail: byarmon@ix.netcom.com   www.partylinepublishing.com
Ragan's Media Relations Report
   Trends, media tips and interviews
   Ragan Communications, 212 W. Superior Ave., Chicago, IL 60610
   Tel: (800) 878-5331

ONLINE RESOURCES

www.artslynx.org/writing
   Artslynx Internatonal Writing Resources lists organizations for writers
   and has links to other sites.
www.awpwriter.org
   Associated Writing Programs includes lists of college writing programs
   and writer's conferences.
www.authorinterviews.com
   An online advertiser that sends information about authors to the media.
   Includes enough info to function as a media kit or Web site.
www.bookflash.com
   Provides links to news releases and other publishing information.
www.booktalk.com
   Booktalk has an archive of articles about publishing and links to other sites.
www.bookzone.com
   Offers links to authors' sites and promotional material.

www.bookwire.com.

Click on *Publishers Weekly* for a free subscription to a daily dose of publishing news. The site also provides links to other helpful sites including dozens of online marketing companies.

www.cluelass.com

A network of mystery writers

www.cspan.org

Information on the cable TV station's book programming

www.frugalfun.com

Shel Horowitz, the author of *Marketing Without Megabucks*, offers free monthly Frugal Marketing Tips and other helpful information.

www.gebbieinc.com

Mark Gebbie provides links and E-mail addresses that will enable you to E-mail the media. Gebbie Press specializes in online promotion.

www.geocities.com/athens/6346

The Writer's Toolbox has resources for novelists and journalists.

www.hwg.org

HTML Writers Guild hosts a network of Web authors and offers help on writing and marketing for the Web.

www.infoproduct.sitesell.com

This site has 1,143 pages of resources for selling your books, products and services online.

www.iuniverse.com

A print-on-demand publisher offering a compendium of helpful links and information.

www.nciba.com

The Northern California Independent Booksellers Association offers a free newsletter by Pat Holt, a former *San Francisco Chronicle* book review editor and publishing's I.F. Stone.

www.pilot-search.com

Lists eleven thousand writing links.

www.profnet.com

Provides a link to authors and other experts for journalists and eleven thousand public relations professionals.

www.publicrelations.com

Edward Segal, author of *Getting Your 15 Minutes of Fame—and More! A Guide to Guaranteeing Your Business Success,* provides a resource for promoting anything.

www.put-it-in-writing.com

Jeff Rubin puts twenty-five years of journalism experience into making newsletters as effective as possible.

www.ralan.com

Ralan Conley's SpecFic and Humor Webstravaganza has information on humor and sci-fi markets, and six hundred writing links.

www.@Harlequin.com

An information-rich network for romance writers hosted by Harlequin.

www.speakersdirect.com

The first online marketplace for speakers.

www.speakernetnews.com

A free weekly newsletter aimed at speakers that also provides valuable ideas for writers.

www.theonion.com

Provides humor breaks and, by example, wisdom about writing it.

www.visualhorizons.com

Designs for "200 On-Screen/MS Word," along with help on using them.

www.writersdigest.com

Includes daily publishing news, information about promotion and writer's conferences.

www.zinebook.com

Chip Rowe's *Book of Zines* provides info about 'zines and a network of 'zine editors.

ORGANIZATIONS FOR SELF-PUBLISHERS AND SMALL PRESSES

Although the primary goal of the organizations below is to help self-publishers and small presses, they are valuable to all authors.

Bay Area Independent Publishers Association (BAIPA)

P.O. Box E, Corte Madera, CA 94976

Tel: (415) 257-8275   www.baipa.org

Small Press Center

20 W. 44 St., New York, NY 10036

Tel: (212) 764-7201   Fax: (212) 354-5365

E-mail: smallpress@aol.com   www.smallpress.org

WORKSHOPS

The following organizations are led by guerrillas who have earned their places in the Guerrilla Marketing Hall of Fame.

They provide a wealth of information, online and offline, about publishing and promotion. They also present workshops.

The Jenkins Group

Jerrold Jenkins, 400 W. Front St., Traverse City, MI 49684

Tel: (231) 933-0445, (800) 706-4636   Fax: (232) 933-0448

E-mail:jenkinsgroup@bookpublishing.com   www.bookpublishing.com

Publishes *Independent Publisher.*

Open Horizons

John Kremer, Box 205, Fairfield IA 52556-0205

Tel: (515) 472-6130, (800) 796-6130   Fax: (515) 472-1560

E-mail: info@bookmarket.com   www.bookmarket.com

John is the author of *1001 Ways to Market Your Book.* He also edits the *Book Marketing Update* listed above.

Para Publishing

Dan Poynter, P.O. Box 8206-146, Santa Barbara, CA 93118-8206

Tel: (805) 968-7277   Fax: (805) 968-1379

E-mail: info@parapublishing.com   www.parapublishing.com

Publishers Marketing Association (PMA)

Jan and Terry Nathan, 627 Aviation Way, Manhattan Beach, CA 90266

Tel: (310) 372-2732   Fax: (310) 374-3342

E-mail: pmaonline@aol.com   www.pma-online.org

Small Publishers Association of North America (SPAN)

Tom and Marilyn Ross, P.O. Box 1306, Buena Vista, CO 81211

Tel: (719) 395-4790   Fax: (719) 395-8374

E-mail: span@spannet.org   www.spannet.com

PUBLICITY ORGANIZATIONS

Book Publicists of Southern California

6464 Sunset Blvd., Room 580, Holywoood, CA 90028

Tel: (323) 461-3921   Fax: (323) 461-0917

Northern California Book Publicity & Marketing Association (NCBPMA)

P.O. Box 192803, San Francisco, CA 94119-2803

Monthly programs. Puts on a tea at Book Expo America. Has a directory.

Public Relations Society of America

33 Irving Pl., New York, NY 10003

Tel: (212) 995-2230   Fax: (212) 995-0757

Has chapters, a newsletter and a directory.

Publishers Publicity Association

299 Park Ave., New York, NY 10017

E-mail: nlatimer@randomhouse.com

Trade group for all publishers and publicists. Monthly meetings and workshops.

TELEPHONE SALES

1 (800) AUTHORS

For an annual fee, you can record a two-minute interview that callers can access around the clock, then order the book. The interview can serve as a demo for talk shows. The company also does a syndicated column and advertises its books.

VIDEO

You're on the Air, a must-have video created by Brian Jud in which producers for major shows discuss how to prepare for and give interviews. Comes with two companion books by Jud:

* *It's Showtime: How to Perform on Television & Radio*

- *Perpetual Promotion: How to Contact Producers and Create Media Appearances for Book Promotion*

Offers other videocassettes and audiocassettes.
Marketing Directions
  PO Box 715, Avon, CT 06001-0715
  Tel: (800) 562-4357

WRITER'S ORGANIZATIONS

For the most part, these are national organizations. *Literary Market Place* lists many others that are statewide or regional.
The Academy of American Poets
  584 Broadway, Ste. 1208, New York, NY 10012
  Tel: (212) 274-0343   Fax: (212) 274-9427
  E-mail: academy@dti.net   www.poets.org
American Medical Writers Association
  40 W. Gude Dr., Rockville, MD 20850-1192
  Tel: (302) 294-5303   Fax: (301) 294-9006
American Society of Journalists & Authors (ASJA)
  1501 Broadway, Suite 302, New York, NY 10036
  Tel: (212) 997-0947   Fax: (212) 768-7414
  E-mail: asja@compuscrve.com
  Has chapters around the country and an annual conference.
Associated Business Writers of America
  3140 S. Peoria St., Ste. 295, Aurora, CO 80014
  Tel: (303) 841-0246   Fax: (303) 751-8593
  E-mail: sandywrter@aol.com   www.nationalwriters.com
  Presents annual conference.
Austin Writers League
  1501 West Fifth St., Suite E2, Austin, TX 78703
  Tel: (512) 499-8914   Fax: (512) 499-0441
  E-mail: awl@writersleague.org   www.writersleague.org
Authors Guild
  330 West 42nd St., New York, NY 10036

Tel: (212) 563-5904   Fax: (564) 8363
E-mail: staff@authorsguild.org   www.authorsguild.org
Publishes a newsletter for its 7,200 members.
California Writers' Club
    2214 Derby St., Berkeley, CA 94705
    Tel: (510) 841-1217
    Has eleven chapters.
Christian Writers Guild
    65287 Fern St., Hume, CA 93628
    Tel: (559) 335-2333   Fax: (559) 335-2770
    E-mail: nvrohrer@spiralcomm.net
    Offers a study course and workshops.
Dog Writers' Association of America (DWAA)
    173 Union Rd., Coatesville, PA 19320
    Tel: (610) 384-2436   Fax: (610) 384-2471
    E-mail: dwaa@dwaa.org   www.dwaa.org
Editorial Freelancers Association (EFA),
    71 West 23rd St., Ste. 1504, New York, NY 10010
    Tel: (212) 929-5400   Fax: (212) 929-5439
Education Writers Association
    1331 "H" St., Ste. 307, Washington, DC 20005
    Tel: (202) 637-9700   Fax: (202) 637-9707
    E-mail: ewa@crosslink.net   www.ewa.org
Freelance Editorial Association
    P.O. Box 38035, Cambridge, MA 02238-0835
    Tel: (617) 576-8797
Garden Writers of America
    10210 Leatherleaf Ct., Manassas, VA 20111
    Tel: (703) 257-1032   Fax: (703) 257-0213
Horror Writers Association (HWA)
    P.O. Box 50577, Palo Alto, CA 94303
    E-mail: hwa@horror.org   www.horror.org
International Association of Crime Writers, North America Branch
    P.O. Box 8674, New York, NY 10116-8674
    Tel. and Fax: (212) 243-8966   E-mail: mfrisque*gc.apc.org*

International Food, Wine, & Travel Writers Association
  P.O. Box 8429, Calabasas, CA 91372-8249
  Tel: (562) 433-5969   Fax: (562) 438-6384
The International Women's Writing Guild (IWWG)
  P.O. Box 810, Gracie Station, New York, NY 10028-0082
  Tel: (212) 737-7536   Fax: (212) 737-9469
  E-mail: iwwg@iwwg.com   www.iwwg.com
Investigative Reporters & Editors
  138 Neff Annex, UMC School of Journalism, Columbia, MO 65211
  Tel: (573) 882-2042   Fax: (573) 882-5431
Media Alliance
  814 Mission St., Ste. 205, San Francisco, CA 94103
  Tel: (415) 546-6334   Fax: (415) 536-6218
  E-mail: info@media-alliance.org   www.media-alliance.org
Mystery Writers of America (MWA)
  17 East 47th St., 6th Floor, New York, NY 10017
  Tel: (212) 888-8171   Fax: (212) 888-8107
  www.mysterywriters.org
National Association of Black Journalists (NABJ)
  University of Maryland, 8701 Adelphi Rd., Adelphi, MD 20783
  Tel: (301) 445-7100   Fax: (301) 445-7101
  E-mail: nabj@nabj.org
National Association of Science Writers (NASW)
  Box 294, Greenlawn, NY 11740
  Tel: (516) 757-5664   www.nasw.org
National Federation of Press Women (NFPW)
  P.O. Box 5556, Arlington, VA 22205
  Tel: (703) 534-2500, (800) 780-2715   Fax: (703) 534-5751
  E-mail: presswomen@aol.com   www.nfpw.org
National Writers Association
  3140 S. Peoria, Ste. 295, Aurora, CO 80014
  Tel: (303) 841-0246   Fax: (303) 751-8593
  www.nationalwriters.com
National Writers Union (NWU)
  113 University Place, 6th Floor, New York, NY, 10003-4527

Tel: (212) 254-0279   Fax: (212) 254-0673

E-mail: nwu@nwu.org   www.nwu.org

California branch:

357 17 St., Ste. 101, Oakland, CA 94612

Outdoor Writers Association of America

RD 1 Box 177, Spring Mills, PA 16875-9633

Tel: (814) 364-9557   Fax: (814) 364-9558

E-mail: eking4owaa@compuserve.com

Overseas Press Club of America

320 E. 42nd St., New York, NY 10017

Tel: (212) 983-4655   Fax: (212) 983-4692

PEN New England (Poets, Playwights, Essayists, Novelists)

568 Broadway, Ste. 401, New York, NY 10012

Tel: (212) 334-1660   Fax: (212) 334-2181

E-mail: pen@pen.org   www.pen.org

Western branch:

PEN Center USA West

672 S. Lafayette Park Pl., Ste. 41, Los Angeles, CA 90057

Tel: (213) 365-8500   Fax: (213) 365-9616

E-mail: pen@pen-usa-west.org   www.pen-usa-west.org

Poetry Society of America

15 Gramercy Park W., New York, NY 10003

Tel: (212) 254-9628, (800) USA-POEM

E-mail: poetrysocy@aol.com   www.poetrysociety.org

Poets & Writers

72 Spring St., New York, NY 10012

Tel: (212) 226-3586   Fax: (212) 226-2963

E-mail: pwsubsw.org   www.pw.org

Romance Writers of America (RWA)

3707 FM 1960 West, Ste. 555, Houston, TX 77068

Tel: (281) 440-6885   Fax: (281) 440-7510

E-mail: info@rwanational.com   www.rwanational.com

Science Fiction & Fantasy Writers of America (SFWA)

P.O. Box 171, Unity, ME 04988-0171

Tel. and Fax: (207) 861-8078

E-mail: execdir@sfwa.org   www.sfwa.org

Society of American Business Editors and Writers (SABEW)

University of Missouri, School of Journalism,

176 Gannett Hall, Columbia, MO 65211

Tel: (573) 882-7862   Fax: (573) 884-1372   www.sabew.org

Society of American Travel Writers

4101 Lake Boone Trail, Ste. 201, Raleigh, NC 27607

Tel: (919) 787-5181   Fax: (919) 787-4916

Society of Children's Book Writers & Illustrators (SCBWI)

8271 Beverly Blvd., Los Angeles, CA 90048

Tel: (323) 782-1010   Fax: (323) 782-1892

E-mail: membership@scbwi.org   www.scbwi.org

The Society of Professional Journalists (SPJ)

3909 N. Meridian St., Indianapolis, IN 46208

Tel: (765) 653-3333   Fax: (765) 653-4631

E-mail: spj@spjhq.org   www.spj.org

The Society of Southwestern Authors (SSA)

P.O. Box 30355, Tucson, AZ 85751-0355

Tel: (520) 296-5299   Fax: (520) 296-0409

E-mail: wporter202@aol.com

Space Coast Writers Guild, Inc. (SCWG)

Box 804, Melbourne, FL 32902

Tel. and Fax: (407) 727-0051

Western Writers of America

1012 Fair St., Franklin, TN 37064

Tel. and Fax: (615) 791-1444

E-mail: tncrutch@aol.com   www.wwa.home.html

Women's National Book Association (WNBA)

160 Fifth Avenue, New York, NY 10010

Tel: (212) 675-7804   Fax: (212) 989-7542

E-mail: skpassoc@cwixmail.com   www.bookbuzz.com/wnba.htm

OTHER ORGANIZATIONS OF INTEREST TO WRITERS

American Booksellers Association

828 S. Broadway, Ste. 625, Tarrytown, NY 10591

Tel: (914) 591-2665   (800) 209-4575   Fax: (914) 591-2720

E-mail: editorial@bookweb.org   www.bookweb.org

Publishes a monthly newsletter. Allied with regional associations. Sponsors ABA Convention and Trade Exhibit, held in conjunction with BookExpo America (BEA).

BookExpo America (BEA)

383 Main Ave., Norwalk, CT 06851

Tel: (203) 840-2840   Fax: (203) 840-9614

E-mail: inquiry@bookexpo.reedexpo.com   www.bookexpo.reedexpo.com

The Center for the Book in the Library of Congress

The Library of Congress

101 Independence Ave. SE, Washington, DC 20540-4920

Tel: (202) 707-5221   Fax: (202) 707-0267

E-mail: cfbook@loc.gov   www.loc.gov/loc/cfbook

Presents exhibitions and events to stimulate interest in books and reading. Has more than thirty affiliated state centers.

Friends of Libraries USA

1420 Walnut St., Ste. 450, Philadelphia, PA 19102-4017

Tel: (215) 790-1674   (800) 936-5872   Fax: (215) 545-3821

E-mail: folusa@libertynet.org   www.folusa.com

Supports Friends of Libraries groups around the country.

Speakers Organizations

National Speakers Association

1500 S. Priest Dr., Tempe, AZ 85821

Tel: (480) 968-2552   Fax: (480) 968-0911   www.nsaspeaker.com

Has thirty-seven chapters and conferences.

Toastmasters International

23182 Arroyo Vista, Santa Margarita, CA 92688-2620

Tel: (949) 858-8255   Fax: (949) 858-1207

E-mail: tminfo@toastmasters.org   www.toastmasters.org

Has 8,900 chapters that meet weekly and a national conference.

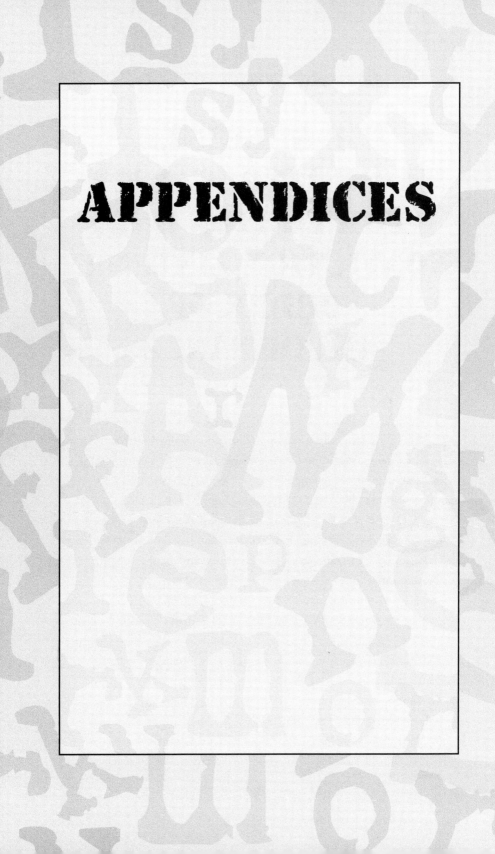

APPENDICES

APPENDIX I

THE GUERRILLA MARKETING WEAPONS FOR FICTION AND NONFICTION LISTED IN ORDER OF IMPORTANCE

hese lists can only be an approximation. We include them because we wanted you to understand that the lists for fiction and nonfiction differ greatly. The importance of these weapons will vary depending on the author, the book and the publisher.

We welcome your suggestions for changing them in the next edition. We encourage you to rearrange your list so that, based on your experience, it makes sense to you, and send it back to us. Many thanks for your help.

Nonfiction	**Fiction**
You: The Ultimate Weapon	*You: The Ultimate Weapon*
1. The Most Powerful Weapon: You	1. The Most Powerful Weapon: You
2. Your Books	2. Your Books
3. Your Identity	3. Your Identity
4. Your Knowledge of Publishing and Promotion	4. Your Ideas
5. Your Professionalism	5. Your Creativity
6. Your Enthusiasm	6. Word of Mouth

7. Your Networks
8. Your Talks
9. Word of Mouth
10. Your Publicity
11. Your Platform
12. Your Grand Tours

13. Your Objectives
14. Nichecraft
15. Creativity
16. Your Ideas
17. Branding Your Books
18. Your Sense of Humor
19. Your Promotion Plan: The First Version
20. Your Budget
21. Your Guerrilla Greenbacks
22. Your Promotion Plan: The Final Version
23. Your Lifelong Promotion Plan: Your Promotion Calendar
24. Your Strategic Alliances
25. Your Competitiveness
26. Your Book Signings
27. Your Titles

28. Your Covers
29. Merchandising
30. Your Smiles
31. Excerpts from Your Books
32. New Editions of Your Books
33. Your Optimism
34. Your Elevator Speech
35. Your Television Interviews

7. Your Networks
8. Nichecraft
9. Branding Your Books
10. Your Courage
11. Your Professionalism
12. Your Knowledge of Publishing and Promotion
13. Your Enthusiasm
14. Your Passion for Books
15. Your Book Signings
16. Your Web Site
17. Your Links and Directories
18. Online Booksellers
19. Your Objectives

20. Your Competitiveness
21. Your Sense of Humor
22. Your Bookmarks

23. Your Business Cards

24. Your Smiles
25. Your Optimism
26. Your Package
27. Your Publisher's Publicity Questionnaire
28. Your Publicity
29. Your Grand Tours
30. Your Talks
31. Your Platform
32. Your Elevator Speech
33. Your Television Interviews
34. Your Print Interviews
35. Your Radio Interviews

36. Your Radio Interviews
37. Your Print Interviews

38. Your Satellite Tours
39. Your Follow-up
40. Your Press/Speaker's Kit

41. Your Web Site

42. Your Links and Directory Listings
43. Your Package
44. Your Column

45. Your Tip of the Day and Weekly Teasers
46. Your Press Release
47. Your Newsletter or 'Zine
48. Trade Shows
49. Professional Conferences
50. The Last Page of Your Book
51. Your Promotional Copies
52. Online Booksellers
53. Bartering Your Stories for Ad Space
54. Per-Order Ads

55. Catalogs
56. Your E-mail Chain Letter
57. Your Special Events
58. Your Contests
59. Book Festivals
60. Your Articles
61. Your Brochure
62. Your Thank-You Notes

36. Your Satellite Tours
37. Your Promotion Plan: The First Version
38. Your Budget
39. Your Guerrilla Greenbacks
40. Your Promotion Plan: The Final Version
41. Your Lifetime Promotion Plan: Your Promotion Calendar
42. Reading Groups

43. Your Follow-up
44. Memberships in Professional Organizations
45. Professional Conferences

46. Book Festivals
47. Your E-mail Chain Letter
48. Your Column
49. Your Newsletter or 'Zine
50. Your Titles
51. Your Covers
52. Trade Shows
53. Excerpts From Your Books

54. Your E-mail and Snail-mail Lists
55. Your Webcasts
56. Your Discussion Groups
57. Your Press/Speaker's Kit
58. Your Promotional Copies
59. Your Press Release
60. Your Stationary
61. Your Thank-You Notes
62. Your Theme

63. Your Memberships in Professional Organizations
64. Cooperation
65. Your Money-Back Guarantee
66. Your Theme
67. Your Logo
68. Your Illustrations
69. Your Book Reviews

70. Your Op-Ed Pieces and Letters to the Editor
71. Your Publisher's Publicity Questionnaire
72. Your Acknowledgments
73. Your Self-Writing Sequels
74. Your Webcasts
75. Your Giveaways
76. Your Surveys
77. Your Discussion Groups
78. Your E-mail Signature
79. Your E-mail and Snail-mail Lists
80. Your Audiocassettes
81. Your Videocassettes
82. Window and In-Store Displays
83. Fundraisers
84. Your Annual Awards
85. Your Memberships in Community-Service Organizations
86. Promotion Potlucks

63. Your Logo
64. Your Book Reviews
65. Bartering Your Stories for Ad Space
66. Your Special Events
67. Your Audiocassettes
68. Your Videocassettes
69. Your Op-Ed Pieces and Letters to the Editor
70. Window and In-store Displays

71. Cooperation

72. Your Contests
73. Your Short Stories or Articles
74. Your Giveaways
75. Your Surveys
76. Your E-mail Signature
77. Your Handouts
78. Your Acknowledgments
79. Raffle Prizes

80. Your Money-Back Guarantee
81. Your Brochure
82. Your Promotion Potlucks

83. Your Broken-In Walking Shoes
84. Your Sense of Balance
85. The Last Page of Your Book

86. Your Memberships in Community-Service Organizations

87. Your Broken-In Walking Shoes
88. Your Stationery
89. Your Business Cards
90. Your Bookmarks
91. Your Handouts

92. Your Bibliographies
93. Raffle Prizes
94. Your Evaluation Form
95. Reading Groups
96. Your Passion for Books

97. Your Sense of Balance
98. Your Courage
99. Your Speed
100. Your Flexibility

87. Per-Order Ads
88. Catalogs
89. Your Speed
90. Your Flexibility
91. Merchandising

More of a Challenge

92. Your Annual Awards
93. Your Evaluation Form
94. Fundraisers
95. Your Strategic Alliances
96. Your Tip of the Day and Weekly Teaser
97. New Editions of Your Books
98. Self-Writing Sequels
99. Your Illustrations
100. Your Bibliographies

APPENDIX II

HOW TO FIND THE PUBLICIST YOU NEED

hen you look for a publicist, take the following factors into consideration:

1. Book publicity is a specialty. You need someone with experience promoting books on a national scale, someone who has contacts with trade and consumer print, broadcast and electronic book media around the country. When you hire a publicist, you are basically paying for four things: ability, contacts, experience and enthusiasm.

   It's not that a publicist who promotes clothing doesn't have the ability to help you. In fact, if you were writing a book about clothing, such a publicist might be your best bet even though he or she has no book experience.

   That concern aside, the ideal publicist for you is the one who
   * is the most successful
   * has the most experience
   * is the most passionate about your book
   * you have the most confidence in

2. The rapport you establish with the publicist is also a key factor in choosing one. As with your agent and editor, try to meet with the publicist before you make a commitment.

   If you can, meet prospective publicists, see their offices, the press materials they produce for their clients and what they have accomplished for clients. Be sure to meet any other publicists in the agency as well as anybody else in the office who will be involved with your book. Talk to present and former clients to learn what it's like to work with the agency. You want someone with whom you will enjoy working with.

Only your books are more important to your success than the personal relationships you create, and no relationship is more important than the one between you and your publicist.

3. Geography may be a factor in your decision. Does a publicist have to be in New York to be effective? Not every publicist in New York is a genius, and there are many excellent publicists outside of New York. Some of them were staff or freelance publicists in New York before they literally headed to greener pastures.

What you need is a publicist who can convince you that, based on the agency's experience and results, he can do the job you want done.

Another factor to consider: If you will hire a publicist whom you will mention in the promotion plan you send to New York publishers, try to make it someone whose name at least the staff publicist will know. Better still, her name should be recognized by the editor and others whose enthusiasm will help convince the house to buy the book.

If nobody recognizes the name, they won't have a clue how effective the publicist is. This diminishes the value of your commitment. This is more of a problem with out-of-town publicists, because publishers may feel that if publicists are in the Big Apple, they must know what they're doing.

If you're going to hire a publicist whose name big publishers won't recognize, solve this problem in advance by including
- how long the publicist has been in business
- whether the publicist has worked in New York
- the titles of successful books from New York houses for which the publicist ran national campaigns
- any other information that will raise the publisher's comfort level
- the publicist's brochure if it's impressive

4. The best time to contact prospective publicists is after you've prepared the first version of your promotion plan. Your plan will benefit

from the practical advice of a pro. Publishers who receive your work will assume that the publicist you mention in your plan assisted you in preparing it. Having your publicist advise you on how to create your promotion plan will increase the likelihood your book will sell.

Ask prospective publicists to advise you on how to prepare a publicity campaign for your book using what's left of your budget after your other weapons are accounted for. Then together, you can integrate your first promotion plan with the plan of your publicist and write the final version.

After you and your publicist agree on the most effective plan for promoting your book, ballpark the cost of every item so you can come up with a reasonably accurate "guesstimate" of the total that is best for your budget. It can't be exact, but it also can't be too far off base, or publishers will think that either the plan or the budget is not realistic.

5. How flexible a publicist is about structuring fees may affect your choice. If publicists are short on experience, they will be more eager to make a mark in the field and perhaps more open to trying new ideas. As in other fields, their fees will reflect their experience.

    Among the questions for you to ask publicists about fees are:
    - Would the publicist be willing to accept being written into the contract to receive a certain percentage of the royalties? This would certainly be an incentive for the publicist to go all-out to make sure your book is successful. Advertising agencies working with high-tech start-ups are taking stock instead of cash. Mint those guerrilla greenbacks any way you can.
    - Would the publicist accept being used on an assignment basis, for example, to create a news release and then let you send it out?
    - Would the publicist be willing to serve only as a consultant? She can
        —share sample press kits with you
        —give you feedback on the publicity materials you create

The basic notion: the publicist shows you what to do, you do it, and the publicist looks over your shoulder to make sure you're doing it right.

The Resource Directory includes contact information for the directories mentioned above. Publicity organizations have monthly meetings with guest speakers and helpful monthly newsletters. Joining one or more of them is a worthwhile investment for building your network and keeping up to speed on new developments in the field.

QUESTIONS TO ASK A PUBLICIST BEFORE HIRING ONE

You need answers to the following questions. But before you ask them, research the answers in directories and in agencies' brochures, media kits and Web sites. Publicists will be impressed with your professionalism if you know about them before you meet.

- How long have you been in business?
- Have you handled any books like mine?
- I have a budget of $X. What's the best way for you to help me within that budget?
- What is your payment schedule?
- Are you a member of any professional associations?
- How do you like to work with your clients?
- When should I expect to hear from you?
- How can I help you?

GUERRILLA TACTICS
Ask if you can intern in the agency to learn about publicity and how the agency works.

FINDING THE RIGHT PUBLICIST FOR YOU

Try using these techniques for finding the publicist you need:

- Find out what publicists your networks know or have worked with and the results they got.

- Check *Literary Marketplace*, which includes a list of book publicists.
- Contact the Publisher's Publicity Association (PPA), an organization of staff and independent publicists in the New York area. Also contact its counterpart in the San Francisco Bay Area, the Northern California Book Publicity and Marketing Association.
- Contact publicity clubs around the country.
- The Public Relations Society of America has a directory that lists publicists by their specialties.
- Check *O'Dwyer's Directory of Public Relations Firms*, which lists all of the publicists in the country.

APPENDIX III

HOW YOUR NETWORKS CAN HELP YOU

Below is an excellent example of how your networks can help make your books successful. When guerrillas Tom and Marilyn Ross published their book *Jump Start Your Book Sales*, they sent this list to their networks.

The list helps prove the proverb: If you don't ask, they won't have it. You can't assume that the people who want to help you promote your books know how.

The list also promotes Tom and Marilyn's business and adds to their credibility as pros who know how to promote books.

"HOW CAN I HELP?"

That's a question we hear often these days when people see *Jump Start Your Book Sales*. Actually, there are many ways you can be of assistance. Here are a few ideas:

- ✓ Tell your colleagues, your friends, (your enemies?) about this new resource. Talk it up over coffee, during phone conversations, at association gatherings, on listservs you belong to, etc.
- ✓ Take your copy when you go to meetings of writers and publishers. Show it to people and give them our toll-free order number ([800] 331-8355).
- ✓ Write a Letter to the Editor or mini-review for newsletters of appropriate professional organizations to which you belong.
- ✓ Go to Amazon.com and write a 5-star review . . . if you think that's deserved, of course.

✓ Give the book as a gift to an aspiring author or a newcomer to publishing.

✓ Ask for *Jump Start Your Book Sales* whenever you go into a bookstore. If they don't have it, suggest they order it. If they do, put it face-out on the shelf (smile). Thanks!

✓ Request it at your local library. Again, suggest they order it if it isn't in stock.

✓ Talk with us about becoming a reseller if you give seminars, speeches or classes in related subject areas and can sell back-of-the-room or via mail. This can be a revenue builder for you.

✓ Recommend it during your speeches; ask for free flyers if your group is holding a conference.

✓ Include *Jump Start Your Book Sales* in bibliographies, recommended reading lists and the text of your own books if they relate to the subject of publishing.

✓ Add a link to your Web site (we're at http://www.SPANnet.org/cc/js).

✓ Include flyers in your mailings to customers (if you're a printer, for instance) or to your vendors (if you're a distributor or wholesaler). This is a win-win-win alliance. The more books sold, the more we all benefit. And we'll even provide the flyers.

Consider hiring the Rosses to keynote your next annual conference, or build a special fundraiser around a full-day seminar with them.

Thank you so very, very much!
Marilyn and Tom Ross

APPENDIX IV

SAMPLE MEDIA KIT

he media kit that Rick created for Harvey Mackay befits a best-selling author. Although you may not have one this elaborate, the kit will give you an idea of what a kit might include and what the parts of it look like.

FOR IMMEDIATE RELEASE

CONTACT:
David Hahn 555/555-1234
Rick Frishman 555/555-4321

PUSHING THE ENVELOPE:
All The Way To The Top
by Harvey Mackay

Harvey Mackay is the premier expert at "pushing the envelope" in every way. In addition to writing two of the *New York Times*'s top fifteen inspirational business books of all time (*Swim With The Sharks* and *Beware The Naked Man Who Offers You His Shirt*), he's built his Mackay Envelope Corporation into an $85 million enterprise that produces more than seventeen million envelopes a day.

When it comes to business advice that gets results, nobody can touch Harvey Mackay. Mackay is the quintessential self-made man who reached the top through brain power, determination and creativity.

In his new book, **PUSHING THE ENVELOPE: All The Way To The Top** (Ballantine Books, Jan. 6, 1999, hardcover/$24.95), Mackay shares his wit and savvy, his common and not-so-common sense, with everyone who wants to succeed . . . at anything.

In **PUSHING THE ENVELOPE,** you'll learn:
• How to get the order,

continued

Sample Press Release

- The art of negotiating the best deals for you,
- The essential qualities all leaders possess,
- Fail-safe ways to move up the corporate ladder,
- Business titans' secrets to achievement,
- The keys to balancing work and family,
- How to use laughter as a productivity tool,
- And much more!

Humor. Honesty. Fairness. The ability to get others to see your vision. Judgement. Guts. Respect for the bottom line—and all the lines that lead to it. These are the values that have made Harvey Mackay the business and civic leader that he is today. A born communicator, Mackay distills the lessons of his forty years in business into pithy, punchy chapters that cut to the heart of everyday problems and situations.

As usual, Mackay has his trademark, no-nonsense lists, including:

- 5 ways to ruin a good sales force,
- 7 things not to do with a friend,
- 10 New Year's resolutions,
- 11 questions to ask you job prospect,
- 12 ways to ruin your next speech.

Both practical and entertaining, charged throughout with Harvey Mackay's inimitable style, humor and entrepreneurial wisdom, **PUSHING THE ENVELOPE** puts the *fun*, the *creativity* and the *challenge* back in business. Whether you're at the top of your company or determined to get there, this is one business book you can't afford to miss.

In his spare time, Mackay writes a nationally syndicated weekly business column that appears in 52 newspapers across the country and he speaks, on average, once a week to a Fortune 500 size organization.

ABOUT THE AUTHOR

Harvey Mackay is the CEO of the $85 million Mackay Envelope Corporation, a business he founded in 1959 in Minneapolis, Minn. In addition, he is a #1 *New York Times* bestselling author, a nationally syndicated business columnist and an internationally acclaimed speaker. In fact, Toastmasters International named him one of the top five speakers in the world. He and his wife of 38 years, Carol Ann, have three children and five grandchildren, and live in a suburb of Minneapolis.

PUSHING THE ENVELOPE: All The Way To The Top by Harvey Mackay
Ballantine Books, Jan. 6, 1999, hardcover/$24.95
ISBN: 345-43295-9

Sample Press Release, continued

HARVEY MACKAY

Harvey Mackay is the author of the *New York Times* #1 bestsellers **Swim With The Sharks Without Being Eaten Alive** and **Beware The Naked Man Who Offers You His Shirt**. Both books are among the top 15 inspirational books of all time, according to the New York Times.

Dig Your Well Before You're Thirsty: The Only Networking Book You'll Ever Need, made the *New York Times* bestseller list 12 days after its release on April 20, 1997, and remained there for five months. **Sharkproof**, Mackay's third book, was a national bestseller.

Now, **PUSHING THE ENVELOPE: All The Way To The Top**, is being published by Ballantine Books on Jan. 6, 1999. It is full of business and life lessons, including how to lick the competition, and is guaranteed to earn your stamp of approval.

Mackay's books have sold 8,000,000 copies worldwide, been translated into 35 languages and sold in 80 countries.

Mackay is a nationally syndicated columnist for United Feature Syndicate, whose weekly articles appear in 52 newspapers around the country, including the *Detroit Free Press*, *Denver Post*, *Orange County Register*, *Minneapolis Star Tribune* and *Arizona Republic*.

He is also one of America's most popular and entertaining business speakers, speaking on average—once a week to Fortune 500-size companies and associations. Toastmasters International named him once of the top five speakers in the world.

In addition, Harvey is a chairman and CEO of Mackay Envelope Corporation, an $85 million company he founded at age 26. Mackay Envelope employs 500 people and manufactures 17 million envelopes a day.

Mackay is a graduate of the University of Minnesota and the Stanford University Graduate School of Business Executive Program. He is an avid runner and marathoner, and former #1 ranked tennis player in Minnesota.

Mackay is the past president of the Minneapolis Chamber of Commerce, the Envelope Manufacturers Association of America, the University of Minnesota National Alumni Association, the Young Presidents Organization (Twin Cities Chapter), to name only a few of the organizations in which he is involved.

He currently is a director of Robert Redford's Sundance Institute, the Minnesota Orchestral Association and the University of Minnesota Carlson School of Management. He has been a guest lecturer at various universities and business schools, including Harvard, Stanford, Michigan, Cornell, Wharton and Penn State.

Mackay played a key role in bringing the 1992 Super Bowl to Minneapolis, along with obtaining an NBA franchise (Minnesota Timberwolves), getting the Hubert H. Humphrey Metrodome built, bringing in Lou Holtz to coach the University of Minnesota football team and many more civic involvements.

All of which is why *Fortune* magazine refers to him as "Mr. Make Things Happen."

Sample Author Bio

CREATIVITY KILLERS

Here are some creativity killers Harvey Mackay has heard at receptions, conferences, seminars, speeches and cocktail parties:

- It's not in the budget.
- The boss will never go for it.
- Great idea! Let's form a committee to tackle it.
- It will never work.
- Who will we get to do it?
- Let's think about it for a while.
- Let's discuss it some other time.
- Why not leave well enough alone?
- We have done it this way for many years, and we still make a profit.
- Why fix it if it isn't broken?
- We tried it five years ago and it didn't work.
- That's not how we do things around here.
- That's the kind of idea that cost your predecessor her job.
- That's not my job.
- Let's let the competition try it first and see what happens.
- It will create more work for the rest of us.
- Sounds like a great idea . . . let's run it by legal.

Sample Document

INTERVIEW QUESTIONS FOR HARVEY MACKAY

What are some of your best negotiating tips?

Why do you feel so strongly about telephone skills?

What's the best way to get a raise?

Why do smart people do stupid things?

What is a manager's single most important task?

How do you pick an expert?

What is the best way to get even?

What makes a good leader?

Why is teamwork so crucial for companies?

What are some of the valuable lessons you learned from your parents?

Can you describe some of your myths of the marketplace?

What are some of the creative gifts you have given?

Sample Document

HARVEY MACKAY'S NEW YEAR'S RESOLUTIONS

Start your New Year today. And remember, anyone can make a resolution. Very few people can keep one.

1. **I will improve my listening skills.** I will remind myself that I can't learn anything when I'm doing the talking. I will abandon my phony "open door" policy, establish specific meetings and set aside specific times so that others can have real access to me. I will break down barriers. I will try to end the "not invented here" syndrome and encourage the free flow of information across departmental and hierarchical lines. I will answer my own phone . . . well, I will answer it more often.

2. **I will improve my professional skills.** I will cease to be a pothole on the information highway. I will not allow myself to become one of these old fuddy-duddies who brags about their inability to operate modern business equipment. I will get up to speed in computers and communications equipment. Nobody should come into the 21st century without being computer literate.

3. **I will improve my reading skills.** Unfortunately, my reading ability has slowed down over the years and it is taking me longer to absorb less. I will take a speed-reading course. Instead of reading what merely confirms my existing prejudices, I will search out material that introduces me to new ideas and new ways of thinking.

4. **I will waste less time.** I will use my commuter time to read more or to listen to audio tapes that can help me improve my skills and broaden my understanding.

5. **I will exercise regularly.** I will exercise regularly to the point where I will become "positively addicted." I know exercise not only improves my health but helps me maintain a high level of performance on the job.

6. **I will encourage risk-taking.** I know that more businesses fail from lack of boldness than from trying something new. I will not punish or ridicule honest mistakes. I love my work. I want others to feel the same about theirs, so I will try to make my workplace a fun and exciting place to be, not just a paycheck.

7. **I will put into practice a plan to become the sole source of supply to my largest customers.** The most important element of my plan is to treat my customers as though I were their most dedicated employee and consultant, ready to serve them in every way so they feel my company is practically a division of their company.

8. **I will be committed to growing and improving every facet of our business.** I want every employee in my company to know we are open for hire eight days a week, 13 months a year. I want them constantly to be on the lookout for good people to become part of our team.

continued

Sample Document

9. **I will contribute to my community.** I will be a giver. I will give money. I will give time. I will try to make a difference. I want to help make the place I live become a better place for everyone.

10. **I will not neglect my family in pursuit of the almighty dollar.** I will never forget that they do more to keep me on an even keel and bring more genuine happiness into my life than any business success I can ever achieve. So Carol Ann, David and Virginia, Mimi and Larry, Jojo and Michael, make room for me. I'm on my way home.

Sample Document, continued

HARVEY MACKAY'S NEGOTIATING STRATEGIES

1. Never accept any proposal immediately, no matter how good it sounds.
2. Never negotiate with yourself. Once you've made an offer, if the other party doesn't accept it, don't make another offer. Get a counter offer. It's a sign of weakness when you lower your own demands without getting your opponent to lower theirs.
3. Never cut a deal with someone who has to "go back and get the boss's approval." That gives the other side two bites of the apple to your one. They can take any deal you are willing to make and renegotiate it.
4. If you can't say yes, it's no. Just because the deal can be done, doesn't mean it should be done. No one ever went broke saying "no" too often.
5. Just because it may look nonnegotiable, doesn't mean it is. Take that beautifully printed "standard contract" you've just been handed. Many a smart negotiator has been able to name a term and get away with it by making it appear to be chiseled in granite, when they will deal if their bluff is called.
6. Do your homework before you deal. Learn as much as you can about the other side. Instincts are no match for information.
7. Rehearse. Practice. Get someone to play the other side. Then switch roles. Instincts are no match for preparation.
8. Beware the late dealer. Feigning indifference or casually disregarding timetables is often just a negotiator's way of trying to make you believe he/she doesn't care if you make the deal or not.
9. Be nice, but if you can't be nice, go away and let someone else do the deal. You'll blow it.
10. A deal can always be made when both parties see their own benefit in making it.
11. A dream is a bargain no matter what you pay for it. Set the scene. Tell the tale. Generate excitement. Help the other side visualize the benefit in making it.

continued

Sample Document

12. Watch the game films. Top players in any game, including negotiating, debrief themselves immediately after every major session. They always keep a book on themselves and the other side.

13. No one is going to show you their hole card. You have to figure out what they really want. Clue: Since the given reason is never the real reason, you can eliminate the given reason.

14. Always let the other side talk first. Their first offer could surprise you and be better than you ever expected.

Sample Document, continued

MACKAY'S MORALS

[NOTE: Chapter numbers refer to Mackay's book, *Pushing The Envelope: All The Way To The Top*]

- Be like a postage stamp. Stick to it until you get there. (Chapter 4)
- Ideas without action are like being all dressed up with no place to go. (Chapter 8)
- Big shots are only little shots who keep shooting. (Chapter 16)
- Time is precious. You can't own it, but you can use it. You can't keep it, but you can spend it. Once you've lost it, you can never get it back. (Chapter 17)
- Put your own little self aside when you make business decisions, or you'll wind up with ego on your face. (Chapter 19)
- In negotiations, as in poker, a superior hand can be beaten by superior knowledge of your opponents. (Chapter 31)
- Making each day count is a tactic. Making each year count is a strategy. You need both to succeed. (Chapter 44)
- The most valuable ability is the ability to recognize ability. (Chapter 51)
- Even the Lone Ranger didn't go it alone. (Chapter 65)
- Friends are made by many acts . . . and lost by only one. (Chapter 66)
- Arrogance is believing you're so high up that you don't have to keep and ear to the ground. (Chapter 75)
- Every dog gets one bite. (Chapter 78)
- When someone says . . . "It ain't the money but the principle of the thing" . . . it's the money. (Chapter 83)
- You can take any amount of pain as long as you know it's going to end. (Chapter 89)
- Nothing will improve a person's hearing more than sincere praise. (Chapter 90)

Sample Document

APPENDIX V

THE TIMELINE FOR A PUBLICITY CAMPAIGN

The timeline of Rick's campaign for Harvey Mackay starts long before publication. There are magazines that close six months in advance. So once your manuscript is accepted and you have a firm pub date, choose the media that you want to approach, find out what their deadlines are and give them enough time to make use of what you have to offer.

Media Campaign Timeline

Galley mailing/manuscript mailing   **JANUARY/FEBRUARY**
(Long lead book reviewers, magazines,
weeklies, appropriate newsletters, national TV
shows)   (Finished Laydown—April 18)
         (Publications Date—May 1)

Network giveaway program with booksellers   **FEBRUARY**
Follow up on review mailing
Development of contest materials
Newspaper feature service (article goes out)

Approach to all national media   **MARCH**
Approach to first ten cities on road tour
Approach to syndicated columnists
Continue to follow up on review mailing
Power promotion leads developed
Follow up on bookseller giveaway program

National media bookings   **APRIL**
Ten-city road tour (April 21-May 2)
Morning drive radio tour
Print placements running
Active promotion of contest
Continue to follow up on review mailing
Power promotion carried out
Other network giveaway programs conducted

National media bookings continue   **MAY**
Ten-city road tour (May 5-May 16)
Continued promotion of contest
Continued print placements
General telephone interviews
Supplemental tour cities decided upon
Satellite TV tour (optional)
Bestseller lists start hitting

National media bookings continue   **JUNE**
Supplemental tour cities (if needed)
Continued print placements
Announcement of contest winners/publicity
Run with bestseller momentum
Rest!

Decide where to go next   **JULY**

APPENDIX VI

WRITER'S DIGEST BOOKS PUBLICITY QUESTIONNAIRE

he publisher's questionnaire you fill out will be your opportunity to impress your publicist with your writing and promotional skills, contacts and experience.

Assuming you are being published by a big house, it's your chance to prove you are ready for the big time. If you sold your book with a proposal, you have already covered some of the same ground but not in the same detail and possibly a long time ago. Nor can you assume your publicist saw your plan. She may not have been working for your publisher when you sold your book.

In any case, don't hold back, include everything about yourself that will convince a publicist that you have what it takes to make your books successful.

GUERRILLA TACTICS

Provide the information this form requests before you write your promotion plan. It will help you marshal the ammunition you need to write your plan. And it will make it easy to fill out your publisher's questionnaire when it arrives.

AUTHOR QUESTIONNAIRE

Name:_____

Title:_____

Season:_____

Biographical Information

Name under which you write:_____

Legal name:_____

Is there a title you prefer with your name? (Mr., Ms., Dr.):_____

Home Address:_____ Telephone:_____

_____ Fax:_____

_____ E-mail:_____

Office or studio address:_____ Telephone:_____

_____ Fax:_____

_____ E-mail:_____

Agent (address and phone number):_____

_____

Book Promotion

Bio information for press releases, book jackets and other promotional materials. Please list any accreditations, university affiliations, other books published or any publications you regularly contribute to (in 100 words).

_____

_____

_____

_____

In your own words, please briefly describe your book. How is your book different from others on the subject; for what audience the book was written; what points you feel should be emphasized in the promotion of your book.

_____

_____

_____

Author Questionnaire

Please list reviewers and/or interviewers you feel would be particularly interested in your book. Include such people as book review editors, features writers, radio and TV commentators and personalities, columnists and editorial writers. Please provide names, street addresses and zip codes for all contacts.

_____

_____

_____

_____

Any affiliations with universities or colleges who may be interested in purchasing your book as a text, include names of professors, the institution as well as a full address.

_____

_____

_____

_____

From time to time members of the community query our office to ask about our author's plans for appearances. If you plan to attend any seminars or conferences as a speaker, or if you will be giving seminars, workshops, etc., please notify our office of such appearances (including the dates and locations), by fax to my attention at (513) 531-7107, or via mail.

Often we receive calls from conferences and workshops, TV and radio shows, newspapers and magazines asking for information about our authors. After my pre-screening, is it OK to give out your:

E-mail _____ -or- Phone Number _____
without contacting you first? Please indicate with a "yes" on each line. If so, indicate the e-mail and phone number where you would prefer to be contacted.
E-mail:_____ Phone:_____

Publishing History
Other books (please list publisher, as well):

_____

_____

_____

_____

Author Questionnaire, continued

Magazine publications (titles, subjects, dates):

_____
_____
_____
_____

Are you a regular contributor to any newspapers or magazines? Has an article/story of yours attracted particular attention?

_____
_____
_____
_____

Hometown newspapers/magazines (list any contacts that you know, plus an address if available):

_____
_____
_____
_____

For our subsidiary rights division, are there any magazines/trade journals/newsletters you feel would be interested in excerpting from your book?

_____
_____
_____
_____

Organizations/Associations
Organizations or associations that would be interested in your book (please provide names and addresses of contacts where possible).

_____
_____
_____
_____
_____
_____

Author Questionnaire, continued

Since we have a variety of direct mail efforts, are there any specific mailing lists that you know of that may be available?

_____

_____

_____

_____

Prizes, awards, fellowships (name the work honored and include the date):

_____

_____

_____

_____

Question & Answer

What is the best piece of advice you ever received? Who gave you this advice?

_____

_____

_____

_____

How did you become interested or get started in your craft? Did/do you have a mentor, special teacher or any other important influences on your work?

_____

_____

_____

_____

What do you find most enjoyable or rewarding about what you do?

_____

_____

_____

_____

Were you ever discouraged in your craft? What did you do to turn yourself around and start again?

_____

_____

_____

_____

Author Questionnaire, continued

What do you do in your spare time? Any hobbies or something else you'd like to share?

_____

_____

_____

_____

Open Letter to Readers

This open letter can resemble the words of advice you'd impart to readers in your introduction.

_____

_____

_____

_____

_____

_____

_____

_____

_____

_____

_____

_____

_____

_____

_____

_____

_____

_____

_____

_____

_____

_____

_____

_____

_____

_____

_____

Author Questionnaire, continued

Top 10 List—Quick Tips for Reprint

When sending information about you and your book to the print media, we often find editors are looking for quick tips: information that they can (with proper credit given) reprint.

Here we would like your suggestions for material found in your book for reprint. For Writer's Digest and Betterway genealogy titles, it can be as simple as "check out tips on formatting your manuscript."

Our art, craft and woodworking authors may find it easier to jot down a few ideas here, instead of needing to use photos to illustrate their points. For example, "Six Tips for Getting Brushes to Last," "Best Ideas for Finding Time to Paint" or "Advice for Keeping the Home Shop Safe."

Any input is greatly appreciated!

APPENDIX VII

THE TOP 100 MARKETS IN THE UNITED STATES

Want to know where to go on your grand tours? Start with this list and adapt it to suit your book. If, for example, you are writing about technology, you will want to get to New York, Los Angeles, San Francisco, San Jose and Boston. But you will also want to include technology centers like Seattle, Austin and the golden triangle of Raleigh, Durham and Chapel Hill.

Talking to authors who are writing the kind of books you are will ensure that you are heading in the right direction. The more you travel, the clearer it will become which are the most receptive cities for your books. Here's a tip from Harvey Mackay: big name authors are more interested in going to the big markets than second-tier cities. This makes smaller markets more receptive to authors who don't yet have big names.

And a tip from us: look at the country as having two coasts and everything in between. From Seattle to Portland, Sacramento, San Francisco, San Jose, Los Angeles and San Diego is one coast.

From Boston to New York, Philadelphia, Baltimore, Washington D.C. and Atlanta to Miami is the other. Chicago in the Midwest and Dallas in the Southwest are the suns for a constellation of cities around them. Think clusters.

Top 100 Markets in the United States

1 New York	5 San Francisco-San Jose
2 Los Angeles	6 Boston
3 Chicago	7 Dallas-Ft. Worth
4 Philadelphia	8 Washington, D.C.

9	Detroit	44	Buffalo
10	Atlanta	45	Oklahoma City
11	Houston	46	Harrisburg-York/Lancaster
12	Seattle-Tacoma	47	Greensboro—Winston-Salem
13	Tampa-St.Pete (Sarasota)	48	Louisville
14	Minneapolis-St.Paul	49	Albuquerque-Santa Fe
15	Cleveland	50	Providence-New Bedford
16	Miami-Ft.Lauderdale	51	Wilks-Barre—Scranton
17	Phoenix	52	Jacksonville, Brunswick
18	Denver	53	Las Vegas
19	Sacramento-Stockton	54	Fresno-Visalia
20	Pittsburgh	55	Albany-Schenectady
21	St. Louis	56	Dayton
22	Orlando-Daytona Beach	57	Little Rock
23	Portland, OR	58	Tulsa
24	Baltimore	59	Charleston-Huntington
25	San Diego	60	Richmond
26	Indianapolis	61	Austin
27	Hartford-New Haven	62	Mobile
28	Charlotte	63	Knoxville
29	Raleigh-Durham	64	Flint-Saginaw
30	Nashville	65	Witchita-Hutchinson
31	Kansas City	66	Lexington
32	Cincinnati	67	Toledo
33	Milwaukee	68	Roanoke-Lynchburg
34	Columbus	69	Green Bay-Appleton
35	Greenville-Spartanburg	70	Des Moines
36	Salt Lake City	71	Honolulu
37	San Antonio	72	Tucson
38	Grand Rapids-Kalamazoo	73	Omaha
39	Birmingham	74	Paducah-Cape Giradeau
40	Memphis	75	Shreveport
41	New Orleans	76	Syracuse
42	Norfolk-Portsmith	77	Rochester, NY
43	West Palm Beach-Ft. Pierce	78	Spokane

79 Springfield, MO

80 Portland-Auburn, ME

81 Ft. Meyers-Naples

82 Huntsville-Decatur

83 Springfield-Decatur, Il

84 Chattanooga

85 Madison

86 Columbia, SC

87 South Bend-Elkhart

88 Davenport, RI

89 Jackson

90 Cedar Rapids-Waterloo

91 Burlington-Plattsburg

92 Tri-Cities, TN-VA

93 Colorado Springs-Pueblo

94 Waco-Temple-Bryan

95 Johnstown-Altoona

96 El Paso

97 Baton Rouge

98 Evansville

99 Youngstown

100 Savannah

APPENDIX VIII

MIKE'S
EVALUATION FORM

eel free to alter this to suit your needs. Continue to improve all of your handouts whenever you find a way to make them more helpful to your students or yourself. Note the "400" in the lower right corner. It helps Mike to be sure he's using the latest version of the form.

PRESENTATION EVALUATION

Our students are our best teachers, so please take a moment and help us improve our presentation. Many thanks for your help.

Overall Rating

Hated It					OK				Loved it
I	2	3	4	5	6	7	8	9	10

What I liked best about this presentation:

This is the idea or information that helped me the most:

Here are my suggestions for improvements:

This is what I think that you should add to your presentation:

Are there any books or articles on the subject that you would like to read?

Other comments (please use the other side of the page if necessary):

Optional:

Name_____

Phone number_____

E-mail address (for our use only)_____

Would you like to discuss your comments?   Y   N

Would you be interested in hearing about future events?   Y   N

400

Sample Evaluation Form

ABOUT THE AUTHORS

JAY CONRAD LEVINSON

 Jay Conrad Levinson has authored or co-authored twenty-eight books. He writes a bi-monthly newsletter, wrote a monthly online column for Microsoft and for his own Web site, and writes regular online columns for several marketing and small business Web sites.

A former vice president and creative director at J. Walter Thompson Advertising and Leo Burnett Advertising, Jay is chairman of the board of Guerrilla Marketing International, a marketing consulting organization serving large and small businesses around the world.

His awards for creativity in marketing include First Place in television at the Venice Film Festival, First Place in graphics at the American TV Commercial Festival, First Prize in videotape at the London Daily Mail Awards, First Prize in television at the Hollywood International Film Festival, Radio Commercial of the Year from The Chicago Copywriters' Club, Award of Merit in consumer magazines from the American Advertising Federation, Honorable Mention for televison advertising at the Cannes Film Festival, Automotive Ad of the Month from *Automotive Age*, Most Important Advertisement of the Year from *Advertising Age*, First Prize for most creative campaign at the Aqua Awards, and First Prize in print advertising from the San Francisco Society of Communicating Arts.

Jay spent ten years as an instructor of marketing for the extension division of the University of California in Berkeley and has served on the Microsoft Small Business Council and the 3Com Small Business Advisory Board. He is a marketing partner of Adobe Systems.

The guerrilla series includes *Guerrilla Marketing, Guerrilla Marketing Attack, Guerrilla Marketing Weapons, Guerrilla Financing* (with Bruce Jan

Blechman), *Guerrilla Selling* (with Bill Gallagher and Orvel Ray Wilson), *Guerrilla Marketing Excellence, Guerrilla Advertising, Guerrilla Marketing Handbook* (with Seth Godin), *Guerrilla Marketing Online* (with Charles Rubin), *Guerrilla Marketing for the Home-Based Business* (with Seth Godin), *Guerrilla Marketing Online Weapons* (with Charles Rubin), *The Way of the Guerrilla, Guerrilla Trade Show Selling* (with Mark S.A. Smith and Orvel Ray Wilson), *Get What You Deserve: How to Guerrilla Market Yourself* (with Seth Godin), *Guerrilla Marketing with Technology* (he first wrote as a monthly online column for Microsoft), *Guerrilla Teleselling* (with Mark S.A. Smith and Orvel Ray Wilson), *Guerrilla Negotiating* (with Mark S.A. Smith and Orvel Ray Wilson), *Guerrilla Saving* (with Kathryn Tyler) and the forthcoming *Guerrilla Creativity*. There are more than a million copies of the Guerrilla books in print.

Jay's other books include *The Most Important $1.00 Book Ever Written, Secrets of Successful Freelancing, San Francisco: An Unusual Guide to Unusual Shopping* (with Pat Levinson and John Bear), *Earning Money Without a Job, 555 Ways to Earn Extra Money, 150 Secrets of Successful Weight Loss,* (with Michael Lavin and Michael Rokeach), *Quit Your Job!, An Earthling's Guide to Satellite TV, The Investor's Guide to the Photovoltaic Industry* and *The 90-Minute Hour.*

Jay and his wife Pat, to whom he has been happily married for forty-four years, have a daughter named Amy.

In addition to being an author and speaker, Jay is a marketing consultant. He can be reached at

170 Seaview Drive, San Rafael, CA 94901

Tel: (415) 453-2162   Fax: (415) 453-0899

E-mail: jayview@aol.com   Web site: www.gmarketing.com

RICK FRISHMAN

Rick Frishman received a B.F.A. in acting and directing and a B.S. from the Ithaca School of Communications. After working as a producer for radio station WOR-AM in New York, he joined Planned Television Arts (PTA) in 1976 and became president in 1982.

PTA is the oldest and largest book publicity firm in America. PTA has several specialty divisions, including PTA Faith, PTA Satellite, PTA Entertainment and PTA Solutions Group, which builds Web sites for authors and specializes in internet promotion and publicity.

In 1993 PTA merged with Ruder Finn, the second biggest public relations firm in New York. Rick is also executive vice president at Ruder Finn.

Rick works with the top agents, authors, editors and publishers including HarperCollins, Hyperion, Random House and Simon & Schuster. Among the authors he has worked with are Bill Moyers, Richard Preston, Hugh Downs, Alan Dershowitz, Arnold Palmer, President Jimmy Carter, Harvey Mackay, Jack Canfield and Mark Victor Hansen.

Rick is a member of the National Speakers Association and the Public Relations Society of America and is a sought-after lecturer on publishing and public relations. He and his wife Robbi have three children, Adam, Rachel and Stephanie, and a cockapoo named Rusty.

Rick can be reached at

Planned Television Arts, 1110 Second Avenue, New York, NY 10022

Tel: (212) 593-5845   Fax: (212) 715-1667

E-mail: FrishmanR@RuderFinn.com

Web site: www.PlannedTVArts.com

MICHAEL LARSEN

 Born and educated in New York, Michael Larsen worked in promotion for three major publishers: William Morrow, Bantam and Pyramid (now Jove). He and his wife Elizabeth Pomada moved to San Francisco in 1970.

They started Michael Larsen/Elizabeth Pomada Literary Agents, Northern California's oldest literary agency, in 1972. Since then, the agency has sold books, mostly by new writers, to more than a hundred publishers. Both principals are members of the Association of Authors' Representatives.

The agency represents book-length fiction and nonfiction for adults. Michael handles most of the agency's nonfiction, while Elizabeth represents novelists and nonfiction directed to women.

Mike is the author of *How to Write a Book Proposal* and *Literary Agents: What They Do, How They Do It and How to Find and Work with the Right One for You*, a selection of the Writer's Digest and Quality Paperback Book Clubs.

He also wrote *The Worry Bead Book: A Guide to The World's Oldest and Simplest Way to Beat Stress* and *How to Write with a Collaborator* with Hal Zina Bennett.

In 1972, Mike and Elizabeth created California Publicity Outlets, which is now called *Metro California Media*. They also coauthored the six books in the Painted Ladies series: *Painted Ladies: San Francisco's Resplendent Victorians*; *Daughters of Painted Ladies: America's Resplendent Victorians*, which *Publishers Weekly* selected as one of the best books of 1987; *The Painted Ladies Guide to Victorian California*; *How to Create Your Own Painted Lady: A Comprehensive Guide to Beautifying Your Victorian Home*; *The Painted Ladies Revisited: San Francisco's Resplendent Victorians Inside and Out*; and *America's Painted Ladies: The Ultimate Celebration of Our Victorians.*

Mike has reviewed books for the *San Francisco Chronicle*, and his articles have appeared in the *San Francisco Examiner*, *Writer's Digest*, *Publisher's Weekly*, and Writer's Digest's *Guide to Literary Agents*.

Michael and Elizabeth give talks on writing, agenting, proposals, publishing and guerrilla marketing for writer's groups and conferences. They also present talks and seminars on "How to Make Yourself Irresistible to Any Agent or Publisher" based on the last part of Michael's book on agents.

If you have completed a novel and tried it out on your professional network to make sure it's 100 percent, Elizabeth will be glad to see the first ten pages and a synopsis. If you have had a novel published, please send the whole manuscript and a synopsis.

Parcels weighing more than two pounds must be brought to the post office. To help ensure a faster response, enclose a prepaid return label from United Parcel Service or Federal Express. Please include a self-addressed, stamped envelope with correspondance, and allow two weeks for a reponse to a letter and six to eight weeks for a reading.

For a free brochure about the agency, please send a stamped, self-adressed #10 envelope to

1029 Jones St., San Francisco, Californa 94109

The agency can also be reached at larsenpoma@aol.com or at www.larsen-pomada.com.

WWW.GMARTKETING.COM

The guerrilla Marketing Web site, www.gmarketing.com, is a valuable resource for new information that can help you promote your books and keep you up to date on marketing news and trends.

We are always on the lookout for creative new promotion ideas and outstanding examples of printed materials to share with our readers. We welcome the chance to learn about your experiences with the ideas in the book and how we can make the next edition of the book more helpful.

Because we wanted the bibliography to be as comprehensive and up to date as possible, we are making it available on the Web site where we will update it with new books. We will also include a glossary on our Web site.

THE GUERRILLA MARKETING NEWSLETTER

The Guerrilla Marketing Newsletter provides state-of-the-moment insights to maximize profits online and offline. The newsletter offers the cream of new guerrilla marketing information from around the world, along with new perspectives on existing wisdom about marketing. It's filled with practical advice, the latest research, upcoming trends, brand-new and valuable marketing techniques—all designed to pay off in handsome profits.

A yearly subscription costs $59 for six issues and includes this risk-free guarantee: If you aren't convinced after examining your first issue for thirty days that the newsletter will raise your profits, your subscription fee will be refunded—along with two dollars just for trying it.

To subscribe, write, call, fax or E-mail us at:

Guerrilla Marketing International

260 Cascade Dr., P.O. Box 1336

Mill Valley, CA 94902

Tel: (800) 748-6444   Fax: (415) 381-8361

E-Mail: GMINTL@aol.com

Our Web site, www.gmarketing.com, is the largest small-business site on the Internet and makes offers too generous to miss. For example, you can sign up to receive a daily Guerrilla Marketing Communique for only two dollars a year!

INDEX